ISBN 978-1-332-25774-4
PIBN 10305351

1 MONTH OF
FREE
READING

at

www.ForgottenBooks.com

By purchasing this book you are eligible for one month membership to ForgottenBooks.com, giving you unlimited access to our entire collection of over 1,000,000 titles via our web site and mobile apps.

To claim your free month visit:

www.forgottenbooks.com/free305351

English
Français
Deutsche
Italiano
Español
Português

www.forgottenbooks.com

Mythology Photography **Fiction**
Fishing Christianity **Art** Cooking
Essays Buddhism Freemasonry
Medicine **Biology** Music **Ancient**
Egypt Evolution Carpentry Physics
Dance Geology **Mathematics** Fitness
Shakespeare **Folklore** Yoga Marketing
Confidence Immortality Biographies
Poetry **Psychology** Witchcraft
Electronics Chemistry History **Law**
Accounting **Philosophy** Anthropology
Alchemy Drama Quantum Mechanics
Atheism Sexual Health **Ancient History**
Entrepreneurship Languages Sport
Paleontology Needlework Islam
Metaphysics Investment Archaeology
Parenting Statistics Criminology
Motivational

S. HRG. 104–532, PT. 4

DEPARTMENT OF DEFENSE AUTHORIZATION FOR APPROPRIATIONS FOR FISCAL YEAR 1997 AND THE FUTURE YEARS DEFENSE PROGRAM

HEARINGS

BEFORE THE

COMMITTEE ON ARMED SERVICES
UNITED STATES SENATE

ONE HUNDRED FOURTH CONGRESS

SECOND SESSION

ON

S. 1745

AUTHORIZING APPROPRIATIONS FOR FISCAL YEAR 1997 FOR MILITARY ACTIVITIES OF THE DEPARTMENT OF DEFENSE, FOR MILITARY CON-STRUCTION, AND FOR DEFENSE ACTIVITIES OF THE DEPARTMENT OF ENERGY, TO PRESCRIBE PERSONNEL STRENGTHS FOR SUCH FISCAL YEAR FOR THE ARMED FORCES, AND FOR OTHER PURPOSES

PART 4
AIRLAND FORCES

MARCH 15 AND 29, 1996

MAR 19 1997

Printed for the use of the Committee on Armed Services

U.S. GOVERNMENT PRINTING OFFICE

26–504 CC   WASHINGTON : 1997

For sale by the U.S. Government Printing Office
Superintendent of Documents, Congressional Sales Office, Washington, DC 20402
ISBN 0-16-054023-2

S. Hrg. 104–532, Pt. 4

DEPARTMENT OF DEFENSE AUTHORIZATION FOR APPROPRIATIONS FOR FISCAL YEAR 1997 AND THE FUTURE YEARS DEFENSE PROGRAM

HEARINGS

BEFORE THE

COMMITTEE ON ARMED SERVICES
UNITED STATES SENATE

ONE HUNDRED FOURTH CONGRESS

SECOND SESSION

ON

S. 1745

AUTHORIZING APPROPRIATIONS FOR FISCAL YEAR 1997 FOR MILITARY ACTIVITIES OF THE DEPARTMENT OF DEFENSE, FOR MILITARY CONSTRUCTION, AND FOR DEFENSE ACTIVITIES OF THE DEPARTMENT OF ENERGY, TO PRESCRIBE PERSONNEL STRENGTHS FOR SUCH FISCAL YEAR FOR THE ARMED FORCES, AND FOR OTHER PURPOSES

PART 4
AIRLAND FORCES

MARCH 15 AND 29, 1996

Printed for the use of the Committee on Armed Services

(II)

CONTENTS

CHRONOLOGICAL LIST OF WITNESSES

TACTICAL AVIATION ISSUES

MARCH 15, 1996

Page

Eberhart, Lt. Gen. Ralph E., USAF, Deputy Chief of Staff for Plans and Operations 3

McGinn, Rear Adm. Dennis V., USN, Director, Air Warfare Division, Office of the Chief of Naval Operations 7

Steidle, Rear Adm. Craig, USN, Director, Advanced Strike Technology Program 13

Magnus, Brig. Gen. Robert, USMC, Assistant Deputy Chief of Staff for Aviation 19

ARMY AND UNMANNED AERIAL VEHICLE (UAV) MODERNIZATION EFFORTS

MARCH 29, 1996

Decker, Gilbert F., Assistant Secretary of the Army for Research, Development and Acquisition, accompanied by Dr. Fenner Milton, Deputy Assistant Secretary f the Army for Technology 58

Griffith, Gem Ronald H., USA, Vice Chief of Staff 101

Heber, Charles, Director, High Altitude Endurance/Unmanned Aerial Vehicle Advance Research Projects Agency 116

Strong, Rear Adm. Barton D., Program Executive Officer for Cruise Missiles and Unmanned Aerial Vehicles 125

DEPARTMENT OF DEFENSE AUTHORIZATION FOR APPROPRIATIONS FOR FISCAL YEAR 1997 AND THE FUTURE YEARS DEFENSE PROGRAM

FRIDAY, MARCH 15, 1996

U.S. SENATE,
SUBCOMMITTEE ON AIRLAND FORCES,
COMMITTEE ON ARMED SERVICES,
Washington, DC.

TACTICAL AVIATION ISSUES

The subcommittee met, pursuant to notice, at 9:39 a.m., in room SR–222, Russell Senate Office Building, Senator John W. Warner (chairman of the subcommittee) presiding.

Committee members present: Senators Warner and Levin.

Committee staff members present: Romie L. Brownlee, staff director; and Christine K. Cimko, press secretary.

Professional staff members present: Stephen L. Madey, Jr., and Eric H. Thoemmes.

Minority staff members present: Creighton Greene, professional staff member.

Staff assistants present: Shawn H. Edwards.

Committee members' assistants present: Judith A. Ansley, assistant to Senator Warner; Glen E. Tait, assistant to Senator Kempthorne; John F. Luddy II, assistant to Senator Inhofe; Patty Stolnacker, assistant to Senator Santorum; Andrew W. Johnson, assistant to Senator Exon; Richard W. Fieldhouse, assistant to Senator Levin; Steven A. Wolfe, assistant to Senator Kennedy; John P. Stevens, assistant to Senator Glenn; Mary Weaver Bennett, assistant to Senator Bryan; and Melanie DeMayo, assistant to Senator Cohen.

Committee members' fellows present: CDR Thomas A. Vecchiolla, fellow to Senator Cohen; MAJ Sharon K.G. Dunbar, fellow to Senator Coats; Brian Levengood, fellow to Senator Santorum; LTC Max H. Della Pia, fellow to Senator Levin.

OPENING STATEMENT BY SENATOR JOHN WARNER, CHAIRMAN

Senator WARNER. The subcommittee will come to order.

We have before us a very distinguished array of aviators this morning. Our subcommittee, as the first hearing, leads off with some of the toughest challenges. We welcome them. I am going to put brief remarks into the record.

(1)

Just sitting here thinking back over a lifetime of my own, if I had to figure out, Senator Levin, one or two disappointments in my lifetime the first one was not achieving Navy gold wings. Unfortunately, World War II had ended, and they did not need youngsters in the pipeline anymore and we all went home. But ever since then I have been highly envious of those of you who sought as your professions aviation. It is a very challenging and high-risk occupation. I realize, and I think most realize, that every day you get in that cockpit there is a certain measure of personal risk. I want to thank each of you, and the tens of thousands like you wherever they are today, for having made this contribution to our Nation's security.

The work of this committee, however, is to try and evaluate the various programs brought forth by the Commander-in-Chief, the President, the Secretary of Defense, and the Secretaries of the Air Force and Navy. Therein, again, I have had the privilege of having a good deal of experience through the years. It is particularly sad for me to address this morning the F–14 program, a program that was brought in while I served in the Department of the Navy, and have spent a good many hours in the rear seat of that aircraft in the early days. But it is a fine airplane, it served the country well, and I hope that we can put fixes in to allow it to continue that service to the Nation with such service life technically that we can get out of it.

The JAST program—I was just sort of sitting here scratching a note or two—the challenges here are almost like going to the moon, and this time it is Tac Air. There is a high technical risk, there is a high financial risk, and there is a high political risk, all three of them wrapped up in this program. We are very anxious to hear from you this morning on that, General.

So I will not take further time. We are anxious to hear from the witnesses, but I would like to turn to my distinguished colleague. We have been together now—we came together some 18 years ago to the United States Senate, and we have worked side by side and traveled the world together to some very challenging assignments. Who knows? With a little luck we might be sitting here a while longer.

I am privileged to have you here as the ranking member of our subcommittee.

[The prepared statement of Senator Warner follows:]

PREPARED STATEMENT BY SENATOR JOHN WARNER

Today's topic—Tactical Aviation—is one that has a record of magnificent achievements but also of terrible program failures, for I hope to address both side of this record in today's hearing.

Several items are of particular interest to me. Last year Senator Levin and I closely examined the issue of concurrence in the F–22 program, as well as program difficulties at critical design review. I look forward to receiving an update on this program.

The joint advanced strike technology program is a promising start at rationalizing tactical aviation program. Unfortunately, it is one of many starts in recent years, not all of which got off the ground, sometimes at great cost. Indeed, many of those programs had less ambitious goals than JAST. Now, with the services answering their needs with separate programs for the present, we hear that the future under jar will be better. I hope so. However it will take more than hope to provide the Navy with a deep strike capability from its carriers, and to provide a vertical take off jet for the Marines, or to provide an F–16 replacement for the Air Force.

We look forward to your testimony as we begin the search, once again, to rationalize the requirements for tactical aviation and make the best use of the development work already done.

I hope your testimony will address the single role and high cost of the F–22 program, as well as what should be done about electronic warfare shortfalls.

Thank you all for your efforts to provide for America's aviation striking power. As seen in the Desert War, tactical aviation can be a *decisive* capability. However, important as it is, tactical aviation is also expensive, and deserves careful scrutiny.

STATEMENT OF SENATOR CARL LEVIN

Senator LEVIN. I just want to thank you, Senator Warner. It has been indeed a privilege to work with you for these many years, whether I am chairing a subcommittee and you are ranking member or you are chairing and I am ranking member, or we are working on so many other things, we have always worked together in a spirit of cooperation. Some of these people ask me about the U.S. Senate, how it must be difficult to work in the U.S. Senate these days, and I always say no, you must be thinking of the House of Representatives. [Laughter.]

We really do work together very well as a team in the Senate, and we have alternated who has been the majority over this decade and a half, and regardless of who is in the majority and who is in the minority, it has worked out very well and our staffs have worked together consistently.

So that is going to be the order of the day again, and it is necessary because of the challenges we face, not as challenging as what you folks have faced in the cockpits over the years, but nevertheless a different kind of challenge, and the chairman has mentioned a number of them including the JAST program and some of our other acquisitions.

Why, for instance, are we buying more F–15's and F–16's at this time? That is a question that is very much on my mind as to whether that makes sense for us to do that. But I agree with the chairman. I think the JAST program is one that we are going to have to pay a lot of attention to because of the number of challenges that it presents.

I am interested in the digitization issue as to why we are not making as much progress with our situational awareness in the air as the Army has done with its digitization program on the ground, which has given it tremendous situational awareness. That is something that this subcommittee has been pressing for many, many years, as well.

So, Mr. Chairman, I also will put some remarks in the record which are in more detail, but I just wanted to join you in welcoming our witnesses and thanking them for their presence and for their contribution over the years, and again saying how much I look forward to working with you this year again.

Senator WARNER. Fine. All right, General. Turn up the engines.

STATEMENT OF LT. GEN. RALPH E. EBERHART, USAF, DEPUTY CHIEF OF STAFF FOR PLANS AND OPERATIONS

General EBERHART. It is an honor to be with you this morning and talk about issues that are so important to our great Nation, because in my view they are key to joint war-fighting today, and to our success in the future. That is air power.

With your approval, what I would like to do is submit my opening remarks for the record.

Senator WARNER. Without objection.

General EBERHART. In those remarks, as well as in the other prepared statements that we have submitted to the committee, we address those questions you asked in your letter of invitation to appear before the committee.

[The prepared statement of General Eberhart follows:]

PREPARED STATEMENT BY LT. GEN. ED EBERHART

Mr. Chairman and distinguished members of the committee, thank you for the opportunity to discuss our nation's Air Force. This written statement supplements my verbal testimony before your committee.

To echo General Fogleman's comments early this week: the Air Force is ready and capable to meet the challenges of the Post-Cold War environment. Today, more than 10,000 of our people are deployed supporting operations around the world. In Bosnia, we have flown thousands of sorties to get our troops and equipment in theater and then to provide round-the-clock air superiority, close air support, surveillance, and command and control. In Southwest Asia, our airmen are maintaining an "air occupation" to force continued Iraqi compliance with United Nations' mandates.

Our airmen operate the finest equipment in the world, thanks to continued Congressional support. It was Congressional decisions to support modernization during the 1970's that insured the United States dominates the skies today. It will be your foresight today that ensures we dominate the skies in the 21st Century.

Our modernization program is a coherent, **time-phased** effort to develop what we need, delivered when we need it. Our programs balance today's readiness with modernization-leading to our readiness in the 21st Century.

In the **near-term**, our focus is on airlift with a multi-year procurement of the C–17; replacing 250 C–141s with 120 C–17s. The C–17 had a very successful year. The program won the Collier Trophy for excellence in aviation in May, earned great marks on its reliability, maintainability, and availability evaluation (RM&AE) in July, and in December, proved its versatility supporting operations in Bosnia. During the peak of our buildup, 12 C–17s hauled 47 percent of cargo into the theater while maintaining a departure rate of 97 percent. The cargo included bridge sections for the Sava River bridge. All told, the C–17 is a great success story, making accelerated multi-year procurement well worth it. In the **mid-term**, we are working to bolster our conventional deterrence by equipping our bombers with conventional upgrades.

We are also working with the Navy on the Joint Air-to-Surface Standoff Missile (JASSM) to provide precise, long-range, standoff capability.

Our **long-term** effort includes maintaining our dominance of the skies with the F–22. It will replace the F–15, which will be in its fourth decade of service by the time the F–22 reaches IOC in 2005.

F–22. The F–22 is the future centerpiece of America's ability to achieve air superiority over any battlefield. Desert Storm and Bosnia have taught us that air superiority is the essential ingredient of any policy option that includes the use of military force. That is why one of our top funding priorities continues to be the F–22.

The F–22 will be the backbone of America's fighter force out into the years 2020–2030. It's our long-term insurance policy. It will be taking the fight to the enemy's airspace. Simply put, we are going to operate in it, and they will not. Parity is not acceptable. The F–22 will give us sustained advantage in a very unfair fight.

The F–22 combines supervise, maneuverable stealth, and exciting advances in integrated avionics. These things work together to revolutionize air superiority.

Supercruise, which is the ability to sustain supersonic speeds without resorting to afterburner, gets you to the action quickly without leaving a red-hot plume in your wake. It gets you there economically, meaning you can go farther and stay in the fight longer.

Stealth limits the enemy's detection and weapons engagement envelopes—we are nearly invisible. Maneuverable stealth does all that, while leaving you the freedom to put your airplane where you want, when you want.

Integrated avionics leverage very high-speed integrated circuits, revolutionizing the display of vital information. Information from many sources, both on and off the airplane—AWACS, JSTS and ELINT—come into the cockpit, forming an incredibly —detailed "air picture" for the pilot's situational awareness. This situational awareness is continuous, and extends to the other aircraft in the formation. Furthermore, since the F-22 will be able to receive data from external sources passively, it will not compromise its stealth advantage.

That is what the F-22 is bringing to the warfighter—air superiority over all our military operations well into the 21st Century. Let's not forget that air superiority is job one for us.

Joint Strike Fighter (JSF). Five years after the F-22 reaches IOC, the JSF will enter the force to replace our F-16s and A-10s. As the F-16 complements the F-15—providing an affordable multi-role complement—so the JSF will complement the F-22, both operationally and technically. We have structured the JSF program to take full advantage of the technical advances developed by the F-22, and to leverage its operational capabilities as well.

Like the F-15, the F-16 will be entering its fourth decade by the time its replacement arrives on the scene. Like the F-15, it has been upgraded continually during its lifetime—but it is reaching the extent of useful development that can be done within the limits of its airframe. The JSF will fill its place in our inventory and provide the advanced avionics and reduced signatures necessary to survive the battlefield of the 21st Century.

Because we will need a large number of these aircraft, they must be affordable. This joint Air Force, Navy, and Marine program is proceeding well and we are confident that it will produce a superb, affordable next generation fighter. The JSF will also provide an affordable front-line fighter for our allies as their fleets age.

Our ongoing modernization efforts also include keeping our technological edge in terms of electronic countermeasures, munitions, and command and control.

Electronic Countermeasures (ECM). Electronic jamming provides important protection for our aircraft. Due to maintenance costs, we are in the process of phasing out the Air Force's EF-111. In an unprecedented action, we have collaborated with the Navy and Marines to operate jointly the EA-6B wherever it is needed—at sea or over land. There are also several other programs focused on improving self-protection capability. The F-15E and B-1 ECM upgrades will increase their survivability and reduce reliance on off-board jamming support and lethal suppression of enemy air defense (SEAD).

Protection of our aircraft will improve with advances in the ability to locate, target, and destroy surface-to-air missiles, particularly those that can move quickly. The recent addition of the High Speed Anti-Radiation Missile (HARM) Targeting System (HTS) to our block 50/52 F-16s provides a good capability to target and kill surface-to-air missiles (SAM's) that are actively emitting radar signals. The F-16 HTS allowed retirement of the aging F-4G, Wild Weasel, aircraft.

Munitions. Once air superiority is achieved, our air forces can focus on attacking the enemy's infrastructure and fielded force. We will employ stealth and stand-off capabilities to eliminate the enemy's ability to defend targets. This will allow less stealthy forces to operate more safely over enemy territory. To successfully execute this strategy, our forces must be able to deliver standoff and precision weapons, from a safe altitude, and in adverse weather.

Our ability to deliver precision guided ordnance has improved significantly since Desert Storm. However, improvement is needed in our capability to deliver ordnance during periods of adverse weather (i.e. through the clouds) without visually acquiring the target. Just as the enemy was denied the cover of darkness with the introduction of our night systems, we will deny a weather sanctuary.

To do this, we are developing a new class of weapon, with internal guidance using the Global Positioning System (GPS), inertial guidance, or a combination of both. We have already added GPS capability to our AGM-130 stand-off weapon. Two follow-on weapons, the Air Force/Navy Joint Direct Attack Munition (JDAM) and Joint Stand-off Weapon (JSOW), also rely on internal guidance systems. Both of these programs are vital to our future deep strike capability. The precision capabilities of these weapons allow employment through the weather, on multiple targets per attack. This maximizes combat effectiveness while minimizing risk to our airmen and the danger of collateral damage.

The bomber force will also be able to deliver these weapons. Within a few years the B-52 and the B-2 will carry JDAM and JSOW. The B-1 is being modified by a Conventional Munition Upgrade Program (CMUP) to get this capability. These platforms enable us to fly missions from the United States and attack targets or stop an advancing enemy early in a conflict, before deploying friendly forces arrive in theater.

The Joint Air to Surface Stand-off Missile (JASSM), the follow-on to TSSAM, will give the Air Force and Navy a long range, precision, stand-off weapon delivered by bombers and fighters. We will use this to hold heavily defended, high-value targets at risk. JASSM is slated for the B-52 in 2001, the F-16C/D in 2002, and, potentially, the B–1 and B–2 by 2003. Other platforms include F/A–18, F–15E, F–117, and JSF.

The wind corrected munitions dispenser (WCMD) program will equip cluster bomb units (CBUs) with inertial guidance systems that can guide them to targets from medium altitude. CBUs can be loaded with anti-armor, combined effects munitions (anti-personnel and vehicles) and area denial munitions. An improved delivery capability provides greater close air support (CAS) to our ground troops.

All of these programs are designed to invest limited resources in areas that will yield the greatest returns towards a ready and capable future joint warfighting force.

Command and Control. Upgrades in command and control and surveillance aircraft, such as AWACS, Joint STARS, and Rivet Joint, will insure our continued ability to control the airspace. In the near term, Joint Tactical Information Distribution System (JTIDS) terminals in command and control and air superiority aircraft will greatly increase battlefield awareness and combat effectiveness while reducing the possibility of friendly fire incidents. We are also committed to widespread deployment of tactical data links on virtually all Air Force aircraft, a move which will vastly improve our ability to keep track of and to effectively employ all our forces.

To better support operations in Bosnia, we have "pushed" some systems still under development to the field. Joint Surveillance Target Attack Radar System (Joint STARS) made its operational debut in Desert Storm and is now operating in Bosnia, providing surveillance, targeting, and battle management information to the joint force commander. We also accelerated the Contingency Airborne Reconnaissance System (CARS) which—takes data from the U–2 and in less than 15 minutes converts it to information ready for the joint force commander—near real-time intelligence at the commander's fingertips. In early March, the Predator, an unmanned aerial vehicle (UAV), redeployed to the United States European Command in support of the Implementation Force. The UAVs have great potential and complement our manned reconnaissance.

All these efforts—the F–22, the Joint Strike Fighter, improved ECM, munitions, and command and control—mean we will be able to provide our forces the airpower we need to conduct successful surface combat. Comprehensive defense, however, calls for a theater missile defense system.

Theater Missile Defense. We are working with the other services and BMDO to provide theater missile defense. The Air Force is pursuing the airborne laser (ABL) which will complement terminal defenses and attack operations with the capability to destroy missiles in their boost phase. By killing a missile early in flight, submunitions and weapons of mass destruction fall in enemy territory instead of continuing towards friendly forces or population centers. Continued development of ABL (capable of detecting, tracking, and destroying the missile using a speed of light, high power laser) is one of our highest priorities. This technology continues to show great promise. We are providing funding to support demonstration flights by 2002.

This picture of the Air Force would be incomplete without addressing those who fly and maintain our aircraft and missiles, those who support the mission in hundreds of locations around the world. Our people are the key to our success.

People. Since 1986, we have reduced our ranks by 36 percent, with our overseas strength down by 40 percent. On the other hand, our humanitarian and contingency operations quadrupled. Some units like Red Horse civil engineering squadrons and tanker airlift control elements experience very high operations tempo, shared by specialties like security police and command and control. This increased operations tempo called for steps to make sure we share the work and continue to support our people as we ought. In cases like AWACS, ABCCC, and Rivet Joint, we asked for and received relief from some taskings to allow us to regenerate our forces. In addition, we have increased our use of the Guard and the Reserves. For example, we have taken steps to establish an AWACS Reserve Associate unit to help ease the active duty load. We are seeing the pay off for our investments in front-line equipment and training for the Guard and Reserves.

On a recent trip to Aviano and Vicenza, I was impressed with the total focus and dedication of our men and women. They knew what they were doing was important—bringing the hope of peace was worth their commitment.

Bottom line. The United States Air Force is ready today. With your continued support, we can maintain the world's premier air force into the 21st Century.

We thank you for the opportunity to discuss tactical aviation and associated issues. We look forward to working with you.

STATEMENT OF REAR ADM. DENNIS V. McGINN, USN, DIRECTOR, AIR WARFARE DIVISION, OFFICE OF THE CHIEF OF NAVAL OPERATIONS

Admiral McGINN. Mr. Chairman, members of the committee, it is a privilege and a pleasure for me to appear before you to present an overview of naval aviation's present tactical capabilities and our vision for the future. I would also like to abbreviate my time here in opening remarks and submit them for the record.

Senator WARNER. Without objection.

Admiral McGINN. I would like to, Senator Warner, make an offer if you can find the time. I will talk to Adm. T-Ball Hayden, the Chief of our Naval Air Training, and see if we can get you to come down to Pensacola for training.

Senator WARNER. I hate to tell you, I started in the "Yellow Peril", which was the old biplane with canvass—whatever was in it, I do not know. I know those days are gone. Thank you very much.

Admiral McGINN. I would like to also recount just briefly that I had a phone conversation this morning with Adm. Hank Giffin, the Commander of the *George Washington* battle group. He is preparing that aircraft carrier and his battle group to transit the Suez Canal later on today. They are in route to the Persian Gulf to work for the CINC Central Command. Adm. Lyle Bien and his battle group on the *Nimitz* are steaming across the Indian Ocean enroute to the vicinity of Taiwan, where they will join Adm. Jim Ellis and the *Independence* battle group in providing that tremendously capable aircraft carrier battle group presence to hopefully stabilize that area.

With that, sir, I look forward to answering any questions that you and the subcommittee members may have.

[The prepared statement of Admiral McGinn follows:]

PREPARED STATEMENT OF REAR ADM. DENNIS V. McGINN

INTRODUCTION

Mr. Chairman and distinguished members of the subcommittee, thank you for this opportunity to appear before you to discuss the Department of the Navy's plan for Tactical Naval Aviation. I would like to update you on initiatives to ensure that Naval Aviation continues to fully support our expeditionary force strategy contained in the White Paper "Forward . . . From The Sea." The value of the inherent mobility, flexibility and adaptability of Naval Aviation forces continues to grow as a cornerstone of our National military strategy during a time of diverse threats and uncertain scenarios.

SHIFTING WORLD ORDER

"Forward . . . From the Sea" sets forth the Department's vision of Naval expeditionary force strategy by addressing the unique contributions of our forces in peacetime operations, crises, and regional conflicts. This document clearly defines the role of the Navy and Marine Corps for the next several decades.

In this regard, Naval Aviation is exactly on the right track. Our current and future plans provide for the right mix of flexible forces tailored for an uncertain future. Our Carrier Battle Groups and Amphibious Readiness Groups constitute the main battery of Naval Expeditionary forces. They are at the very heart of our Navy and Marine Corps mission. These formidable Naval combat units possess a vast array of aviation capability providing strike, support, surveillance and intelligence gathering for the fleets all around the globe. Indeed, Naval Aviation's inherent power, flexibility and adaptability are the core characteristics at the center of our naval strategy. "Forward . . . From the Sea" is a concept that is turned into reality on a daily basis just as it is occurring today near the Taiwan Straits, in the Arabian

Gulf and in the Mediterranean Sea. The demand by our National Command Authority and Unified Commanders-in-Chief (CINCs) for a wide spectrum of warfighting capabilities in a dangerous and uncertain world is met every time, in every way by Naval Aviation. The Unified CINCs continue to be Naval Aviation's most important customers and our most ardent supporters.

As you know, the Bottom-Up Review concluded that the United States Navy needs 12 aircraft carriers and 11 carrier air wings. For Naval Aviation, this means fixed and rotary wing aircraft and ships that are *expeditionary* in nature; i.e., those best suited for power projection and joint strike, battle space dominance, command and control, force sustainment and forward presence. I believe we bring all of those characteristics to the joint arena in ample measure and that our future plans continue to set out the right mix of Naval Aviation ships, aircraft, systems and weapons.

BUDGET OVERVIEW

Supporting our long-range vision for Naval Aviation is a well conceived acquisition strategy. We have crafted a plan that strikes a very careful balance between maintaining today's readiness, modernizing systems and aircraft, and planning for tomorrow's readiness through force recapitalization. Although future funding is always a serious concern, we will continue to aggressively pursue acquisition of the right mix of Naval Aviation capabilities in a prudent and cost-effective way.

Naval Aviation has moved responsibly to restructure itself within the environment of Defense downsizing. In order to meet mandatory budget reductions and to provide funding for Naval Aviation modernization, the Department has taken decisive measures. We have reduced force structure and associated infrastructure without jeopardizing our core warfighting capabilities or incurring an unacceptable level of mission risk.

This restructuring or "rightsizing glide slope" is almost over, however. Now is the time to focus and build for the future with such important programs as the F/A–18E/F, MV–22, and CVN–77. Additional Naval Aviation funding priorities are the Helicopter Master Plan; continued procurement of precision strike weapons; improved Command, Control, Communications, Computers and Intelligence (C⁴I); and Joint Strike Fighter research and development. With clear political support for a balanced budget, the inherent flexibility and value of Naval Aviation will provide the maximum "Bang for the Buck." I am certain that the competition for future defense dollars will create an even greater need and appreciation for the tremendous return on investment that Naval Aviation forces provide to our Nation's security interests.

In view of Defense budget projections, we are continuing with the following major changes:

- Leveling the carrier force to 11 active aircraft carriers and 1 conventionally-powered reserve/training carrier that will also be available for periodic deployments.
- Leveling the carrier air wing force level to 10 active and 1 reserve air wings. The reserve air wing has been restructured to reflect a more dynamic and functional strike-fighter mix.
- Reducing, in the near term, the number of tactical aircraft planned for each of our carrier air wings. This is based on the ability to meet presence requirements with a more efficient mix of strike-fighter aircraft. Carrier air wings will transition during this decade from a desired combination of 60 single and multi-mission aircraft to 50 multi-mission strike-fighters. This 50 aircraft strike fighter air wing will consist of three F/A–18 squadrons with a total of 36 aircraft and a single F–14 squadron of 14 aircraft. It is important to note that our air wings still retain the flexibility of previous years. We will continue to exercise the option of tailoring the specific composition of deploying air wings to meet task-oriented and geographical requirements for the Unified CINCs.

Continuing our list of changes and initiatives, we are:

- Removing A–6 aircraft from the active inventory by the end of fiscal year 1997.
- Updating our most critical weapon systems such as the F/A–18, F–14, AV–8, E–2, and EA–6B, as well as incorporating safety and survivability upgrades to all aircraft.
- Recognizing the virtues and flexibility of carrier based air forces, we are integrating four Marine F/A–18 strike fighter squadrons and a Marine EA–6B Prowler squadron into Navy carrier air wings. In turn, we will provide Navy aircraft to support Marine commitments where necessary. That we

can even contemplate doing this is strong testimony to the adaptability and professionalism of our Marine Naval Aviators and maintenance personnel.
• Supporting a variety of options for basing Navy and Marine Corps EA-6B squadrons in carrying out their critical emergent tasking as our Nation's tactical electronic warfare force.
• Emphasizing Joint Systems Development to support multi-mission aircraft and deploy weapon systems such as the Joint Advanced Strike Technology (JAST) Program, Joint Primary Aircraft Training System (JPATS), Joint Direct Attack Munitions (JDAM), Joint Standoff Weapon (JSOW), and the Joint Air to Surface Standoff Missile (JASSM).
• Expanding the roles and responsibilities of the H-60 helicopter series aircraft and moving toward a common SH-60 series.
• Reducing the Maritime Patrol forces to a level of 12 active and 8 reserve squadrons. This recognizes the reduced ASW threat, and allows us to retire older P-3B aircraft in our Reserve force and replace them with P-3Cs in order to avoid significant operating and maintenance costs.
• Adjusting pilot training rates to account for force structure reductions while reducing aircrew training pools.
• Making aggressive, yet sound, infrastructure reductions, including single-siting all tactical aviation Fleet Readiness Squadron (FRS) with the exception of the F/A-18 community which will remain at three FRSs.
• Continued active use of the reserve force which was recently tasked to provide a USNR EA-6B aircraft and crews aboard aircraft carriers off-shore Bosnia.

AIRCRAFT PROCUREMENT PLAN

Aircraft Procurement, Navy (APN) provides aircraft, spares, modifications, and support equipment for the diverse missions of Naval Aviation. Aircraft force structure and modernization have focused on multi-mission aircraft to meet Major Regional Conflicts (MRCs). All F/A-18 Series, F-14, H-60 series, E-2C, MV-22, P-3, S-3, ES-3, EA-6B and AV-8B have been, and remain high priority platforms. Of concern, the average age of all Naval aircraft continues to increase, achieving 17.4 years by fiscal year 2000. Our APN account addresses the force level requirements of 10 active and 1 reserve carrier air wings, 12 active and 8 reserve MPA squadrons, 3 active and 1 reserve USMC aircraft wings, and all Naval Aviation supporting aircraft. Our APN modifications account also will cover the USAF EF-111A EW replacement requirements with USN/USMC EA-6Bs. Funding for Vertical Replenishment (VERTREP) mission replacement helicopters is programmed late in the FYDP. We will also begin studies to determine a common follow-on airframe called the Common Support Aircraft, or CSA, to replace the S-3, ES-3, E-2, and C-2 aircraft.

The Navy Department's aircraft procurement budget submission for fiscal year 1997 is $5.88 billion and is based on realistic defense spending projections. Of this amount, the budget provides $3.4 billion for procurement of 40 aircraft in fiscal year 1997 which includes the remanufacture of 10 AV-8Bs as well as modifications and upgrades to other aircraft. The Navy budget rationale for aircraft procurement is based on our continued strategy to "neck-down" to two primary tactical strike aircraft, the F/A-18E/F Series and the F-14, and our long-term strategy to achieve an air wing composition of F/A-18E/Fs and the JAST derived Joint Strike Fighter (JSF).

NAVAL AVIATION STRIKE FORCE PLAN

Clearly, the programming challenge for Naval Aviation is to restructure our forces for the 21st Century in an era of scarce defense resources, to balance force structure with modernization, re-capitalization and readiness requirements and, most importantly, to avoid a hollow force structure. Past budget cuts and downsizing plans for the Department of the Navy, coupled with the redefinition of the Navy's air power role as described in "Forward . . . from the Sea" forced us to review the structure of our carrier-based strike force.

To remain within budget limits while maintaining the best possible fighting force on our forward deployed carriers and to maintain the unique power projection capability from the sea that separates us from other services, we are eliminating an entire type/model/series aircraft the A-6E. To partially offset this loss of key warfighting capability until the arrival of the Navy's next generation strike aircraft, the F/A-18E/F and JSF, we are continuing modest strike upgrades as well as safety and survivability modifications to the F-14 aircraft. The proposed combat lethality and survivability modifications will enable a safe and effective, day/night smart weapon strike capability, fulfilling the Tomcat's potential as a self-escorting, multi mission aircraft. F–14 precision strike upgrades will incorporate a FLIR/laser guided bomb capability which has already proved to be a force multiplier in the Bosnia peacekeeping efforts. These changes will result in a multi mission carrier strike force of F–14s and USN/USMC F/A–18s and which expands the flexibility of our air wings and greatly enhance combat capabilities. Now I will briefly discuss our strike aircraft recapitalization for the 21st Century.

CARRIER BASED AIR (F/A–18E/F & JAST)

An indispensable part of this recapitalization is the development and fielding of two platforms—the F/A–18E/F Super Hornet and the JSF. Together, these two aircraft will provide future Battle Group and Joint Force Commanders the flexibility to deal with any crisis in an uncertain threat environment. The F/A–18E/F is our highest warfighting priority in Naval Aviation. It is a significant improvement to the demonstrated, combat proven excellence of the current F/A–18C/Ds being flown by our Navy and Marine Corps aircrews. Despite its proven combat capability, the C/D is approaching some limitations in the future battle space that the E/F will correct. These include: limited mission radius & endurance, insufficient carrier recovery payload, vulnerability in high threat scenarios and, most importantly, extremely limited potential for growth and flexibility—the key to exploiting full combat effectiveness from our future precision air launched weapons.

The F–18E/F will greatly expand on the proven capabilities of the C/D model as well as provide 90 percent commonality with C/D avionics, software, and weapon carriage. Mission radius will increase by 35 percent, endurance by 50 percent, and weapons carriage by 22 percent. The F/A–18E/F will carry an additional 3600 pounds of internal fuel, increasing target coverage by 52 percent. It will increase carrier recovery payload to 9,000 pounds, a significant improvement in payload flexibility and bring back. The Super Hornet has enhanced self-protection capabilities through a balanced investment in signature reduction and self defense systems, increasing survivability by one order of magnitude. The E/F is optimized for high intensity power projection operations from both carriers and expeditionary airfields. In addition, an aerial refueling buddy store capability is included for added strike package flexibility. The FA–18E/F program is on schedule, on cost and is executable within the Congressionally imposed RDT&E cap of $4.88 billion. The first flight was flown in November, 1995 and the F/A–18E/F Program Team recently received the very first DOD Acquisition Excellence Award from Dr. Kaminski.

The JAST development is a joint Navy, Marine, and Air Force effort initiated to serve as DOD's focal point for defining future strike systems. The JAST program will identify, promote, and demonstrate key leveraging technologies for the reduction of life cycle costs for each services' next generation strike-fighter aircraft. The JAST derived Joint Strike Fighter (JSF) will complement the F/A–18 E/F and will allow the Navy to transition to two tactical aircraft types. The JAST program Concept Demonstration Phase will commence in early fiscal year 1997 with competitive award of two contracts for ground and flight demonstrations. The Navy is firmly committed to JAST as the key to fulfilling both the Navy's requirement for a "first day survivable, stand-alone, strike-fighter" and the Marine Corps' requirement to replace both their AV–8s and F/A–18s with a highly capable ASTOVL aircraft.

Together, the Super Hornet and JSF will optimize tactical Naval Aviation for the new direction envisioned in "Forward . . . From the Sea." They provide a flexible and dominant capability for any contingency. The cooperative interaction of these multi-role aircraft in the AAW role will ensure battle space dominance. Power projection is optimized by their unprecedented sortie generation rate and strike firepower in concert with other joint forces. Force sustainment is enhanced by the high reliability and survivability of both the E/F and the JSF. The F/A–18E/F and JSF are precisely the type of aircraft required to execute our Navy and Marine Corps strategy well into the 21st Century.

V–22

As the Marine Corps' top aviation priority, the MV–22 is an integral component of our recapitalization plans. In order to conduct Operational Maneuver From The Sea (OMFTS), amphibious forces must be able to project forces inland at great distances from the shore, and continue to maneuver flexibly once over land. The MV–22 provides the precise solution to the problem of an aging H–46 fleet and meets the Marine Corps' requirement for Medium Lift. It represents significant improvement in comparison to current rotary wing technology and will provide the battlefield commander with increased tactical mobility, range, speed, and survivability. It will replace both the CH–46E and CH–53D, providing increased passenger and payload capacity, as well as increased growth potential for emerging missions.

TACTICAL AIRCRAFT MODERNIZATION

A centerpiece of Naval Aviation is a robust modernization program which enables us to maintain our warfighting edge. In addition to combat capability improvements, modernization allows us to incorporate new technology in our older platforms which increases their safety, reliability, effectiveness, and maintainability. Our primary modernization efforts are focused on the following platforms: the F–14, AV–8B, E–2C, P–3C, and EA–6B.

As discussed earlier, the F–14 aircraft will continue to be upgraded to partially compensate for the loss of the A–6 strike capability and to bridge the gap to an FA–18E/F and JSF carrier air wing. All necessary safety, structural, survivability, and interoperability improvements will be made simultaneously with the "precision strike" capability upgrade. This day/night precision strike capability (FLIR/laser) will significantly increase the number of true multi-mission aircraft available to the force commander and will add great flexibility to air wing operations.

To increase our Marines' expeditionary capabilities, the Department has embarked on a limited AV–8B remanufacture program that will provide 72 upgraded aircraft. This will enhance USMC night fighting/close air support capability, as well as provide inherent improvements in safety, reliability, and maintainability. The first aircraft was delivered in January of this year.

The E–2C aircraft continues to be a carrier battle group command and control mainstay and force multiplier. The E–2C Group II modernization program will enable the Navy to meet AEW mission requirement to 2015 and beyond, and will upgrade radar range and processing, connectivity, as well as incorporate GPS and structural and avionics improvements. Further improvements, including the addition of TMD Enabling Cooperative Engagement Capability (CEC) and Mission Computer Upgrades, will increase the overall mission capability of the aircraft.

In recognition of an ever present foreign submarine threat and in working to improve our capability to meet Unified CINCs' requirements, the Navy Department has developed a modernization plan for our Maritime Patrol force. Our plan sustains operational capability, reduces multiple configurations, and provides system upgrades. A key element of the program is the Sustained Readiness Program (SRP) which will extend the projected operational airframe life of the P–3C an average of 8 years. We are investigating additional options to safely and effectively extend the service life of the aircraft to 48 years. We also continue the conversion of the P–3C aircraft to one common fleet configuration, Update III. To ensure that the P–3C will remain highly effective in joint littoral and battle group operations, the Department also plans to modify a part of the force with an enhanced Antisurface Warfare Improvement Program (AIP), consisting of command, control and surveillance capabilities.

Our Nation's tactical jamming asset, the EA–6B, is an aircraft that remains the premier tactical electronic warfare platform in the world. Projected to be in the inventory until 2015, ICAP II (Block 89A) will require an upgrade planned to begin in 1998. Based on the Lower Cost Alternative to ADVCAP Study, planned modifications will address aircraft structure and supportability, as well as enhanced warfighting capabilities, including a receiver upgrade. Beginning this year, the EA–6B will assume the role of standoff jammer for the Air Force, as well as for the Navy and Marine Corps, totally replacing the EF–111A by the end of fiscal year 1998. A Tri-Service Memorandum of Understanding covering this transition is due for signature by the Service Chiefs this month.

These key modernization programs, in conjunction with our new procurement plans, will result in a tremendous amount of capability for our forward deployed forces. They will ensure that Naval Aviation maintains its robust spectrum of crisis and warfighting capabilities in support of the Unified CINCs.

AIRCRAFT CARRIERS

Despite all the post-cold war changes to our National and Naval Strategy, one element of our national security policy that has not changed is our continued reliance upon aircraft carriers. Each one of them represents "four and one half acres of American sovereignty," able to range over 70 percent of the earth's surface and to rapidly respond to regional crises. Our aircraft carriers with their embarked air wings are, and will continue to be, the centerpiece of the United States Navy. Since last year, we have again witnessed the utility of the aircraft carrier in our enforcement of the UN no-fly zones over the Adriatic Sea and the Balkans. Their participation in NATO air strikes in Bosnia was central to bringing the warring factions to the peace table. Most recently, our nation's response to increasing tensions in the Taiwan Straits was the stabilizing effect of immediately sending an aircraft carrier battle group with another on the way. In order to continue to meet National tasking with a carrier force level of 12 (11 active and 1 reserve/training), it is essential that follow-on planning for the next carrier begin now. Presently, a study of alternative aircraft carrier concepts for the 21st Century is being planned to develop and assess a range of affordable technologies for future design aircraft carriers. In support of near and long term plans, the Future Carrier Project will define, develop and evaluate the key technologies for incorporation in future aircraft carrier platform design concepts (CVX) that will support deploying tactical Naval aviation in the future. Our ability to continue to provide the National Command Authority with a wide range of tailored response options in future crises rests on maintaining a modern and highly capable aircraft carrier fleet. They are the key to sovereign combat operations and crisis response throughout the oceans and seas of the world.

WEAPONS MODERNIZATION

The same focused strategy that applies to aircraft procurement also pertains to our procurement of future weapons. Of specific note, nearly all future weapons will be jointly procured. Currently under development are two new families of precision guided weapons: the Joint Direct Attack Munition (JDAM) and the Joint Standoff Weapon (JSOW). These two programs are designed to significantly increase capability with precision accuracy and survivability with standoff, as well as to reduce the types of weapons in the Navy's inventory.

With the cancellation of Tri-Service Standoff Attack Missile (TSSAM), we are also rapidly proceeding with a retrofit program to provide significant survivability and performance improvements. We are using the existing inventory of the Navy's only long-range, man-in-the-loop, air-launched standoff missile. The Standoff Land Attack Missile-Expanded Response (SLAM–ER) will provide precision strike against fixed, high value land targets and ships in port. Development of the Joint Air-to-Surface Standoff Missile (JASSM) will also provide a Standoff Outside Area Defense (SOAD) weapon that can attack heavily defended, high value, time sensitive targets.

Additionally, we continue to integrate our precision strike weapons development efforts with our Intelligence, Surveillance and Reconnaissance (ISR) and C4I plans. This information integration will help to achieve synergism amongst all of the elements which comprise the Sensor-to-Shooter architecture developed by the Services and Joint Staff and which was recently approved by the Joint Requirements Oversight Council (JROC).

RESERVE FORCE INTEGRATION

With downsizing of the active forces, it has become even more necessary and critical to increase the contribution of our Naval Reserve forces to Naval Aviation. Our goal has been to expand the reserve mission from a mobilization force to one that is actively contributing to the daily operation of fleet missions. As a result, today Naval Air Reserve forces are more closely integrated with their active counterparts and providing more daily fleet support than at any time in fleet history.

PERSONNEL

Undoubtedly, the changes caused by reducing and reorganizing our forces cause turmoil and a certain amount of consternation among our fine Naval Aviation people. I want to emphasize that these people are clearly our most important asset. They make the machines of technology work, and work well. We are not making reductions and changes to force structure without carefully considering the impact on our people. Every possible consideration has been given to transitioning personnel from those aviation communities most affected by force structure reductions to other aircraft communities. We have, for the most part, been very successful in doing this. Naval Aviation is the better for integrating fresh perspectives and ideas across aircraft community lines into traditional ways of doing business. We are absolutely committed to retaining, training and promoting our best and brightest. We remain committed to avoiding involuntary reductions in forces as we finish what has been the greatest changes in Naval Aviation in over 40 years. TRAINING

In consonance with our commitment to our people, we are also committed to preserving a quality training program. Underscored by our continued success in recent operations, highly trained and motivated professionals remain the linchpin of a responsive, viable, and lethal force. As our force structure changes, we will continue to balance our program with the proper mix of classroom, simulation, and operational training. Technology and jointness offer efficiencies in these areas, and we intend to take full advantage of them. In the evolutionary process of maintaining a quality training program for aviation professionals, we allow our best and brightest men and women to achieve their full potential. We have accepted the challenges inherent in a much more technologically advanced force, and our training programs emphasize innovative computer technologies required by combat in the information age.

SUMMARY

In summary, we are committed to maintaining robust Navy and Marine Corps expeditionary forces fully capable of operating "Forward . . . From the Sea." By capturing the savings realized by program reductions and selecting high priority investments, we will continue our procurement and modernization strategies. Through these efforts, we will ensure that Naval Aviation will always be a force in readiness, a forward force, able to respond with flexibility and lethal precision. By careful investment in emerging technology, we will take advantage of the ongoing revolution in military affairs—a revolution that we recognize is as much about people as it is about machines.

Naval Aviation has made extraordinary contributions to our national security in the past, and we will continue to do so for the foreseeable future. In partnership with out sister services and with the sustained support of Congress, we will continue to ensure that our Navy/Marine aviation forces lead the way, flexibly, affordably and, most importantly, successfully.

STATEMENT OF REAR ADM. CRAIG STEIDLE, USN, DIRECTOR, ADVANCED STRIKE TECHNOLOGY PROGRAM

Admiral STEIDLE. Good morning, sir. I am Craig Steidle. I am the Program Director for the JAST program. Sir, I thank you very much for your invitation to be here to discuss the Joint Advanced Strike Technology Program, a program that has just transitioned to the Joint Strike Fighter Program.

Because it has been so dynamic, I have a short, brief statement. I also have a more detailed longer version I will submit, sir.

Senator WARNER. All statements in their entirety will be admitted to the record, and you may proceed with your short statement.

Admiral STEIDLE. Thank you.

Sir, we have matured from the JAST program and are now converging on an affordable solution that meets the requirements of all three services plus our allies—the Navy, Marine Corps, and the Air Force, as well as our allies. Specific focus on the program remains affordability, reducing the development costs, production costs, costs of ownership of the joint strike fighter family of airplanes.

We fully merged the Advanced Research and Project Agency's ASTOVL—advanced short takeoff and vertical landing program—into the joint strike fighter program, and additionally the United Kingdom Royal Navy has joined the program as a collaborative partner. They are committing $200 million to the program in accordance with an MOU that signed in December of 1995. Interest has been extremely high in other foreign countries. We have provided several different briefings, and I expect the interest to continue at a high level.

The program focuses on a new approach for weapons systems acquisition. We applied the recommendations of the Packard Commission and other experts in acquisition reform. We created an environment that provides early interaction between the war-fighters and the technologists, in order to be able to make cost and performance trades early. That has been a significant part of the program. We have done this by utilizing the integrated product development team process. Industry is a full partner in this process, and they welcome this tremendously. They have been very positive in our process and in our way of doing business.

The first formal product that came out of this integrated industry war-fighter technologist group continuing relationship was our initial requirements document that was signed by all three services last August, and was submitted and approved and endorsed by the JROC in August of last year.

We continue to be the role model for acquisition reform and streamlining, a lot of initiatives in coherence with our industrial partner. We are just completing the concept definition phase. We will finish that phase this summer, and then move on into the concept development phase where we will downsize from three teams that we have today to two teams. Each one of the teams will build demonstrators demonstrating commonality, hovering transition, flying qualities, as well as continue with our research and development technology maturation programs.

Each one of the contractors will demonstrate two aircraft, and demonstrate the particular attributes that I just mentioned. In conclusion, sir, we strongly——

Senator WARNER. Let us stop a minute. That is a total of what, six aircraft?

Admiral STEIDLE. No, sir. That will be two aircraft. We will downsize to two concept development teams, and each one of those teams will fly two airplanes each.

Senator WARNER. So that is four?

Admiral STEIDLE. Yes, sir. Four airplanes. Yes, sir.

In my concluding remarks, sir, the services stand extremely committed to the program, as does OSD and industry, and I stand by to answer any of your questions, sir.

[The prepared statement of Admiral Steidle follows:]

PREPARED STATEMENT BY REAR ADM. CRAIG STEIDLE

INTRODUCTION

Mr. Chairman and distinguished members of the subcommittee, I appreciate your invitation to present the Joint Strike Fighter Program (JSF), formally the Joint Advanced Strike Technology (JAST) Program. I will highlight key aspects of the program and describe how we are converging on an *affordable* solution to meet the next generation strike warfare needs of the Air Force, Navy, Marine Corps and our allies. The specific focus of the program is affordability—reducing the development cost, production cost and cost of ownership of the Joint Strike Fighter family of aircraft.

BACKGROUND

The Secretary of Defense's Bottom-Up Review (BUR) in fiscal year 1994 acknowledged the Services' need to replace their aging strike assets in order to maintain the Nation's combat technological edge. The JAST Program was consequently established as the focal point for defining *affordable* next generation strike aircraft weapon systems for the USAF, USN, and USMC and our allies. The program is chartered under the signatures of the Secretary of the Navy, Secretary of the Air Force, and the Deputy Secretary of Defense. The program is jointly manned and funded. I became Program Director last summer, replacing Lt. Gen. George Muellner, and the Service Acquisition Executive role then shifted from the Navy to the Air Force. My deputy is an Air Force g r l officer (select) who will take over the program when I leave and report to the Navy Acquisition Executive. This program structure ensures strong program support and balanced input from both Departments.

Subsequent fiscal year 1995 legislation merged the Advanced Research Projects Agency (ARPA) Advanced Short Take-off and Vertical Landing (ASTOVL) program with the JAST Program, and ARPA now also provides personnel and funding for JAST Program execution. The United Kingdom Royal Navy is also participating in the JAST Program, extending a collaboration begun under the ARPA ASTOVL program. They are committing $200 million to the program in accordance with the terms of a Memorandum of Understanding (MOU) signed in December 1995. Numerous other countries have expressed interest in the program, and I expect foreign participation to increase.

Due to the structural age-out of the F–14 and the F–16 and the expected attrition of the AV–SB, the JAST Program is designed to support transition to Engineering and Manufacturing Development (E&MD) of the Joint Strike Fighter in fiscal year 2001. First deliveries of operational aircraft are planned in 2008. Attachment 1 summarizes the Services' mission needs that will be met by the JSF.

PROGRAM STRATEGY

This program forges a new approach to weapon systems acquisition. In designing the JAST Program, we applied recommendations voiced by the Packard and Carnegie Commissions and other experts on Acquisition Reform. We created an environment that provides early interaction between the warfighter and developer to ensure cost versus performance trades are made early when they can most influence weapon system cost. Our strategy recognizes that key technologies must be adequately demonstrated before entering E&MD in order to reduce development risk and control cost. We understand that to significantly reduce the cost of our weapon systems, we must learn from the commercial sector and apply specific technologies aimed at reducing cost as well as increasing performance. Finally, we are meeting the Deputy Secretary of Defense's challenge to be the catalyst in implementing acquisition reform and streamlining within the aerospace industry.

PROGRAM PROCESS

The JAST Program office, working with the requirements staffs from the Air Force, Navy, Marine Corps, and the United Kingdom, and teamed with industry, is facilitating requirements definition efforts. The JAST Program Integrated Product Teams of warfighters and technologists use the disciplined strategy-to-task process supported by an extensive underpinning of Modeling, Simulation and Analysis to help the Services evaluate joint strike warfare needs and potential solutions to meeting those needs. This process permits development of a set of requirements with maximum focus on jointness and consistent with technology's ability to support them affordably. I would like to point out that industry is a full participant on these teams and their response has been overwhelmingly positive. We have run three Major Regional Conflict campaign level simulations. Over 90 representatives from government and industry participated in each of these exercises.

The first formal product of the requirements definition process was the Joint Initial Requirements Document (JIRD), signed by all of the participating Services and briefed to the Joint Requirements Oversight Council (JROC) in late summer. The JROC endorsed the JAST process and "family of aircraft" strategy and emphasized "the great potential towards achieving an affordable solution to meet our joint warfighting capability." Completion of the Services' Joint Operational Requirements Document (JORD) is anticipated in fiscal year 1998.

Numerous Technology Maturation demonstrations in leveraging areas are being pursued to reduce risk prior to entering E&MD and lower the Life Cycle Cost of the JSF family of aircraft. At the outset of this program we reviewed and catalogued over 585 technology programs and used that information in formulating our initial investment plan. We continue to refine our Technology Maturation investment plans based on the results of our cost and performance trades. We have contracted for multiple technology demonstrations that will enable us to quantify the savings and technical efficiencies of specific initiatives. JAST demonstration results are made available to all of our industry participants. Achievement of affordability objectives for the prime contractors preferred weapon system concepts depends on availability of these technologies for platform incorporation in E&MD and production. Some examples of successful demonstrations to date include:

- Carrier suitability of tailless configurations evaluated using the X–31 aircraft
- J–1,000 improved capabilities in an advanced penetration weapon
- Virtual manufacturing—reduces the manufacturing cycle time and cost; validated by real-world application (F–15 Class II frame change)
- Virtual maintenance trainer technology—Virtual Environment trainer will reduce redundancy and increase simulator commonality
- Avionics demonstrations of shared apertures, Virtual Avionics Prototypes, and software common applications.

On-going demonstrations with high technical and affordability payoffs include:

- JAST/Integrated Subsystems Technology (J/IST)—will demonstrate aircraft weight savings (over 1000 pounds) and increased durability due to in-

tegrating aircraft functions such as heating/cooling, power generation and distribution, and aircraft control functions presently controlled by separate subsystems
• Advanced Lightweight Aircraft Fuselage Structure (ALAFS)—will demonstrate weight and cost savings of 20 percent and 30 percent, respectively, based on innovations in advanced composite materials structural design and manufacturing processes for improved fabrication and assembly
• Multi-function Integrated RF Systems (MIRFS)—will demonstrate a light weight, low cost multi-function array which supports radar and other sensor functions.

The JAST Program continues its role as a leader in the area of DOD acquisition streamlining and reform and use of "paperless" processes. We are encouraging the use of commercial standards and best practices in weapon systems development; teaming with industry to create a common cost model to improve government and industry understanding of weapon system life cycle cost; and will minimize the number of contractor deliverables through on-line access to the contractors' management systems. We continue to emphasize electronic processes as the standard means of communication. We have an extensive database which exploits the Internet for efficient, real-time dissemination of program information including information related to program procurement solicitations. Response from Industry, Academia and Government continues to be extremely enthusiastic.

PROGRAM STATUS

The program schedule is provided as Attachment 2. We are nearing completion of our *Concept Development Phase*. This phase focused on (a) developing designs that take advantage of the "family of aircraft" concept and (b) defining the necessary leveraging technology demonstrations that will lower risk prior to entering E&MD of the JSF. The "family of aircraft" concept allows a high level of commonality while satisfying unique service needs. Our Concept Exploration Phase results underscored the possibility and benefit of commonality as a viable means for achieving significant savings in next generation strike aircraft. Concept Development Phase efforts have ratified the conclusion of the program's competing weapon system contractors that a *family of aircraft can meet tri-service needs*, with overall significant Life Cycle Cost savings. The degree of commonality varies with individual contractor designs. This approach brings with it the cost benefits of a common Depot, commonly supported logistics trail, and increased joint service interoperability.

PROGRAM PLANS

The *Concept Demonstration* Phase commences in early fiscal year 1997 following the competitive down select from three potential weapon system concept teams to two—the Request for Proposals will be released in the near future. This phase will feature flying concept demonstrators, concept unique ground and flight demonstrations, and continued refinement of the contractors' preferred weapon system concepts. Specifically, the two winning contractor teams will demonstrate commonality and modularity, Short Take-off and Vertical Landing (STOVL) hover and transition, and low speed handling qualities of their concepts. Risk mitigating Technology Maturation demonstrations will continue as well.

Let me describe the acquisition strategy for this phase of the program. This fall we will competitively award two weapon system concept demonstration contracts. Each winning contractor team defines those demonstrations it believes are crucial for its concept vis a vis providing concept assessment and insuring a low risk technology transition to E&MD. All three of the JAST Program weapon system prime contractors independently selected either the basic or a derivative of the Pratt and Whitney F119 as the cruise engine for their Preferred Weapons System Concepts and demonstrator aircraft. We will therefore award a contract to Pratt and Whitney to provide hardware and engineering support for the Weapon System Concept Demonstration efforts. We will also award a propulsion contract to General Electric for technical efforts related to development of an alternate engine source for production.

Each contractor team will produce two demonstrator aircraft; one aircraft from each team will demonstrate the STOVL concept. Aircraft designations have already been assigned—X–32A, B, and C and X–35A, B, and C, denoting two concepts with variants for the USN, USAF, and USMC. The concept demonstration approach is depicted in Attachment 3. This strategy has several advantages:

(1) it maintains the competitive environment prior to E&MD and provides for two different STOVL approaches and two different aerodynamic configurations

(2) it provides for the demonstration of the viability of a multi-service family of variants—high commonality and modularity between conventional take-off and landing (CTOL), aircraft carrier capable (CV), and STOVL variants is expected

(3) it provides affordable and low risk technology transition to the JSF E&MD in fiscal year 2001.

This phase of the JAST Program will complete the foundation the Joint Strike Fighter program will build on beginning in fiscal year 2001 when E&MD for a single, affordable family of multi-service variants commences.

SUMMARY

In conclusion, the Services remain strongly committed to this joint program to develop an affordable solution to their future strike warfare needs—the Joint Strike Fighter. The government and industry team is converging on a design concept for a family of strike aircraft weapon systems which, coupled with the other technology "building blocks," will yield continued technological superiority for our warfighters but much more affordably. As we prepare to meet the fiscal and threat demands of the next century, the Department of Defense clearly recognizes that we must optimize our tactical air modernization and focus on jointness and commonality. The Joint Strike Fighter will achieve these goals (Attachment 4).

Mr. Chairman, that concludes my statement. I stand ready to answer your questions.

SERVICE NEEDS

- USN
  - FIRST DAY OF WAR, SURVIVABLE STRIKE FIGHTER AIRCRAFT TO COMPLEMENT THE F/A-18E/F

- USAF
  - MULTIROLE AIRCRAFT (PRIMARY A/G) TO REPLACE THE F-16 AND A-10

- USMC
  - ASTOVL AIRCRAFT TO REPLACE THE AV-8B AND F/A-18

- ROYAL NAVY
  - SUPERSONIC REPLACEMENT FOR THE SEA HARRIER

Attachment

JSF PROGRAM SCHEDULE

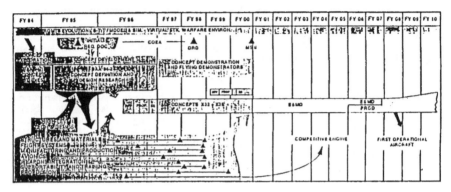

CONCEPT DEMONSTRATION APPROACH

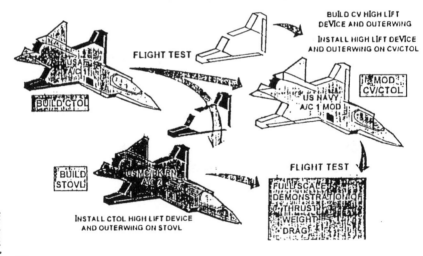

TACAIR ROADMAP

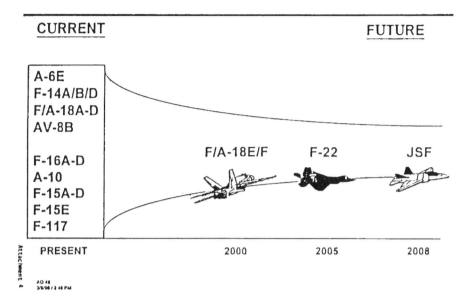

CURRENT			FUTURE

A-6E
F-14A/B/D
F/A-18A-D
AV-8B

F-16A-D
A-10
F-15A-D
F-15E
F-117

F/A-18E/F   F-22   JSF

PRESENT   2000   2005   2008

AO 48
3/8/96 / 3 48 PM

Senator WARNER. One of the questions I will ask, and I was going to send this up so you could read it if you have not, I am sure you have read the New York Times article.

Admiral STEIDLE. Yes, sir, I have.

Senator WARNER. I am going to ask you momentarily if you would sort of give us a side-by-side as to it appears to me to be very well written and researched, but since it is a significant piece on this article, and I commend the paper and the writer, I want to make sure our record shows any areas in which you as the manager disagree.

Admiral STEIDLE. Yes, sir.

Senator WARNER. Do you have it there?

Admiral STEIDLE. No, sir, I do not, but I do remember the article.

Senator WARNER. Well, I will tell you what I will do, I will get it reproduced for you and sent right up there.

Admiral STEIDLE. Thank you.

Senator WARNER. General.

STATEMENT OF BRIG. GEN. ROBERT MAGNUS, USMC, ASSISTANT DEPUTY CHIEF OF STAFF FOR AVIATION

General MAGNUS. Mr. Chairman, Senator, good morning. I thank you for the opportunity to appear before you to discuss Marine Corps tactical aviation. I also have, in addition to the formal statement, some short opening remarks which I would prefer to submit for the record, and I would like to also add that on behalf of the strong support of the Congress and the people of the United States, the Marine Corps has always been ready, whether it is forward deployed or on bases in the United States, to continue to be America's 9–1–1 force.

In addition to the forward-deployed forces that Admiral McGinn has mentioned and of course my Air Force wing man has around the world, today you have Marines and F-18B's and EA-6B's poised in Aviano to support American and allied forces in Bosnia. There are Marine forces forward deployed in Okinawa and on the main islands of Japan, ready to support contingencies there.

Senator WARNER. I met the Marines in Aviano on my last trip there.

General MAGNUS. Yes, sir. There are Marines embarked on amphibious ships across the globe supporting the carrier battle forces with our Vietnam era helicopters, prepared to do the Nation's bidding. All I can say to echo our commandant is readiness is our business, and we stand by to answer your questions.

[The prepared statement of General Blot follows:]

PREPARED STATEMENT BY LT. GEN. HAROLD W. BLOT

INTRODUCTION

Mr. Chairman and distinguished members of the Subcommittee, I thank you for the opportunity to appear before you to discuss Marine Corps Tactical Aviation and our plan for aircraft procurement in fiscal year 1997. Our portion of the Presidential Budget submit balances acquisition of combat-proven weapons systems with the upgrading of existing systems for economy, while developing new technologies to fight on and above tomorrow's battlefields.

The end of the Cold War may have changed life for some in the business of national defense, but the Marine Corps' daily tasks have altered little. You see proof of this in the way in which—and the tools by which—your Corps operates. In short, we're still the same "Force in Readiness"—popularly coined as the Nation's "911 Force"—Congress rescribed in law over four decades ago—albeit a little smaller, a little leaner and—as a result, your Marines are much busier. Deterrence of aggression, peacekeeping, containment of regional conflicts, assistance in international drug interdiction, humanitarian assistance, and domestic emergency relief are continuing demands. The Marine Corps has been mandated by Congress to be the most ready when the Nation generally is least ready—and the Marine Corps carries that weighty responsibility proudly. The Marine Corps is foremost an expeditionary force-in-readiness which provides a unique capability that combines air, land, and naval forces from the sea—the Marine Air-Ground Task Force (MAGTF). In preparing Marine Corps Aviation for its future missions, we recognize the need to retain capability and credibility across the full spectrum of contingencies by striving to maintain the combat advantage generated by superior mobility, flexibility, lethality, and speed. As we concentrate on achieving a high return for our investment dollars, major programs of interest to Marine Aviation in the fiscal year 1997 Budget Request include:

MS-22 (OSPREY)

The MV-22 OSPREY remains the Marine Corps' highest acquisition priority and is necessary to implement our doctrine of Operational Maneuver from the Sea. Recognizing the tremendous operational advantages of such an innovation, the Marines have long championed the development of tilt rotor technology. The advent of the MV-22 can be compared in importance with previous capability advances associated with the first helicopter and the jet engine. The MV-22 gives our Marine Air Ground Task Forces improved strategic and tactical mobility to fly significantly farther and faster with a far greater payload than our current aging fleet of medium lift CH-46E/CH-53D helicopters.

In terms of strategic mobility, the advantages are numerous; self-deployability (2100 NM with one aerial refueling), faster Maritime Prepositioning Force closure, and a reduced deployment footprint. Tactically, the s eed, combat radius, payload and survivability features of the tilt rotor will greatly expand the maneuver space of the sea, allow greater stand-off distances, provide greater operational tempo, and will reduce both the operational risk and, most of all, friendly casualties in battle. This combat multiplier allows Marines to strike deeper in the littoral and allows Navy ships adequate stand-off distance for response to shore-to-ship missiles, underwater mines, and other developing threats.

In today's regional environment, the expeditionary Marine is the most cost-effective deterrent we have. As a result, the support our Marines receive must be as comprehensive as possible to fight and win on tomorrow's battlefield. With the arrival of the MV-22 in the Fleet Marine Force, this unique American technology will provide the decisive edge needed to prevail against the increasing sophistication of regional aggressors.

The joint V-22 program is a success story. Unit recurring cost is down 23 percent over the past year and expected to be further reduced as production efficiencies are achieved. Additionally, the aircraft has completed over 1,080 flight hours and 948 flights of development risk reduction flight testing and envelope expansion. Currently, the MV-22 is 489 pounds under its projected design weight, has lower projected drag, higher projected reliability and maintainability, and meets or exceeds all of the Joint Requirements Oversight Council approved Key Performance Parameters for both the USMC MV-22 and the USSOCOM/USAF CV-22 aircraft. Long-lead procurement for the first low rate initial production (LRIP) will be approved by the Defense Department, contingent upon meeting the relevant exit criteria. LRIP is scheduled to begin in 1997, with deliveries commencing in 1999. Initial Operating Capability (IOC) of the MV-22 for the Marine Corps is scheduled to occur in fiscal year 2001. While the current program is constrained by a very low rate of procurement, consideration should be given to the significant saving and production efficiencies to be gained by investing in a higher procurement rate for the MV-22.

AV-8B (HARRIER) REMANUFACTURE

The MAGTF has limited organic artillery and tanks and relies heavily on its complementary aviation assets. The AV-8B's Short Take Off/Vertical Landing (STOVL) design gives it the capability to operate from a variety of land and sea-based areas to provide additional fire support. The Harriers will remain in service until replacement by the STOVL variant of the Joint Strike Fighter (JSF) which will begin in 2008, with an IOC about 2010. Current production AV-8Bs are built to the radar/night attack standard, which incorporates an improved engine, and the APG-65 multi mode radar. The AV-8B is undergoing a remanufacture program in which 72 older "day attack" aircraft will be rebuilt to the current radar/night attack standard at only 77 percent of the cost of a new aircraft. The STOVL capability of the AV-8B is well suited to the needs of expeditionary forces, both ashore and from the sea. The addition of night attack and radar capabilities will allow the AV-8B to be responsive to the needs of the MAGTF for expeditionary, night, adverse weather offensive air support. The seventy-two (72) day attack aircraft programmed to be remanufactured though fiscal year 2001 will add increased capability, reliability and operational safety to the overall AV-8B program and the MAGTF.

CH-53E (SUPER STALLION)

In the 1995 Defense bill, the 103rd Congress provided the latitude and flexibility to use appropriated funds to procure CH-53E heavy helicopters. This action avoided closing America's only heavy helicopter production line. In the 1996 Defense Bill, Congress provided National Guard and Reserve Equipment Account (NG&REA) funds for the procurement of two heavy helicopters for the Marine Corps Reserve. These new aircraft will replace the aging 23-year old, medium lift RH-53D's we currently operate in the Marine Reserves. Based on the Congressional support as expressed in the fiscal year 1996 NG&REA funding, the Marine Corps will initiate the stand-up of the first of two Reserve CH-53E heavy helicopter squadrons this summer.

AH-1W (COBRA) MID-LIFE UPGRADE

The AH-1W Super Cobra is a two place, tandem seat, attack helicopter. The aircraft is capable of carrying a versatile mix of ordnance which includes: Hellfire, TOW, Sidewinder, Sidearm, 20mm turreted gun, and assorted rockets. The aircraft's missions include rotary-wing close air support (CAS), enroute escort/protection of assault helicopters, landing zone preparation and fire suppression, anti-armor and anti-helicopter defense, as well as command and control of supporting arms. The AH-1W is currently being equipped with the Night Targeting System (NTS), which incorporates a three field-of-view forward looking infrared (FLIR) sensor with onboard laser range finding and designator, and video recorder.

The 4BW remanufacture program is a key modernization effort that will significantly improve performance and operational effectiveness until the All-1W can be replaced in the 2020 timeframe. The 4BW is a four-bladed rotor system using existing General Electric T-700 engines, with new gear boxes, tail empennage, and tail rotor to provide performance that will double range/payload allowing the carriage of up to 16 precision guided munitions. The 4BW will also include a modern, integrated cockpit with digital weapons capability which solves an operational safety deficiency. Enhanced deployability, supportability, and maintainability will be achieved as the program fields engines, gearboxes, and rotor systems common to both the AH-1 and UH-1 aircraft. Modern avionics will also improve joint interoperability by providing the capability to transmit, receive and display digital information from aircraft or ground units of other services. The program will remanufacture 180 AH-1W's with initial fielding scheduled to commence in fiscal year 2005.

UH–1N (HUEY) MID–LIFE UPGRADE

The UH-1N is a two-place, side-by-side combat utility helicopter. Its primary mission is airborne command and control with additional missions of supporting arms control, medical evacuation, maritime special operations, troop insertion/extraction, and search and rescue. Like the AH-1W, the UH-1N is scheduled for a phased midlife upgrade. Communications/Navigation (Comm/Nav) upgrades will include a Global Position System (GPS), Inertial Navigation System (INS), lightweight TACAN, a digital moving map display, satellite communications, and a FLIR system. The UH-1N will also receive a four-bladed performance upgrade (4BN) which will re-engine the aircraft and use the same dynamic component remanufacture kit as the AH-1W's.

The 4BN program is a key modernization effort that will significantly improve performance, solve an operational safety deficiency, and increase operational effectiveness. Enhanced deployability, supportability, and maintainability will be achieved as the program fields General Electric T-700 engines, gearboxes, and rotor systems common to both aircraft. Modern avionics will also improve joint interoperability by providing the capability to transmit, receive and display digital information from aircraft or ground units of other services. The program will remanufacture 100 UH-1Ns with initial fielding scheduled to commence in fiscal year 2003.

CH–46 UPGRADE

We continue to proceed with the CH-46 Dynamic Component Upgrade (DCU). This program replaces portions of the flight control, drive train, and rotor systems. Specifically, this effort will replace aged rotorheads, pitch change shafts, and other dynamic components which have surpassed their original service life. You may recall that our forward deployed forces have been restricted to 10 hours of flight between rotorhead inspections and have had to operate under a plethora of operational restrictions over the past few years. While the Dynamic Component Upgrade will not enhance the performance characteristics of the CH-46, it will remove many current operational restrictions and provide enhanced flight safety and reliability for this almost 30 year old workhorse until it is replaced by the MV-22.

JOINT STRIKE FIGHTER (JSF)

The Short Takeoff/Vertical Landing variant of JSF program, which we call the STOP Strike Fighter (JSF/SSF), is critical to our long range plan. The Marine Corps depends heavily upon the use of integrated air in its combined arms scheme of warfare. This in turn, has allowed us to maintain our expeditionary nature by radically reducing our dependence upon armor and artillery, and in so doing, has helped ens re that we have the strategic mobility necessary to remain the "Nation's 911 Force".

We base as far forward as possible to provide deep strike and rapid CAS for our ground combat forces. The tactical benefits of being close can be measured in two ways: decreased response time and increased sortie generation. Thus, Marines can fly from amphibious decks close to shore, from captured or damaged airfields, or when needed, from highways in or near the battlefields of the future. In Desert Storm, the STOVL capabilities of the AV-8B Harrier allowed us to "shoehorn" eighty-six (86) more tactical aircraft into theater when there was no room at traditional airfields. We did this by operating sixty (60) AV-8Bs from an expeditionary airfield located in a soccer stadium at Jubail, Saudi Arabia while basing an additional twenty (20) AV-8Bs aboard the U.S.S. Nassau and six aboard the U.S.S. Tarawa. These aircraft were the closest fixed-wing assets of any service to the Kuwaiti border. From some of these bases, we were able to provide close air support within 7 minutes—from receipt of the request to bombs on target!

The JSF/STOVL Strike Fighter (JSF/SSF) will allow Marine Aviation to continue to support our ground forces without restricting the CinCs' courses of action. Because the SSF can operate from almost any location, we can launch from amphibious platforms or aircraft carriers, rearm and refuel at forward sites, then recover at sea bases or ashore as necessary. To meet our warfighting requirements, and modernize the force in a timely manner, we plan to begin replacing our AV-8B and F/A-18 aircraft with the SSF beginning about 2007. The SSF will merge the latest technology in a low signature, multi-mission strike fighter with the capability to operate from any austere location. Additionally, its modern technology and tri-service commonality will provide greatly reduced supportability and deployability requirements. This will complete the tactical fixed wing neck-down strategy we embarked upon in the early 1980's; a plan that improves operational efficiency and affordability by relying upon fewer, but more capable type/model/series aircraft.

EA-6B (PROWLER)

Since WWII and the large scale introduction of electronics for military use, Marine Corps Aviation has recognized the need for our Nation to lead the way in electronic warfare while controlling the electromagnetic spectrum. From the beginning, the Marine Corps has recognized the urgency to develop tactics and set apart resources to meet this rapidly developing area of combat. The first electronic warfare aircraft to be built "from the ground up"—was our own EA-6A "Electronic Intruder" of the mid-1960s. Today we have our combat proven Marine Tactical Electronic Warfare Squadrons equipped with EA-6Bs.

With the retirement of the Air Force EF-111 by the end of fiscal year 1997, the Navy and Marine Corps EA-6Bs become the DOD's only tactical airborne electronic warfare platforms capable of providing lethal and non-lethal suppression of enemy command and control air defenses well into the 21st century. A Tri-service memorandum of understanding covering this transition is due for signature by Service Chiefs later this month. To maintain a viable platform through the year 2015, the Marine Corps is pursuing, in concert with our Navy counterparts, a two-step approach.

Our first step is to address the structural and supportability problems associated with our aging EA-6B fleet. This includes the integration of numerous avionics upgrades for improved safety of flight, reliability/maintainability, and joint interoperability. The majority of these items will be included with the Block 89A modifications, due to be incorporated into all EA-6B aircraft. With the completion of Block 89A, there will be one standard configuration of EA-6Bs in the inventory. Second, we are working with the Navy to investigate an incremental approach to upgrading the warfighting capability of our Prowlers. Additionally, we are studying technological alternatives, manned and unmanned, for performing the full spectrum of tactical EW missions beyond 2015.

AUTOMATIC TARGET HAND-OFF SYSTEM (ATHS)

Marine Aviation's number one priority has always been, and will remain, supporting the Marine on the ground. TACAIR efforts, such as the F/A-18D and AV-8B Remanufacture, focus on increasing aviation's capability to support that Marine. As we move into the 21st century, the Marine Corps' STOVL Strike Fighter (SSF) will multiply the capabilities of Marine aviation as an integral part of the MAGTF.

One of the most difficult areas in providing offensive air support, particularly close air support, is locating and designating enemy ground targets for aviation to attack. To answer this challenge, the Marine Corps is pursuing the Target Location, Designation and Hand-off (TLDH) system for the Ground Combat Element and the complementary Automatic Target Hand-off System (ATHS) for the ACE. The TLDH will enable the Marine on the ground to provide digitized precise target location, via Global Position System (GPS) and laser ranging, to airborne platforms. This system will be transmitted into an "on-board" ATHS, which will allow Marine airborne platforms to receive and display this vital information in the cockpit. Along with target location, ATHS also displays other essential mission information, to include aircraft routing, in order to facilitate target attack. This information will serve to reduce aviation response time to Marines on the ground, and improve identification of targets.

ATHS will provide the capability to electronically mark the target, replacing the visual target marks that are required. In essence, ATHS provided with digital TLDH information passed to GPS aided munitions, will enable aircraft to precisely attack targets in or through adverse weather conditions. This capability was not possible when targets required visual marking. The Marine Corps begins installing ATHS in AV-8B aircraft in fiscal year 1997. Along with fixed wing aircraft, Marine aviation is installing ATHS in the AH-1W and is considering other rotary wing aircraft. Incorporated in our TACAIR and Assault Support aircraft, ATHS will enhance Marine aviation's ability to put bombs on target, and will help ensure we do not endanger our own forces.

ADVANCED TACTICAL AIR RECONNAISSANCE SYSTEM (ATARS)

A shortfall of Operation Desert Storm was a lack of adequate tactical battlefield reconnaissance capability. The Advanced Tactical Air Reconnaissance System (ATARS) addresses this problem and provides a capability for transitioning to digital, real-/near-real-time tactical reconnaissance. It is presently the only funded tactical reconnaissance system under development in DOD. The Marine Corps F/A-18D will be equipped with ATARS for responsive tactical airborne reconnaissance for both sea or expeditionary land based operations.

ATARS is a self-contained, palletized reconnaissance sensor suite containing three electro-optical/infrared sensors and associated electronics and recorders. Low and medium altitude electro-optical sensors provide dawn-to-dusk high-resolution, vertical or oblique imagery. An infrared line scanner provides day or night, high-speed, low altitude, high-resolution infrared imagery. The Phase II upgrade to the APG–73 radar, when added to the ATARS suite, will provide high-resolution ground maps in a stand-off capability. The upgraded APG–73 is capable of gathering both wide-area coverage (10mm-wide strip) and point-target (small area spot) reconnaissance imagery during all-weather conditions. A data link, now under development, will allow aircrew to transmit imagery to a ground-based image processing station thereby giving ground commanders a real-time tactical battlefield reconnaissance capability.

Our requirement for ATARS is 31 suites. The IOC is planned for 1st Qtr, fiscal year 1999 with delivery of four sets to Marine Aircraft Group-31 at Marine Corps Air Station Beaufort, South Carolina. Full Operational Capability is planned for fiscal year 2002 with four suites delivered to each of our six F/A–18D squadrons; the remaining seven ATARS suites will be used for aircrew training and logistical spares.

JOINT MUNITIONS

Advanced joint munitions are very important to the Marine Corps. The Joint Direct Attack Munitions and Joint Standoff Weapon provide USMC aircraft with needed standoff range. This increased range, coupled with increased accuracy and lethality, decreases the cost per kill equation of enemy forces.

Marine aviation is designed to operate in an expeditionary, mobile, dynamic environment, and weapons must be designed to meet this requirement. In these circumstances, current advanced weapons, and those under development, have limitations which constrain their ability to extensively replace existing programs. Specifically, they have limited capabilities to maintain lock in dynamic, maneuvering environments and are suited to only a select target set. In summary, while advanced weapons programs have a place in Marine aviation, their wide spread replacement of lower priced weapons should depend on a case-by-case assessment of their operational cost-effectiveness. In many cases, the use of lower-priced weapons remain the most cost-effective way to conduct war.

THEATER MISSILE DEFENSE

Theater missile threats, be it ballistic or cruise missile, remain a high priority for us to counter. We've made tremendous progress in engineering the necessary system modifications to combat this quickly growing and deadly threat. By using our Phase III Mobility Hawk missile system in conjunction with our long-range surveillance radar, the AN/TPS–59, we now possess the only proven short-range theater ballistic missile defense capability in the world. These same systems have also demonstrated that cruise missile defense is possible, and in conjunction with additional long range cueing from other systems such as the Navy's AEGIS, we have enough reaction time to detect, track and kill sea-skimming or terrain following missiles. We tested these systems at the White Sand Missile Range and at the Barking Sands Pacific Missile Range in Hawaii during this past 12 months with great success. The TPS–59 radar set modifications will be fielded during this, and the next fiscal year, to give our forces the additional protection they need in the littoral against the growing theater missiles threat.

Working closely with the Army, Navy and the Ballistic Missile Defense Office, we are maximizing the Hawk's capabilities as a counter missile defense as well as improving our TPS–59 radar as a missile defense detector. We consider ourselves an integral part of the Navy's Lower Tier missile defense system. We will, however, continue to support a Marine organic missile defense system closely tied to the Navy until such time as another capability or service can defend our Marines.

COMMAND AND CONTROL SYSTEMS

Continuing to comply with the Joint Staff mandate requiring all services to adopt the US Air Force's Air Tasking Order system, we have installed and are currently operating the Contingency Theater Automated Planning System (CTAPS) in our Marine air wings. We recently upgraded our Tactical Air Command Centers to operate the CTAPS by providing additional work stations, and we are in the process of fully integration the CTAPS functionality. Now, Marine aircraft wings, including our Reserve air wing, are capable of standing up an Expeditionary Joint Forces Air Component Commander Center (JFACC) from which all joint aviation activities can be planned, coordinated, and executed.

Also, we are capable of operating under the Navy's sea-based JFACC, moving into the littorals, establishing our own expeditionary JFACC to conduct joint air operations until such time as the U.S. Air Force's systems arrive in-country to assume JFACC responsibility. In our aviation command and control system, we are also necking down. We plan to take our many stove-piped and closed architecture command and control systems and down size them by integrating their functions while making them compatible with the Global Command and Control (GCCS) architecture. Our vision is to develop a common aviation command and control system that integrates with the GCCS/Joint Maritime Command Information System (JMCIS). This will provide the necessary functionality required for air control, assault support, air defense, and close/deep air support operations. Additionally, we plan to implement the Joint Tactical Information Distribution System (JTIDS) into our command and control platforms to enhance control of the air war, coordinate with other joint forces, and improve our combat ID capability. These initiatives will take us into the 21st century with efficiency and operational relevance. Our system will insure that we can participate as part of the joint team, and, most importantly, allow us to effectively command and control our own aviation assets.

EXPEDITIONARY AVIATION LOGISTICS

To be responsive to the CinCs warfighting needs, Marine Aviation truly maintains an expeditionary character which allows it to operate anywhere in the world. Whether operating aboard carriers, or air-capable amphibious ships, or ashore at a remote airfield or hastily constructed runway, we have the ability to supply, maintain, command and control, load ordnance, and provide automated data processing support for our aircraft. The Marine Aviation Logistics Support Program SP) and the Expeditionary Airfield (EAF) system are the two unique programs, not duplicated by any other service, and are the linchpins of our aviation logistics support capability.

MALSP

The cornerstone of our aviation logistics support strategy is the Marine Aviation Logistics Support Program. The MSP encompasses a number of other programs that, together, enable aviation logisticians to integrate the people, support equipment, mobile facilities/shelters, and spare parts to support any given number and mix of aircraft. Among those programs encompassed by MSP are the: (1) Fly-In Support Package (FISP) Program; (2) Contingency Support Package (CSP) Program; (3) Aviation Logistics Support Ships (T–AVBs); and (4) Marine Aviation Logistics Squadron (MALS).

MALSP provides many advantages, not the least of which are: standardized support packages, reduced embarkation and strategic lift footprint, rapid deployment and employment, and the ability to operate in austere environments. However, the single biggest benefit provided by the MALSP is the ability to tailor and phase our logistics support for a particular mission. To ensure that it continues to meet our operational needs, we continue to refine the conceptual framework of MSP and invest resources to upgrade and modernize MALSP equipment. These efforts include: (1) drafting a study for a follow-on T-AVB design; (2) restructuring the FISPs and CSPs to decrease strategic lift requirements; and (3) fielding state-of-the-art logistics automated information systems to improve the effectiveness and efficiency of our logistics management.

EAF CAPABILITIES

We are Naval by nature and expeditionary by character—this is our ethos. However, we also have the tools to bring this ethos from principle to application—the Expeditionary Airfield (EAF). The EAF allows us to quickly transfer ashore and operate from austere bases and hastily constructed runways without the need for host-nation support, basing rights, and permanent infrastructure. With the EAF, Marine Aviation has a capability unique among the Services to provide a flexible, reusable, aircraft operations support system that can be built to accommodate the entire spectrum of Marine aircraft.

The major components of the EAF are: AM–2 aluminum matting, visual landing aids, arresting gear, and airfield lighting. These assets can be rapidly deployed and employed to enhance and exploit existing facilities or to construct, from scratch, a forward operating base.

As we prepare to cope with the demands of the next Century, we recognize that Marine aviation will be called upon to operate, and succeed, in a myriad of environments. Future contingencies are likely to be highly unpredictable, unconventional, regionally oriented, and centered in the world's littorals. The EAF provides the capability to meet these dynamic requirements and support any type of aircraft and mission, such as:

● Vertical take-off/landing (VTOL) pads to support AV–8B Harriers; helicopters; and, in the future, our proposed JSF/STOVL Strike Fighter.
● Available roadways can be exploited with EAF material to construct bare-base airfields.
● EAF 2000—our most recent enhancement in the EAF Program—allows for the construction of entire airfields. In addition to a 3,840 foot runway, EAF 2000 provides parking space for 75 tactical aircraft and three KC–130 transport aircraft. If needed, the runway can be expanded to support larger strategic lift aircraft and wide-body commercial aircraft.

The EAF represents a significant aviation support capability that has no equal. Each of our three Marine Expeditionary Forces (MEFs) has the capability to construct and operate two expeditionary airfields, two bare-base airfields, and multiple VTOL pads. Much like the movie "Field of Dreams", the EAF officer is confident in knowing that once he builds it, "they will come!"

MARINE AVIATION'S THREE-PRONGED STRATEGY

Marine Aviation will continue to move the Corps' Air-Ground Team into the 21st Century through a three-pronged strategy of procurement, upgrading, and development. The Marine Corps views readiness as the synergistic result of many elements, one of which is procuring combat-proven weapons systems for our Marines. F/A-18Ds and CH–53Es are examples of this approach. Second, the Corps continues to save American taxpayer dollars by upgrading existing systems like the AV–8B, Cobra and Huey through remanufacture. Third, new technologies currently under development; such as ATARS, the MV–22, and Joint Strike Fighter (JSF) are being pursued as tools of America's future battlespaces. Thus, our strategy dovetails with our time-embraced aircraft neck-down plan.

The present problem is: how can we render the same quality of service that our infantry brethren have come to expect in the current era of fiscal austerity? Efficiency is the key. We embarked upon a strategy about 10 years ago wherein multiple type/model/series aircraft would be replaced by a single aircraft. In the fighter-attack community, we have come far from an inventory of F–4s, AV–8As, and A–4s to a fleet of F/A–18s and AV–8Bs. We also necked down from RF–4s, OA–4s, and A–6s to F/A–18Ds. As a Corps, we want to see the process culminate in the advanced short takeoff, vertical landing variant of the JSF, advanced the STOVL Strike Fighter which will replace all F/A–18C/Ds and AV–8Bs in the Marine Corps.

CONCLUSION

Our fiscal year 1997 budget request, represents a long range investment strategy designed to provide the highest possible combat readiness within resource constraints. The plan focuses on the most urgent equipment modernization and sustainability requirements. As the Nation's premier expeditionary force in readiness, the Marine Corps stands ready to protect American interests, influence, and ideals throughout the globe. As we have always done, we will accord first priority to our operating forces with the objective of assuring their success on the modern battlefield while conserving our most treasured resource . . . our individual Marines and Sailors.

With your assistance, Marine Aviation will remain the ready, relevant, and capable force multiplier that helps to make the Corps a model of joint effectiveness and efficiency. We are ever mindful that our success is found in the synergy of the Marine Air Ground Team and in the courage, honor, and commitment of the individual Marine. We will continue to wisely invest the tax dollars that you entrust to us, giving America a Corps of Marines that responds quickly when called and wins—every time—in any clime and place. On behalf of Marines everywhere and our Commandant, I thank you again, Mr. Chairman, for permitting me to speak to you today, and I thank you, as well, for the steadfast faith and trust that your Committee places in our Corps.

Senator WARNER. All right, gentlemen, what I would like to do is to start with you, General Eberhart. I presume you have had an opportunity to have reviewed to some extent the record of this subcommittee as it reviewed the 22 program last year, and our major concern with the subject of concurrency. Would you start sort of as a threshold where we left off last year, how the 1996 program has unfolded to date, and what you would hope to do on the concurrence issue in 1997?

General EBERHART. Sir, I have reviewed the concurrency issue. With your permission I would like to go back just a little bit further, though. We were concerned with concurrency from the very beginning, to make sure that we were going to get this correct. As such, we looked at what the Packard Commission said about concurrency. We think this program complies with what was pointed out in the Packard Commission. Rand looked at the concurrency issue. They commented favorably in terms of concurrency in the F–22. Just to make sure that we had it right, as you know, the Defense Science Board looked at this issue and submitted a report in 1995 which, in our view, supports the fact that it is not too concurrent.

There is some concurrency. We think there will be concurrency in most all programs today. But we are comfortable with that concurrency. We think it is under control.

Senator WARNER. We questioned whether there should be 70-odd aircraft operational before the last milestone was completed under the—is it the T&E program?

General EBERHART. Sir, before we go to full rate production there will be 70 some odd airplanes. As you know, when we looked at the acquisition reform of 1994, they recommended approximately 10 percent, which had we stayed with the original buy of about 700 and some odd, 10 percent would have been 70 some odd. But as we have drawn down the total buy and also extended the period of EMD, we think that is a natural consequence that we will in fact have more airplanes as we go to full-rate production than this 10 percent guideline talks about.

But we think the important parts, and they have been once again authenticated by the reports that we have talked about, first of all the DT&E which we think is most important will be finished essentially by the time we have four airplanes.

Senator WARNER. For the record, spell out what DT&E is.

General EBERHART. Development, test, and evaluation. Then the initial operational test and evaluation, the Rand Corporation said most problems unfold between the 10 and 20 percent point in DT&E. We will in fact have 27 percent of DT&E.

For these reasons, sir, we believe that concurrency is just about right in this program. We will continue to watch it. We are concerned about it just as you are. But we think it is on the mark.

Senator WARNER. Now, each of us have different views. I think it is really one of the highest rates of concurrency that I have experienced. But that, in your judgment, and General Fogleman has testified this week before this committee, that degree of concurrency is driven by the threat assessment that has been made by a variety of sources, traditional sources, such that to have U.S. air dominance in the theater in the time frame when this plane is scheduled to come in, you essentially have to have that number of aircraft and that design of aircraft to meet that threat. Is that a fair summary?

General EBERHART. Sir, we are concerned about air dominance, we are concerned about ensuring that we have air dominance as quickly as possible, and in our view the F–22 does that for us. But again, when you look at the number of airplanes, the 70 some odd, by the time we go to full rate, we go back to some of the other fac- .

tors we talked about in terms of an extended EMD and having a profile that makes sense.

Senator WARNER. Well, but it is the threat scenario that is driving that quantum of concurrency, and it depends on the individual as to how you want to quantify it. I mean, you very carefully have quantified it from a technical perspective. I just quantify based on past experience. I mean, this committee has gone through a number of aircraft programs that have not materialized as originally envisioned.

Let us talk about your fly-away costs for the 22. Considering the changes in the program to date, and there has been a reassessment of weight—General Fogleman went into that—have you had an opportunity to be debriefed on what he said on weight?

General EBERHART. Yes, sir, I did.

Senator WARNER. To capsule the weight issue, as I recall it, it was that he decided he could make a degradation in the envelope and thereby allow an increase in the weight, and that degradation in his professional judgment would not substantially in any way affect the performance of this aircraft to meet the threat, is that correct?

General EBERHART. Yes, sir, that is essentially correct. There is a little more to it.

Senator WARNER. Well, why do you not put that in the record?

General EBERHART. Yes, sir. I think that when you look at the weight of the airplane it is still about 2,500 pounds below what we think the max allowable weight would be for this airplane. We did look at, and I think you know, and you have referenced the testimony last year, that in fact, at that time we were concerned about the weight growth that we had seen to that time, and we have taken very aggressive measures to bring this under control, and we think we have today, to include weighing and reviewing it every other week, reporting it to the program manager.

We have actually had the opportunity now to weigh some of the parts. In fact, we have weighed about 10 percent of the parts, the actual parts that we have cut, and we are plus 20 pounds on the 3,000 pounds that we have weighed. Then when we looked at avionics, we have weighed hundreds of pieces, and we are minus 16 pounds. So we think we have good understanding that our model is on track.

The situation you are talking about is where we looked at the weight that we had at that time and what it was going to take in terms of thrust to get us the G available at one point on the performance curve. We looked at what that would cost us in terms of dollars to ensure a very small change in G available. I am talking point-zero-something in terms of G's, very negligible. We looked at what that meant in terms of operational capability, and we believe that was negligible, and it was not just the Air Force, sir. We vented this through the JROC process, with the other Vice Chiefs, the Vice Chairman, the Chairman, and the CINC's, to make sure everyone understood what this meant, negligible in terms of operational capability.

I guess the bottom line is we looked at it based on what it would cost us to keep that point-zero-X amount of G at this one point on the performance curve, and we did not think the cost was worth it.

Senator WARNER. Now, let us return momentarily, and then I will yield to my colleague, about the fly-away cost. What do you estimate the fly-away cost of the 22 in fiscal 1996 dollars?

General EBERHART. Sir, I get the fly-away costs confused a little bit here, so let me make sure that I understand it. I think it is around $70 million, but let me check that number to make sure I have it right. It is 71.2, sir. For the record, 71.2

Senator WARNER. 71.2.

General EBERHART. Yes, sir.

Senator WARNER. That is predicated on 442 units?

General EBERHART. Yes, sir.

Senator WARNER. Senator Levin.

Senator LEVIN. Thank you, Mr. Chairman.

On the F–22 concurrency issue, first, is there more or less concurrency with a reduced buy?

General EBERHART. Sir, in terms of the reduced buy coupled with stretching out EMD, there is less concurrency.

Senator LEVIN. So that even though we are buying a greater percentage—no, even though the full rate production of the F–22 is for a smaller percentage of the total buy, the concurrency has actually been reduced?

General EBERHART. Sir, I believe that once you stretch out EMD and you have longer to work these issues, and the IOC moves right—the initial operational capability, and you have more time to work this test and evaluation phase, reduces the concurrency.

Senator LEVIN. You, in answer to the chairman's question as to whether or not the schedule for the F–22 is threat driven, answered, as I understand it, that it is in fact not being driven by the threat, but I would like you to put that in your own words. Are we producing this based on what is a proper, safe rate of development, or are we producing this quicker than that in order to meet some kind of a presumed threat that we are going to face in the out-years?

General EBERHART. Sir, I think that in every case this is a balance between the threat that we anticipate and what we think is acceptable concurrency and acceptable and affordable rate of production. So I think we balance those two things and that is how we decide what the IOC is.

Senator LEVIN. Has the concurrency rate changed in the last 2 years for the F–22?

General EBERHART. Sir, I have not addressed the question specifically like that, and I am not an acquisition expert. I will provide for the record my view that we have stretched out EMD over the last couple of years; we have moved the IOC right; so to me as an operator, that means that the concurrency is not as concurrent. Now, I will have to ask the acquisition experts if they agree, and if their definition of concurrency is the same as mine.

Senator LEVIN. OK, so that from your operator's perspective there is less concurrency now in this program than there was 2 years ago?

General EBERHART. That would be my view as an operator, yes, sir.

Senator LEVIN. I think it would be useful to give us those charts showing us those timelines, comparing for us the milestones that exist now to what they looked like 2 years ago. I think it would be helpful to do that for the record.

General EBERHART. Yes, sir.

[The information referred to follows:]

F-22

The level of concurrency in the F-22 program has remained essentially unchanged for the last 2 years. Despite three program rephases due to funding reductions, we've been careful in replanning to keep our development and production efforts properly phased. For comparison between the exact event dates 2 years ago to the current schedule, please reference the attached chart.

F-22 PROGRAM MILESTONE COMPARISON

Key Program Milestones (selected OSD Prod Exit Criteria)	Master SCH 16 (Nov. 93) Date/Lead Time to Lot Awd	Master SCH 18 (Nov. 95) Date/Lead Time to Lot Awd
PPV Long Lead	Dec. 95	Feb. 97
Critical Design Review	Nov. 94/13 Mo	Feb. 95/24 Mo.
Initial Prod Readiness Review	Nov. 94/13 Mo	Feb. 95/24 Mo.
Engine Initial Flight Release	Aug. 95/4 Mo	Dec. 96/2 Mo.
PPV CA/Lot 1 Long Lead	Dec. 96	Feb. 98
Interim Prod Readiness Review	Jun. 96/6 Mo	Apr. 97/10 Mo.
EMD First Flight	Jun. 96/6 Mo	May 97/ Mo.
Lot 1 CA/Lot 2 Long lead	Dec. 97/Nov. 97	Feb. 99
Final Prod Readiness Review	Jun. 97/6—5 Mo	May 98/9 Mo.
Engine Full Flight Release	Apr. 97/8—7 Mo	Mar. 98/11 Mo.
Lot 2 CA/Lot 3 Long Lead	Nov. 98/Dec. 98	Feb. 00
Engine Initial Service Release	Dec.97/11—12 Mo	Sep. 99/5 Mo.
Lot 3 CA/Lot 4 Long Lead	Dec. 99	Feb. 01
PPV First Flight	Apr. 99/8 Mo.	Jun. 00/8 Mo.
Lot 4 CA/Lot 5 Long Lead	Dec. 00	Feb. 02
Start Dedicated IOT&E	Jul. 00/5 Mo	Oct. 01/4 Mo.
Milestone III (High Rate Decision)	Jul. 01	Sep. 02
Complete IOT&E—AFOTEC Rpt	Mar 01/4 Mo	May 02/4 Mo.

Lot 2 begins at aircraft #5; Lot 1 contained four aircraft. Overall, we expect to have high confidence in the status of the avionics due to extensive subsystem hardware and software test, subsystem qualification and integration tests, subsystem verification test, avionics level integration lab tests, Flying Test Bed (FTB) tests and flight tests. The operational avionics software will be built incrementally in a "block" approach, and be comprised of Blocks 1, 2, 3 and 3.1. At Lot 2 contract award, Block 1 flight testing is complete, Block 2 flight test is 88 percent complete, Block 3 FTB flight testing is 25 percent complete and Block 3.1 development and integration tests at the vendor facilities are complete.

Senator LEVIN. The Science Board found for the F-22 that engine development and passive avionics were the highest risk areas in terms of concurrency. Could you comment on that?

General EBERHART. Yes, sir. In fact, I had the privilege of going down to Pratt & Whitney at West Palm a couple of weeks ago and looking at the engine on the stand and receiving extensive briefings on where they were a year ago and where they were 2 years ago and where they are now. It is very impressive the steps they have taken to make sure that this airplane and this engine will be ready for first flight in May of 1997, and I am convinced that it will.

But the types of redesign work we have done, to include the advances with the hollow blade, we are convinced that that will in fact work. It has tested so on the test stand, and it is a go for May of 1997 for the maiden flight.

Senator LEVIN. The Science Board report indicated that about 20 percent of the avionics testing was going to be completed before the Lot 2 contract award. As I understand, Lot 2 begins at what plane?

General EBERHART. Sir, I do not have that in front of me. We will see if we can get that information now. If not, we will submit that for the record.

Senator LEVIN. Well, my question does not depend on the answer to that. So whatever the plane number is where Lot 2 begins, it was our understanding from the Science Board report that the avionics testing would be 20 percent completed before that point.

Now, in terms of the engine testing, we did not have a specific number. Do you know what that number is? That is, what percentage of the engine testing was to be completed prior to Lot 2 production?

General EBERHART. I do not know, sir. I will have to submit that for the record.

Senator LEVIN. Do you know how much of the testing, the engine testing, is going to be actual testing as compared to modeling and simulation? Is that something you would know offhand?

General EBERHART. No, sir. I am sorry.

Senator LEVIN. That is fine. There is no problem. Just submit that for the record.

General EBERHART. Yes, sir.

[The information referred to follows:]

F–22

By Lot 2 contract award, Feb. 00, the engine is scheduled to have accomplished over 7,500 hours of ground testing or nearly 90 percent of the planned total. This level of ground testing will have given us the data to complete the Initial Service Release milestone for production qualification. We will have verified nearly 95 percent of the requirements in the engine specification. in addition, over 5,000 engin flight test hours will have been accumulated through the flight test program. One hundred percent of the engine test hours planned is actual engine testing in test cells at Arnold AFB and Pratt and Whitney's testing facility located in West Palm Beach, FL.

General EBERHART. Again, as an operator, going down there, visiting Pratt & Whitney, I was very impressed with what I saw.

Senator LEVIN. There was a question, Admiral McGinn, on concurrency on the F–18E/F, and even though, it is a concurrency question so let me use this moment to ask you about that. I think that at yesterday's hearing Senator Warner noted that there would be 76 F–22's that would be authorized and appropriated by Congress when the operational testing on the F–22 is completed. I believe that was the figure that was used. Now, the F–18E/F program, it would appear that Congress will have authorized and appropriated funds for 114 E/F's before operational testing is completed. Now, is that not even a greater concurrency issue than on the E/F's than it would be on the F–22's, if those numbers are correct or approximately correct?

Admiral McGINN. Senator Levin, I would like to turn to my colleague Craig Steidle, who was the former Program Manager for the F/A–18E/F, and I think he can give you a more informed answer on that.

Admiral STEIDLE. Sir, if you do not mind I will answer that. When we put that program together it was a nonconcurrent program with demonstrated performance at every milestone. Before we had approval to go on with the first LRIP buy we had first flight. Before we were allowed to go for the second one we had demonstrated two fatigue lives and flying of all seven test articles. Before we went on for the third LRIP we had another demonstrator performance. So it was a very nonconcurrent program with demonstrated performance.

The operational testing of that particular aircraft started very early in the simulators with an op assessment, first of all, and there was a long string. The operational testing finishes when we have a full suite of aircraft, full suite of weapons in the inventory, but the airplane is fielded before that with a list of required weapons suites that the services provided for us. It has demonstrated performance during milestones which continues on throughout the process.

Senator LEVIN. Has there been any change in those milestones or in the level of concurrency in the E/F's?

Admiral STEIDLE. No, sir, there has not. We have been on schedule, on performance, all the way through, and it has worked well.

Senator LEVIN. Thank you, Mr. Chairman.

Senator WARNER. Let me go back to the F–22 concurrency, referring to the Science Board report of April 1995, page 35. Do you have a copy of that with you, General?

General EBERHART. I do now, sir.

Senator WARNER. Now, just a rough calculation, American taxpayers are going to have about a half a billion dollars invested in airplanes flying during this current concurrency cycle. That is a lot of money. It occurs to me that we should have some assurance in Congress that if you, in the course of this program, discover there are problems, and that is going to exacerbate the concurrency problem, what procedure do we have in place for, first, addressing those problems internally and making such adjustments to the program as may be required; and second, informing the Congress promptly of what you intend to do?

General EBERHART. Sir, in terms of specific procedures in place, I do not know. I will have to submit that for the record.

[The information referred to follows:]

F–22

At the initiation of the F–22 Engineering and Manufacturing Development (EMD) program, the Milestone 11 Acquisition Decision Memorandum (August 1991) created a requirement for exit criteria to proceed from EMD to production. The exit criteria, which were approved by the Under Secretary of Defense for Acquisition, established a series of exit conditions, both schedule events and performance goals, that must be satisfied prior to awarding each low rate production contract. In addition, numerous schedule metrics and technical performance measures are in place to help identify problems early and track corrective measures before they result in a serious program impact. Periodic reports on program progress are provided to DOD in the Defense Acquisiton Executive Summary (DAES), and to Congress in the Selected Acquisition Report (SAR). Most importantly, the Air Force will continue to inform Congress of program issues as they arise. The approach has been, and will continue to be, one of keeping all major stake holders in the program, including the Congress, fully aware of issues and their resolution in a timely manner. Recent examples of this approach include issues involving radar cross section, engine turbine re-design and our Key Performance Parameter change. The Secretary of the Air Force continues to endorse this approach.

General EBERHART. I can tell you when the issues that you have talked about earlier that reference that point on the performance curve where we were looking at what that would cost us to stay with it, and also when we looked at a range issue, that in both cases as soon as that was found out that came forward to Air Force leadership, immediately went into the JROC process, and we were over talking to members of your committee and yourself, sir, to discuss those with you.

I pledge to you that we have learned from other programs, and other issues, that bad news does not get better with age, that we need to go ahead and address the issue, and everybody who has a stake in the action needs to know about it and be involved in the corrective action.

In terms of the specific process or procedures that are in place, I will have to go check with the Acquisition Community. But watching that first-hand, at that time I was the J–8 on the Joint Staff, and I saw that unfold, which really gave me a good feeling. I think it is tied to the new Acquisition Reform Process and those types of things.

Senator WARNER. Just reading from page 35, quote: If there are significant delays in the accomplishment of these key events—and they are described earlier—or if the performance levels achieved are unacceptable, the program could be adjusted by staying at the four-aircraft-per-year production rate for an additional year. You are giving the committee the assurance that they are in place, procedures to make that prompt adjustment, is that correct? You will provide them for the record?

General EBERHART. Sir, I believe they are in place. I will provide for the record what they are. If they are not, I will provide for the record that they are not in place, and then what we need to do to satisfy that requirement.

[The information referred to follows:]

F–22

The F–22 Program is committed to an event-driven philosophy. The Integrated Master Plan is a contractual document which establishes, using key events, the significant accomplishments for both the products and processes necessary to produce a weapon system and engine that meet performance specifications. By contract, the program will not proceed without successful completion of these events.

Senator WARNER. I would like just a sentence in the letter that this matter has been reviewed by the Secretary of the Air Force. I just think it is very important that on a matter of this seriousness that the Secretary would give you the full support to which you are entitled to make that tough decision for the Department.

General EBERHART. Sir, I agree, and I am sure she will.

Senator WARNER. That is a very important representation to the committee.

Let us proceed on to another issue.

Senator LEVIN. May I ask a question?

Senator WARNER. Certainly.

Senator LEVIN. We are going to need to be satisfied on this concurrency issue. I am not particularly satisfied with the answer that you gave to the chairman about whether or not this was threat-driven or not. We are not going to take risks, I hope, in this program that are going to be driven by a threat, when it seems to me we should make sure that we do not make mistakes in the building of this plane. I, for one, would rather it be done right and a year or 2 later than to find that we have got to do a bunch of fixes on this plane.

So when you were asked whether or not it was threat driven, and then when you told me, and your answer to that was non-committal when the chairman asked it, and then when I asked you the question about the level of risk and the concurrency and the same issue that the chairman raised, you talked about a delicate balance between getting there as soon as possible, which was your words, I am a little concerned when you say as soon as possible. I think I would have put a qualifier before possible, like as soon as reasonably possible, or with reasonable degree of certainty, or something there to give us some assurance on the concurrency issue.

But let me phrase a question this way, and you may not be able to answer this, General, and of so that is fine, you can then do it for the record. You do not have to worry about that. But the Science Board's findings about the acceptable overlap in the F–22 program between testing and production depends upon requiring that the development in a testing must pass certain key events which are identified, and this was what the chairman was referring to.

In the C–17 program, which was also supposed to be operating on an event-based schedule, the production imperative kept us signing contracts even though the events were slipping. Now, Admiral Steidle, on the F–18 description, said that we must meet key events before releasing procurement funds. It was a very clear answer on that question. I think the chairman's question may have been—I may be duplicating the chairman's question, but if I am let me put this in my own words. Is the Air Force committed to sticking to achieving testing events as a necessary prerequisite to signing the F–22 contract?

General EBERHART. Sir, we certainly are, yes. We have to go through those wickets, we have to establish those goals before DAB's and pre-DAB's and DRB decisions. So we will have those milestones before we can move from one portion of the program to another, and we are committed to that.

Senator LEVIN. Our contracts provide for that, our existing contracts provide for that?

General EBERHART. Sir, I assume they do. Again, I will have to provide that for the record.

Senator LEVIN. Let us know that for the record.

[The information referred to follows:]

F–22

The F–22 Program is committed to completing approved OSD Exit Criteria which are consistent with our event-driven philosophy and consistent with the Integrated Master Plan (IMP) which is an Engineering and Manufacturing Development (EMD) contractual document. These are not simply "square filler" events, but objective-based events whose completion is dependent not only on meeting schedule constraints, but also meeting performance objectives. The program will not proceed without successful completion of these events. Future production contracts will not be signed until their respective Exit Criteria have been met.

Senator LEVIN. We want to be moving here according to testing events having been met, and not according to a schedule which is set forth in a contract with the contractor. That is the point here, and if you can give us that assurance for the record, I think that will at least help me out some. Thank you.

General EBERHART. Back to your original question, I think your choice of words is probably much better than mine, but I think the bottom line is that we are comfortable with the concurrency. We think that the risk is acceptable, that we are not letting the threat drive us to do something stupid, something dumb. We are comfortable with that balance, and as you said, as soon as reasonably possible is probably a better choice of words.

Senator LEVIN. My memory goes back here not just to the C–17 but to the B–1 and B–2 where we had—somehow or another there was a window of vulnerability and we had to rush the B–1, and we made a mistake, made a lot of mistakes. As a result it did not have the capabilities that we wanted it to have. Instead of saying, look, let us build the B–2 and do it right and take—if we have a little more vulnerability for a few more years, my God, we have got enough capability in that area anyway, let us do it right. Instead, we, I think, and I do not want to rehash the whole B–1 battle, but I think the chairman's point is, and I would agree, is that we really want to do the F–22 right, and we do not want a high level of concurrency. If that means we get it done a year or 2 years later, so be it.

General EBERHART. Sir, those lessons that you referenced are not lost on the Air Force, either, and we are very concerned about those as we move forward. Bottom line is we are comfortable with the concurrency we see in this program.

Senator WARNER. Well, everybody has his own view. In my view, it is a very high degree of concurrency associated with a high degree of risk. I have always been of the impression that the threat was driving this, not in a stupid area, but just we were at the outer edge of the envelope, as you say, as you fly, on the area of risk and concurrency, and that was driven by the surface to air threat. I seem to have gained that from General Fogleman's testimony, because it is this program that is very, very expensive, it is consuming an ever-larger amount of the overall budget of not only the Department of the Air Force, of the across-the-board Tac Air program, and that likewise concerns me.

Let us go to you, Admiral, and the JAST. Have you had a chance to look at the *Times* article?

Admiral STEIDLE. Yes, sir.

Senator WARNER. Are there areas in which you feel that you would like to put information and comments and revising the record?

Admiral STEIDLE. Yes, sir, I would.

Senator WARNER. Fine. Because it is an important piece, and I want to make sure that our record reflects any thoughts that you have.

Admiral STEIDLE. Yes, sir. I think Mr. Shannon did an outstanding job with the article in total, sir.

Senator WARNER. Did he interview you, by any chance?

Admiral STEIDLE. Yes, sir. He did.

Senator WARNER. Well, that is why it is outstanding. [Laughter.]

Admiral STEIDLE. There was one area——

Senator WARNER. You should teach us politicians how you do it. [Laughter.]

Admiral STEIDLE. He had linked me to the $750 billion estimate that he had, and I in fact went back to him after the session that we had and said I cannot add my numbers up to get to that particular figure. Mr. Blackwell from Lockheed mentioned a trillion dollar program, and a Wall Street analyst recommended $750 billion. They probably have more experience in this particular field than I have, but 3,000 airplanes at $30 million a copy comes out to $90 billion, and this is an order of magnitude above that. So I told him I had difficulty with that particular figure.

Another area here in the article I just noticed, and I am sorry I did not the first time I read this, airplanes will roll out in 2005. That is true of the test articles. The first operational airplane will be available in 2008.

The third piece that he brings in is alluding to the fact that perhaps the Navy would possibly in the future not support the program as strongly as the other services. I think I disagree with that. Admiral Boorda has told me several times that he fully supports this and needs the aircraft and the Navy is fully behind it.

Other than that, sir, I think it is on target.

Senator WARNER. All right. Let us address, then, the funding profile, $131 million in fiscal 1996. Excuse me, that was a cut of $131 million off a baseline of what figure?

Admiral STEIDLE. Approximately 331, sir. It brought us down to about $200 million in 1996.

Senator WARNER. Those figures, you are going to stick with them?

Admiral STEIDLE. I am going to refine them in just a second, sir. I will give you the exact figures. They are within plus or minus $2 or $3 million, sir.

Senator WARNER. Now, while he is getting through the figures I have to recount when I used to testify as Secretary of the Navy we would have literally two dolly carts full of records behind us. Now I guess with the modern computer and brighter officers we are able to do it with a handful of papers. [Laughter.]

General EBERHART. Or submit a lot for the record. [Laughter.]

Admiral STEIDLE. Sir, the exact figures, we started out with $345 million and went to $206 million.

Senator WARNER. Okay, tell us what was the impact of that cut, then. Those are some fairly hefty bucks.

Admiral STEIDLE. Yes, sir. If I could just step back just a second from where the program started, it started in the Bottom-Up Review in 1993. At that particular time the AFX program and the multirole fighter airplane were canceled, were rolled into one in this particular program. Mr. Deutch, in August of that year, established the program with a memorandum and laid in a wedge at that particular time in 1993 for the program.

Since that particular time we have merged the ASTOVL program into it, we have gone from a technology demonstration to an actual strike fighter program, and the wedge stayed in the same shape, and that is not appropriate for a DEM/VAL program or development program. You need up-front funds, and the shape of the curve should be a bell curve skewed to the left.

I went forward in August and July of last year with redefining the program as we put some more substance on it, went forward and then came on over here through several of the staffs in late August or September time frame, after it had gone past your particular committee, with this new funding profile. I presented a profile that was going to use 1996 funding to be able to do work in 1997. That funding was quickly removed, and the statement was put in that that funding should be applied in 1997. That was 2-year money, we could do that.

The services came forward with a program decision memorandum in September fully funding the program to the new DEM/VAL profile that we are executing today.

So in answer to your question, sir, the bottom line is we have re-shaped the program, we have the money in the right year, and the funding profile is correct to execute.

Senator WARNER. What time sequence was adjusted?

Admiral STEIDLE. We moved the program 4 months to the right. I looked at some tech maturation programs we are doing. We moved those in the out years. We looked for redundances and shelved a few of those particular programs. We moved the end-point out 4 months, and the total program was then reshaped and moved to the right slightly.

Senator WARNER. I may return to that program, and I will have some questions for Admiral McGinn, and then turn to my colleague.

The old EA-6B. What a workhorse. I think the taxpayers got their money's worth out of that plane, would you not say?

Admiral McGINN. They continue to get it, Senator.

Senator WARNER. No question about it.

The committee has waited for some time for the completed studies of airborne electronic warfare requirements. Despite DOD's unresponsiveness, last year's defense authorization bill included generous funding for the electronic warfare upgrade modification. The committee is concerned that delays in making substantial upgrades to the EA-6B will prevent the Navy from capitalizing on prior investing in the advanced capability. Is the navy now ready to move out on this program and make it a substantial commitment to the near term EW capability?

Admiral McGINN. Yes, sir, we are. We continue to wisely use the funds that Congress provided last year, the $165 million. We are spending $100 million of those dollars in upgrading 20 aircraft to the more modern block 89 configuration. We have spent an additional $40 million to get what we call band 9 and 10, electronic warfare transmitter pods, and the final $25 million is going for 30 pods for communications jamming.

In addition to that, we have R&D programs that are ongoing to address the idea of a reactive jamming capability, something that you can use against a variety of threats with a proliferation of first world weapons systems throughout many different areas of interest to the United States. We are concerned that we do not get our systems approach so stabilized and solidified in a particular threat system that we cannot react in an agile way against additional threat systems that could be quickly put together, using money for off the shelf designs, by a nation with interests counter to ours.

So the reactive jamming is one answer to help us to be able to fly with confidence into an enemy air defense system in any uncertain future.

Senator WARNER. I am going to ask General Magnus a question on JAST. Mr. Recorder, can you put the General's response following Rear Admiral Steidle's JAST comments so we have that at one place in the record?

General, in our invitation letter we asked you about the Marine Corps view of JAST programs. How would you describe the relevance of that program to the future of Marine Corps aviation?

General MAGNUS. Mr. Chairman, I am glad that you asked me that question, because I had the opportunity this morning to speak to the commandant, General Krulak, exactly on that topic.

Senator WARNER. This morning?

General MAGNUS. This morning, sir.

Senator WARNER. You guys got off to a good early start over there.

General MAGNUS. Yes, sir. As I said, sir, readiness is your Corps. [Laughter.]

General MAGNUS. The Marine Corps has made the commitment in a very real way to accept near-term risk in our strike fighter communities or our AV–8B Harriers and our F/A–18's. We are putting, literally, our investment, our money, where our mouth is, and the technology leap that we see is in the Joint Strike Fighter program. We believe that we in the Nation, our wingmen in the Air Force, as well as our shipmates in the Navy, urgently need the joint strike fighter, and we believe that from our perspective in the Corps that now is the time to take the incremental degree of risk we think, with the forces that we have looking at the threats that are in the next decade to take that leap to 2008 to the joint strike fighter.

Senator WARNER. You are still on board?

General MAGNUS. Yes, sir. We are in the lead as far as our IOC requirement, and we are joined, welded at the hip, with the Air Force and the Navy in the urgent need for this affordable, survivable, family of over 2800 joint aircraft.

Senator WARNER. Senator Levin.

Senator LEVIN. Just one question on the JAST Program, Admiral Steidle. The press has reported recently there are some problems with the release of proprietary information to competing contractors by the JAST office. Can you describe what has happened and whether this is a significant problem?

Admiral STEIDLE. Yes, I will. There was, indeed, proprietary information. There was an inadvertent disclosure, unfortunately, ad the fax machine. An enclosure with one particular letter was put into two other letters that went out to the competing contractors. So therefore certain pricing and costing information from one contractor went to the other two. The two particular contractors saw that immediately, wrapped it up, I sent my security officer out there after it. We have statements to that effect, and we are providing information to the contractor whose information was sent. I hope to have it completely resolved by Wednesday, and the release of our RFP on Thursday of next week.

Senator WARNER. Would you yield to me?

Senator LEVIN. Sure.

Senator WARNER. I think, Admiral Steidle, you should, even though this is a purple program that you are operating, what is the Navy's perspective on JAST meeting its requirements in the out years, operational requirements?

Admiral STEIDLE. Sir, could I have Admiral McGinn answer that, sir?

Senator WARNER. Sure.

Admiral McGINN. Just as General Magnus stated, we are firmly on board with the JAST Program, Senator. Our need in terms of timing is not as urgent as the Marine Corps' in the 2007–2008 time frame, but we have a roadmap to the future that involves going from where we are today with the types of aircraft in our air wings using the significant increase in capability of the F–18E/F, and then blending that in a complimentary way with JAST when it comes on board Navy aircraft carriers in about the 2010 to 2012 time frame, about 3 to 4 years after the Marine Corps.

Senator WARNER. General Eberhart, for the Department of the Air Force, likewise?

General EBERHART. Yes, sir. It would sound like a recording. We are completely behind it. It is key to the Air Force in the future.

Senator WARNER. In all aspects in this joint program is it working out well? As a matter of fact, I think your deputy Admiral Steidle is a BG selectee.

Admiral STEIDLE. Yes, sir. The Air Force's newest general, sir.

Senator WARNER. Very good. That is fine.

General EBERHART. If he does not mess up JAST. [Laughter.]

Senator LEVIN. So we do not know whether you are really a general for about 10–15 more years, then. [Laughter.]

Senator WARNER. The only thing I can tell you, Colonel, General, or whatever the case may be, I knew General Eberhart when he was in the Navy. Somehow he has made it, in spite of his association with members of Congress. [Laughter.]

Senator WARNER. Thank you, Senator Levin. I just wanted to get that one JAST thing in the record.

Senator LEVIN. Well, the followup on that JAST question would be you say that the competitor whose proprietary information was inadvertently disclosed has now been informed of that?

Admiral STEIDLE. He has been informed, sir, and I will go down on Wednesday of next week and present our investigation to them. That particular contractor issued an Agency protest, rightfully so in my mind. I will present all the information to him and tell him what our investigation and impact of the disclosure of that material has.

Senator LEVIN. So we really do not know yet what the effect is going to be? It has not been resolved yet?

Admiral STEIDLE. No, sir, it has not. No, sir, it is not. By Wednesday, I will have it finished.

Senator WARNER. Just as a follow-on, Senator, your program has recently progressed from concept exploration into the requirements generation and validation process. What will be the critical two or three events between now and the award of the EMD contracts to produce test aircraft? What has to go right, what could go wrong?

Admiral STEIDLE. Yes, sir. We are doing business differently, Senator. We have this group of war-fighters and technologists together that are doing cost performance trades. It has never been done at that level before. Industry is a full partner of this. We are trading off the requirements base. Each one of the services has allowed us a large envelope to work in as we pull it down.

Moving into the development phase we will award the two contracts to the two teams. They will have to demonstrate their ability to build this airplane with high level commonality which significantly reduces the cost, demonstrate hover and transition, demonstrate carrier suitable flying qualities, and continue on with a ground demonstration of technology maturation.

We need to mature the technology before we go into the EMD program. That will be done. Our ORD will be completely finished by the year 1999. That is a process in itself that is being done in the virtual world in modeling and simulation. So it is a significant change from the way we have done business in the past.

Senator WARNER. Senator Levin.

Senator LEVIN. On a different subject——

Senator WARNER. I think we have pretty well wound up on the JAST, with those questions for the record.

Senator LEVIN. Let me get to the datalink issue on the fighter aircraft, General. Apparently getting tactical datalinks into the fighters has been a difficult issue for the Air Force for a number of years. Some have the perception that the Air Force has resisted adding that capability, not just because of cost but because of cultural barriers. I am convinced that the added situational awareness, that sharing the data among various platforms has tremendous potential for us.

Are there fighter datalinks included in the comm links that the Chief of Staff has added to has added to his list, do you know?

General EBERHART. Yes, sir, there are. It is under the guise of sensor to shooter.

Senator LEVIN. Would you just say that again?

General EBERHART. It is under the title sensor to shooter, and under that are the things that you are so concerned of and so are we. Your spot on, it was a cultural problem for a while, and in my view we might have hid behind the money issue. We are committed now. We realize how important it is to joint war-fighting, and we are moving ahead.

Senator LEVIN. All right. General Magnus, are the Marines committed to also adopt that capability?

General MAGNUS. Senator, we are. We, of course, field our aircraft in a common long-range plan with the United States Navy, and a program that is unique to us having taken over the advanced tactical air reconnaissance system, for example, we have added a datalink pod to that system so that when it is fielded it will not only give us the capability to download the reconnaissance when we get to the ground, but we will be able to give near real-time bursts of that critical tactical battlefield information to joint force commanders and forces at sea.

Senator LEVIN. Admiral McGinn, do you want to add anything to that?

Admiral McGINN. Yes, sir. We already are flying digital links in many of our aircraft, including the F–14D, such as the JTIDS or link 16, which we have found provides tremendously increased situational awareness. It allows aircraft in a particular strike package or fighter sweep to coordinate their efforts in a much better way than we have ever been able to do before.

I would like to also say that a Marine digital program that offers a great deal of promise, has been fielded and prototyped, is a digitalization called automatic target handoff system, which allows a marine on the ground under fire to digitally communicate right into the close air support aircraft weapons system, in this case the AV–8B, but we are looking to field it in all of our F/A–18's as well, and it will actually put the symbol of the target that the marine lance corporal in the trenches wants to hit, needs to hit, right on the heads-up display of the fighter aircraft or the AV–8B. It is a tremendous leap forward in close air support capability for the future.

General Magnus might want to comment further on that, sir.

General MAGNUS. I appreciate the comments of my shipmate, Admiral McGinn, on the automatic target handoff system, because exactly right, our forward observers and support air controllers on the ground will be able to take the standard nine-line immediate air support request and beam it up via datalink just as the Admiral said, so the pilot in a strike aircraft that is line of sight but out of visual range will be able to stand off from the threat, receive the information, and roll in on the target.

Coupling that capability with the emerging 1760 bus digital capability in weapons like JDAM and JSAL, we are literally going to be able to deliver close air support to troops on the ground at night through the weather in the future with precision accuracy because of the capability to pass that information up and then load it down into the weapons.

Senator LEVIN. General, I take it from your answer that the Air Force is now committed to having the same kind of reliance on the tactical datalinks in its fighter aircraft as we just heard described by the Navy and the Marines.

General EBERHART. Yes, sir. To put it a little more bluntly, but you referenced it earlier, we are over our cultural problem that we had, and then to take it one step further, exactly what they just discussed, this interface between the digitalization of the ground battle and the air battle is key. In the past, when we did look at it we looked at it more of just digitization of the air and datalink in the air, and working that together is how we really become efficient. Then reduce fratricide.

Senator LEVIN. Well, it is good news to hear your testimony this morning, and the budget numbers will be helpful if you will submit those.

General EBERHART. Yes, sir.

Senator LEVIN. That is an area of top priority for this committee, and has been for a number of years. That is all I have on that subject.

Senator WARNER. General Magnus, would you please pass on to your senior chief of aviation our best wishes on a speedy recovery from his operation?

General MAGNUS. Thank you, Mr. Chairman. The general is recovering well. He has had shoulder surgery, for your information, and the reason why he is not here is obviously he is fairly uncomfortable, doing very well, but could not get into his uniform, so he sent me to speak to you this morning.

Senator WARNER. Let us talk about your CV–22 and the problems that have been expressed by the retiring chief of the U.S. Special Operations Command. What do you have to enlighten us on that? Have you read that article? If not, I will send it up to you and you can skim it for a minute.

General MAGNUS. I am not sure to which article you are referring, although there have been several that I have read in the last few days.

Senator WARNER. Well, let us work off the same baseline, and I will go to another question.

General MAGNUS. Mr. Chairman, I am familiar with this article.

Senator WARNER. Well, why do you not go ahead, then?

General MAGNUS. The joint V–22 program I believe is a success story, and of course like many other large programs that are in engineering and manufacturing development, were constantly challenged by constrained fiscal resources.

When the Department of Defense had a Defense Acquisition Board and a Defense Resources Board in 1994 joining the U.S. Air Force Special Operations Command requirement for a Special Operations Force CV–22 to the Marine Corps' MV–22, the estimate for the development of the CV–22, the U.S. Special Operations Command variant, was $550 million. That estimate came from the United States Air Force, I believe it was Aeronautical Systems Command.

Subsequent to that, the Department of the Navy committed, with Department of the Navy RDT&E money, to fund that $550 million profile that we believe would be adequate to provide—to take the MV–22 baseline aircraft into a special operations variance.

In the succeeding 2 years, Special Operations Command has defined its configuration much more finely than they had in 1994. We, the program office and Naval Air Systems Command, submitted a request for a proposal for the development effort to the Bell/Boeing joint team, and essentially the response from the contractors came in at approximately $200 million over what was allocated in the budget. Clearly, that presented more than a minor challenge, because we did not have in the Department of the Navy that additional $200 million, and something had to move, and we certainly recognized the Special Operations Command requirements as well as their need for a fiscal year 2005 IOC.

There have been a number of meetings between the assistant Secretary of the Navy for Research and Development, Mr. Douglas, and the U.S. Special Operations Command representatives on alternatives in which we believe there are more than one alternative and which within the Navy's commitment to the $550 million we can, with ideas such as preplanned product improvement, provide exactly the kind of aircraft that Special Operations Command and our Air Force wingmen need to be able to accomplish their critical mission.

There are ongoing discussions between Special Operations Command and the United States Navy. OSD has been involved in the over-arching team that is watching this program closely, and we have been, of course, in consultation with our Air Force wingmen. We believe there are more than one solution that will allow us to execute to our $550 million commitment and provide the Air Force Special Operations Command the aircraft that they need when they need it.

Senator WARNER. That is reassuring. Douglas is a very able man. I have a high degree of confidence in him, as do other members.

Do you want to take a question?

Senator LEVIN. Just on the V–22 issue. There has been another press report relating to testing results on the V–22 which indicates some problems, an unacceptable level of down-draft or prop wash below the aircraft when it operates at hover. Is there going to be an opportunity during the operational testing to determine whether or not that condition is real?

General MAGNUS. Senator, thank you very much for that question. We have been aware, and I say we in a personal sense, have been aware of the downwash effect of tilt rotors, not only from our experience with high velocity downwash aircraft such as VSTOL aircraft, but when I was a major I was on the Joint NASA Army-Navy-Air Force and industry team that went out to NASA–Ames and modeled the aircraft that was then being designed called JFX, which has since become the V–22 Osprey tilt rotor.

We were well aware that the velocity and the footprint, if you will, of the air that was moving down was going to be more than we have in the current medium helicopters, but quite frankly, comparable to heavy lift helicopters such as the CH–52 Echo—different, but comparable to it. In other words, we knew that people who were operating in the vicinity underneath the aircraft would have a high velocity downwash, and we anticipated this, so this is not a surprise.

As a result of that, during our operational tests—we have just completed operational test 2B which focused specifically on this issue—we had better understand how ground combat marines, sailors, and soldiers will operate under aircraft that are being flown by Air Force, Navy, and Marine Corps pilots, and we believe—and I have personally read the comments of Marine helicopter support team members, lance corporals who have worked under these aircraft who basically say it is comparable to their CH–53 Echo experience.

What I can tell you is, just like the CH–53 Echo, which went through its op eval in 1979, and there were words in the report there that described it as dangerous and requiring special equipment that we did not have in 1979, we will find tactics, techniques, and procedures that will allow us to safely and effectively utilize this aircraft. We have anticipated this problem, and we are working with our joint wingmen on this, as well as the people who will actually be the real customers of the aircraft, and that is the troops that will be in the back.

I am confident that this will be resolved.

Senator LEVIN. Thank you, Mr. Chairman.

Senator WARNER. This is a question to all three. I will ask General Eberhart, Admiral McGinn, and General Magnus to answer. Over the years, the committee has taken an active interest in airborne—part of this has been addressed. The Senator and I want to make sure that there is nothing left missed, untouched.

The committee has taken an active interest in airborne electronic warfare. An initiative by the committee a few years ago was encouraged by the Defense Department to consolidate airborne EW into one program and to adequately fund that program.

Today we have an aged EA-6B fleet, with much the same capability as in the years past, while the threat expands and becomes more sophisticated. At the same time, the Air Force plans to retire the E/F-111. What is the importance of airborne electronic warfare to your tactical aviation program? What near-term capabilities do you have to address that threat, General, to the extent you have not covered it already?

General EBERHART. Obviously, airborne ECM is very important to our program and the survival of our pilots and our effectiveness on the battlefield. We support the efforts that are ongoing to build the E-6B fleet up, make improvements to it, to provide for our joint ECM requirements. We are part of the solution there, and not part of the problem. We are committed to it.

However, at the same time I have to tell you that we have an insurance policy there, and that as we draw down the EF-111's we keep them around till—the number is classified, but sometime in 1998. We keep an increased crew-to-aircraft ratio, and the airplanes that we do require we do not take to Davis Mountain, we leave on the ramp. So if there is a hiccup or we have a requirement, then we can fall back on it. But we are committed to it, we want it to work, we know it is the right thing to do.

You know and the committee knows as well as I do that we have to approach this problem from many different ways. In addition to airborne ECM, if we have better battle space awareness in terms of increased intelligence, surveillance, and reconnaissance. So we know where the threats are, we know what the threats can do, we know how to either attack them or avoid them using stealth and using PGM.

We also had the nonlethal part of this, and eventually some day we think there will be information warfare ways to get in and help us survive in the battlefield of the future, and we think it is important to work all of these aspects. That is what we are committed to.

Admiral MCGINN. I fully concur with General Eberhart's remarks, sir, and I would just like to add a few of my own. The E/A-6B, as mature an airplane and engine combination as it is, still enjoys a great deal of service life that is available in it. We have an active and ongoing operational safety improvement program that is closely monitored by engineers, air crewmen and maintenance personnel in the field, as well as at the various systems commands. The EA-6B program is a truly joint program in that later this month the three service chiefs will sign a memorandum of agreement that will solidify the progress that we have made in making our E/A-6B fleet truly the Nation's tactical EW force.

I received a report from the wing commander, the E/A–6B wing commander, 2 weeks ago, as well as a report from one of the E/A–6B squadron CO's who had just returned from deployment in the Mediterranean. They are absolutely confident that the program is on track, it is properly resourced in terms of air frames, the equipment upgrades that are going in now, and those that are planned, as well as the air crew upgrades.

We have Air Force air crews flying in E/A–6B's in training as well as in operations. Our EA–6B community leaders have also coordinated at the E/A–6B wing level with all of the services and with all of the unified commanders in chiefs and their staffs to make sure that global coverage exists with EA–6Bs in terms of forward presence, as well as with a very responsive reaction capability, should that be required in any type of a regional contingency.

Senator WARNER. Very good. General Magnus?

General MAGNUS. Mr. Chairman, I agree with the remarks of General Eberhart and Admiral McGinn. The Marine Corps, as you know, has four squadrons of Prowlers in the ICAP 2 configuration. We, along with the Navy, are operating our aircraft to the block 89 alpha configuration. As I told you earlier in the hearing, Marines are on the ground today in Aviano, and earlier last year when there was the need to bring additional tactical aircraft into the theaters to support the strikes that were needed on the ground, a Marine squadron deployed within 48 hours and was flying combat missions on the 3rd day from the time that they got the go order from the Joint Chiefs of Staff.

We are integrated with the Navy in carrier deployments, as well as basing out of our base at Iwo Kuni, Japan. We will support the United States Navy in fulfilling our important responsibilities in the Department of the Navy to provide aircraft not only for our own support requirements, but to support the United States Air Force and our allies.

Of course, the United States Navy has received a budgetary plus-up and some structure to take up the Air Force's E/F–111 mission as those aircraft stand down; nevertheless, and consistent with the tactical aviation integration memorandum of agreement that the Commandant of the Marine Corps and the Chief of Naval Operations have in general about all of our strike and electronic warfare aircraft, we will support the United States Navy in fulfilling our commitments to the Nation.

Senator WARNER. Thank you.

Senator Levin. Gentlemen, I am going to have to absent myself. My distinguished colleague will wrap up the hearing.

Senator LEVIN [presiding]. General, I want to talk to you about F–16's. We have got a new definition of service life of the F–16's, which is now dragging us to purchase some additional F–16's, and there is a real question about whether that is the right way to go given our other needs in the Air Force. But let me try to work through this number with you.

We have a 20-wing fighter force now, and I gather the portion of that force that is made up of F–16's is somewhat more than half. Do you know offhand if that is correct?

General EBERHART. Sir, that sounds correct. I will get the number here.

Senator LEVIN. Well, then maybe I had better get these numbers for the record. Let me tell you what I need, because you may not have them at your fingertips. What I need to know was what was the F–16 requirement when we had a 26-wing force, what is the F–16 requirement now, what would it have been had we gone to a 36-wing force, which was the goal during the early 90's? Those three items I need. How many F–16's would have made up those three different force structures.

Then I need you to translate that into both the old definition and a new definition of service life, terms of how many available F–16's we have got. That is something you can provide us for the record.

General EBERHART. Yes, sir.

[The information referred to follows:]

The F–16 is a fourth generation multi-role fighter that replaced the F–4 and A–7. At the present, 11.4 FWE (57 percent) are multi-role fighters and all are F–16 aircraft. When the Air Force had 26.5 Fighter Wing Equivalents (FWE), approximately 16 FWE were multi-role of which 15.4 (58 percent) were F–16 aircraft. At 38.5 FWE, 21.5 FWE (56 percent) were multi-role F–4, F–16 and A–7 aircraft. Eleven FWE were F–16 aircraft. Had the Air Force sustained 38.5 FWE, all multi-role fighters (21.5 FWE) would have become F–16 aircraft as the F–4 and A–7 reached the end of their service lives.

FIGHTER AIRCRAFT REQUIREMENTS

	Fiscal year 1988	Fiscal year 1993	Fiscal year 1996
Total FWE	38.5	26.5	20
F–16 FWE (percent of total)	11.0 (29%)	15.4 (58%)	11.4 (57%)
Multi-role FWE (percent of total)	21.5 (56%)	16.0 (60%)	11.4 (57%)

The Air Force normally programs about 55–60 percent of its fighter forces into the multi-role category. The length of an aircraft's service life does not affect this requirement and, therefore, the same amounts listed in insert number SS–08–029 are valid for any service life.

Senator LEVIN. Do you know in general whether or not the number of F–16 fighter wing equivalent has changed over the recent past? Do you know that offhand?

General EBERHART. Sir, it has changed, I would say, as we have drawn down some F–16's, and we can think of wings like the 474th at Nellis and other wings that have drawn down, and as airplanes have aged it has certainly changed. Although the other fighter force structure has changed, too, so I do not have on the tip of my tongue what the relationship in terms of proportion of the force is, in terms of change, but would like to show that to you for the record, and the proportion of the different blocks, how they have changed. Because that is what complicates this issue, as you know.

Senator LEVIN. That is fine. Are you familiar with the Coalition Force Enhancement Program? Does that strike a bell?

General EBERHART. No, sir.

Senator LEVIN. This was a program that would have given the F–16 some improved capability, upgraded them, added some service life, and we can find that in a different way.

General EBERHART. Yes, sir, I am familiar with that program.

Senator LEVIN. Was it our plan to use that program and sell those upgraded F–16's to our allies?

General EBERHART. Sir, our hope was to do just that, and then have a device or a procedure where that money, supposed to be returned to the Treasury, would be returned to the United States Air Force to buy these attrition reserve airplanes that we have just discussed.

Senator LEVIN. Do you know the cost of adding 4,000 hours of service life to a plane under that program?

General EBERHART. No, sir, I do not. One of our big problems right now is that as we have looked around on this and how much we would have to sell those for I think the brutal facts are there are no buyers.

Senator LEVIN. They want——

l EBERHART. They would just as soon have a new airplanera

Senator LEVIN. Now, are you familiar with the JSTAR budget request in the current budget?

General EBERHART. Yes, sir.

Senator LEVIN. As I understand it, the budget would cut the JSTARS procurement in half during fiscal years 1999, 2000, and 2001, buying one instead of two during those fiscal years?

General EBERHART. Sir, my recollection was that we did in fact move one airplane right. I was not aware that we moved three right, I thought we moved one right. I will have to provide that for the record.

Senator LEVIN. Can you tell us what the experience with the JSTARS was in the Persian Gulf War and Bosnia? Are the CINCS interested in more JSTARS?

General EBERHART. Sir, the CINCS are very interested in the JSTARS program as it exists today, and the planned improvements as we get on through the production line. Obviously, as you know, the bird that we have today and the production birds will be much more capable than the bird that we had in the Persian Gulf, and that, we were all amazed by what it was able to do on such short notice.

I think that in Bosnia today people are impressed with what it is doing, although it is a different situation because of the topography. We do not have a pool table, if you will, like we had in Desert Storm, or like we imagined in the Central Region of Europe. But we have tools where we can go and take this and show the CINC that if you bring JSTARS here and you put it in this orbit, this is what you are going to be able to see around Sarajevo, this is what you are not going to be able to see. So that the expectations are there, and he fully understands what this tool will bring to him as a CINC.

That is exactly what we did before we deployed JSTARS, so it is living up to the expectations, and it is allowing us to use it in ways in peacekeeping and peacemaking that we had not envisioned using in a major regional contingency. So everybody is very impressed with what they see in terms of JSTARS now, and frankly, the move right was an affordability issue to make sure that everything would fit.

Senator LEVIN. Well, that is what troubles me, is that we have got a new technology and a new platform which is working extremely well, from everything we can learn, and we are moving that to the right for affordability reasons. Then we are spending money buyinggF-16's and F-15's for attrition reserves which are only created by the changing the program life expectancy of planes, and where planes could be upgraded quite easily, as a matter of fact, if necessary in order to extend that program life.

It just seems to me there is a disconnect here where we have got a real need of a new technology that is proving itself every day in Bosnia and has proven itself over many, many months in the Persian Gulf, and that we are delaying, and using money to create a reserve which really, it seems to me, is not a realistic need when you consider the fact that we have reduced the number quite dramatically of how many F–16's we are going to need because of the reduction in fighter wings.

So to me it is a priority which is misplaced, but I am not asking you to agree or disagree with that so much as I need from you for the record the history of the F–16's when we had 26 fighter wings, now that it is down to 20, what it would have been—what the requirement would have been had we gone up to 35, the impact on that requirement when we changed the service life expectancy of the F–16, and then we can put all that together and reach our own conclusion. But at least that is certainly my tentative conclusion.

General EBERHART. Sir, we will certainly provide that, and the chief shares your concerns there, maybe not necessarily versus the F–16, but the importance of that JSTARS, and we are relooking that now as we build the 1998 to the 2003 program.

Senator LEVIN. My last question, General Magnus, has to do with the C–130J aircraft, and I understand that you would like to begin buying a tanker version of that aircraft, is that correct?

General MAGNUS. Senator, our current active force has 37 35-year-old KC–130F's, and an additional 14 slightly younger KC–130R's. Based upon what our projection of the service life of those aircraft are, unfortunately, the bulk of them are going to come due for block service life requirement just exactly when we need to invest in aircraft like the joint strike fighter and V–22 and the Navy's F/A–18E/F.

We have been monitoring the United States Air Force's C–130J program. We are enormously impressed with the improvements in the cockpit and the avionics, in the performance of the aircraft. We believe it would be prudent for us to be able to essentially piggy back on that program. Fiscal resource constraints have not enabled us to do that at this time.

Senator LEVIN. You just completed, did you not, the modernization of your tactical tankers a couple of years ago?

General MAGNUS. That is correct. We still have some other things that are being modernized in terms of radios, global positioning, satellite comm, so there is a continuing stream. But essentially, that is correct.

Senator LEVIN. Despite that recent completion of that modernization program, you want to start buying some new tankers, for the reasons that you gave?

General MAGNUS. Well, essentially, the modernization the Senator is referring to is subsystems. Our concern is service life, fatigue life of the aircraft. These aircraft are 35 years old. We would have to spend an enormous amount more money to basically do a service life extension on these aircraft, when we have aircraft that are being produced for the United States Air Force that are going to have very low ownership costs, just as ours are spiking.

So we believe it prudent not to invest in SLEPing old aircraft when in fact they are going to be very cost effective in terms of life cycle costs and commonality, very cost effective C–130J's being produced for our wing men in the United States Air Force. So we look forward to being able to take advantage of that program.

Senator LEVIN. Thank you all. I appreciate your testimony. We will stand adjourned.

[Questions for the record with answers supplied follow:]

QUESTIONS SUBMITTED BY SENATOR STROM THURMOND

F–22

Senator THURMOND. The F–22 program did not receive the $200M buy back in the fiscal 1996 authorization and appropriation bills. It received only $100M. What was the final financial impact on the program?

General EBERHART. The congressional add in fiscal year 1996 reduced the fiscal year 1997 President's Budget request by $100M across the FYDP. The plus up will be used during fiscal year 1996 to offset cost growth associated with the latest rephase effort. The additional funding will reduce program risk by allowing earlier completion of the design than would have been possible without the earlier infusion of funds. The additional funding from Congress also helped the F–22 program avoid a fourth consecutive rephase.

Senator THURMOND. What is the status of Contractor Change Proposal 0035? Please give a detailed answer as to the final estimates of the rephase cost growth. Negotiations were to have been completed in March. Please provide impact on total program cost, flyaway and procurement unit cost.

General EBERHART. The combination of a $110M fiscal year 1995 congressional reduction and $200M fiscal year 1996 OSD reduction ($310M total) led to the third F–22 program rephase, known to Lockheed Martin as Contract Change Proposal (CCP) 0035. Lockheed Martin CCP 0035 was signed on 27 Mar 1996. The Lockheed Martin rephase cost with base and award fee will increase total program cost by $454M. Pratt and Whitney's portion of the rephase will be signed in June 1996. The total cost of the rephase includes the increase in the Lockheed Martin and Pratt and Whitney contracts as well as Other Government Cost (OGC). The current estimation of the total cost of the rephase is $692M. During the rephase process the contractor also submitted a bill for unavoidable non-rephase cost growth. That cost growth will increase the F–22 program budget request by an additional $200M through the end of EMD. The total impact to the F–22 budget request for RDT&E funds through the end of EMD includes the approximately $692M in rephase cost, $200M cost growth, and $310M payback which brings the total budget impact to approximately $1202M.

The Flyaway and Procurement Unit Costs are not affected by these EMD contract changes.

Senator THURMOND. Last year the program office was projecting the contractor team would incur a total $572M EMD overrun. Based on the CCP 0035, what is the March 1996 overrun projection? The committee has heard the figure will be closer to $700M. What is the current Lockheed Martin overrun? In September it was estimated to be $196M.

General EBERHART. The current estimate of the Lockheed Martin overrun at completion, which incorporates the changes due to the most current rephase, is $255.5 million. Lockheed Martins overrun figure in January 96 (the most current information available) was $35M. The contractors have done a superb job of controlling cost. The F–22 team is committed to effective management of cost. Cost control is incentivized through the Award Fee process and remains one of the highest program priorities.

Senator THURMOND. The F–22 program grew in cost last year from $71 billion to $73 billion. For the record, state why.

General EBERHART. The referenced growth of the F–22 Program is the total program change from the fiscal year 1995 President's Budget to the fiscal year 1996 President's Budget. The major driver of this increase was the rephase cost resulting from the fiscal year 1994 congressional cut of $163M and the fiscal year 1995 DOD cut of $100M. The EMD cost increase due to this rephase was approximately

$570M. In addition, a one year slip in procurement resulted from the rephase which increased production costs by approximately $1.5 billion, all due to inflation.

Senator THURMOND. The F-22 EMD provides for a pool of award fees. The fiscal year 1996 award fee pool is $129M. Since period ending March 1993 Lockheed Martin's award fees performance has dropped from 91 percent to an 83 percent fee payment for the most recent award fee period. The committee would like the SPO's opinion about Lockheed Martin's EMD performance and why its award fees have dropped rather starkly.

General EBERHART. Lockheed Martin's F-22 award fee determinations are based on a comprehensive evaluation of technical performance, schedule performance and cost control. The downward trend in award fee ratings from 91 percent to 83 percent occurred gradually over several award fee periods. No single deficiency or issue is responsible for the trend but rather a number of interdependent cost, schedule, and performance issues identified as a result of the increased program complexity associated with the transition from a paper design to actual hardware. Lockheed Martin's overall award fee performance, in fact, clearly indicates a sustained record of high achievement over nine consecutive award fee evaluation periods.

The award fee pool is based on a straight percentage of the contract value. Every time the program is forced to rephase, the contract value increases, therefore the award fee pool increases as well. Due to the recent signing of the revised ENM contract required by the latest rephase effort, Lockheed Martin's F-22 award fee pool has changed from $129M to $131M.

ANTHROPOMETRICS AND JPATS

Senator THURMOND. I understand the contract for the JPATS aircraft was recently awarded. Will the cockpit meet the operational requirement for the widest range of body sizes available in any aircraft?

General EBERHART. The JPATS aircraft is required to accommodate a minimum of 80 percent of eligible female pilot candidates. The Beech MKII cockpit will accommodate approximately 97 percent of eligible females and its ejection seat will accommodate at least 80 percent. Efforts are underway to examine the feasibility of increasing the ejection seats accommodation range.

Senator THURMOND. What percentage of body sizes for Hispanies, Orientals, African-Americans and women will be accommodated by the JPATS aircraft?

General EBERHART. The JPATS aircraft is required to accommodate a minimum of 80 percent of eligible female pilot candidates. The Beech MKII cockpit will accommodate approximately 97 percent of eligible females and its ejection seat will accommodate at least 80 percent. There is no data currently available for racial or ethnic accommodation distribution.

Senator THURMOND. The services are stressing jointness today as demonstrated in joint training and joint aircraft. Have you also standardized measurement criteria for mapping cockpits and measuring people?

General EBERHART. Yes. In May 1994 The Secretary of Defense established the Joint Primary Aircraft Training System (JPATS) anthropometric accommodation working group. As a result of this direction, there was a 1994 tri-service meeting at Wright Patterson Air Force Base. At this meeting the USAF, USN, USA all agreed on standardized techniques for personnel measurement and cockpit mapping. This agreement only applied to research and database development. It did not apply to the three services pilot entrance screening or aircraft coding techniques.

COCKPIT MODIFICATIONS FOR CURRENT AIRCRAFT FLOW

Senator THURMOND. The cockpit environment of the current aircraft in inventory is much more restrictive than the JPATS primary trainer. What steps have you taken to correct this situation? Have you funded or conducted feasibility studies to determine which cockpit modifications would be necessary in order for these aircraft to accommodate the widest range of body sizes analogous to the JPATS criteria?

General EBERHART. There are no active programs to address modifying current cockpits for the expanded population. The Air Force has not funded or conducted any feasibility studies other than F-22, JPATS, or Joint Strike Fighter (JSF) for the expanded population range for both accommodation and escape.

Senator THURMOND. Provide for the record copies of your plans of action and milestones (POA&M) for cockpit accommodation. Include associated costs required for such modifications.

General EBERHART. There are no current requirements for modifying current inventory cockpit accommodation.

TACAIR

Senator THURMOND. What are your plans for handling aviation career paths, taking into account that other aircraft in inventory are much more restrictive for body sizes than the JPATS?

General EBERHART. The DOD Cockpit Working Group is currently working to address the integration of JPATS. In support of that goal, we plan to evaluate all cockpits in the Air Force inventory. Following this analysis of cockpit parameters, we will begin an evaluation of the costs and benefits of specific modifications which may impact individual pilot career tracks.

Senator THURMOND. How do you propose to handle the incompatibility in cockpits before the necessary cockpit modifications are completed?

General EBERHART. At this time, we are evaluating all Air Force cockpits for compatibility. Following this analysis, a plan will be developed to address all identified limitations. The Air Force will not assign individuals to cockpits incompatible to their body size.

Senator THURMOND. Does a joint services strategy exist for correlating body size and aircraft training pipelines?

General EBERHART. Not currently. However, this issue will be evaluated by the DOD Cockpit Working Group as part of the JPATS integration.

EJECTION SEATS

Senator THURMOND. Which ejection seats currently in use accommodate the widest range of body sizes and what are the anthropometric limits of those seats?

General EBERHART. All the ejection seats currently in use with the Air Force were designed to accommodate the 5th to 95th percentile male flying population. The actual range of personnel that can be safely accommodated for most seats has not been determined. The seats in the T–37 and T–38 have been studied for lighter aircrew with weights down to 104 pounds. In addition, the T–37 and T–38 ejection seats are no longer in production. They also have a limited capability and are not suited for the newer aircraft. There has been a "small occupant study" for light weight (103 pound) occupants in the ACES II seat, but further work is needed. This study only considered personnel with a 64 inch stature and a 34 inch sitting height (JPATS allows a 31 inch sitting height).

Senator THURMOND. Provide for the record a matrix of current and planned ejection seats with the ranges of weights and other anthropometrics that the seats will accommodate for safe ejection.

General EBERHART.

Ejection seat	Aircraft	Design Anthropometry
ACES II	A–10, F–15, F–16, F–22, F–117, B–1, B–2, JSF candidate.	5th to 95th male AF (1967 data base) 140–211
Martin-Baker Mk 7	F–4G	5th to 95th male AF (1950 data base) 132–201 lbs.
Lockheed	SR–71	5th to 95th male AF (1950 data base) 132–201 lbs
Lockheed	U–2/TR–1	5th to 95th male AF (1950 data base) 132–201 lbs.
Martin-Baker Mk16L	JPATS	JPATS cases 1–7 DOD data base) 116–245 lbs.
Martin-Baker Mk14	JSF candidate	3rd to 98th male Navy (1964 data base) 136–213 lbs
Weber B–52	b–52	5th to 95th male AF (1950 data base) 132–201 lbs
Weber T–37	T–37	5th to 95th male AF (1950 data base) 132–201 lbs.
Northrop improved	T–38	5th to 95th male AF (1950 data base) 132–201 lbs.
Zvesda K36 3.5	JSF candidate	JPATS cases 1–7 103–245 lbs
4th Generation technology demonstration.		JPATS cases 1–7 103–245 lbs

The T–37 and T–38 seats were evaluated for female pilot training in 1976 The Mk 16L was designed to meet the JPATS case 1–7 anthropometry. The K–36 3 5 seat is being modified to meet JPATS case 1–7 anthropometry. The "Fourth Generation Program" is conducting a technology demonstration, and has a goal to meet JPATS case 1–7 anthropometry There is no presently funded effort to expand the pilot population accommodation on any other USAF ejection seat

---

QUESTIONS SUBMITTED BY SENATOR DIRK KEMPTHORNE

AIRSPACE

Senator KEMPTHORNE. General Eberhart, can you describe the airspace requirements that will influence the basing decisions regarding the F–22?

General EBERHART. The amount of airspace an aircraft needs to practice its mission is determined by three factors: (1) aircraft speed and maneuverability (2) aircraft avionics (3) weapons. When the F-15A entered the inventory 21 years ago, it needed airspace 40 NM by 40 NM. Since 1975, the F-15's avionics, designed to detect, identify, and engage enemy aircraft has been upgraded. Its missiles were improved. With the advent of our most advanced/long range air to air missile, and improved radar technology, today the F-15C requires airspace 70 NM by 60 NM, 500 feet AGL to 50,000 feet. When the F-22 enters the inventory, it will fly supersonic for sustained periods of flight at a higher mach number than the F-15C. The F-22's avionics will be better than the current F-15C, and it will also employ AMRAAM. Since the F-22 has greater speed and improved avionics as compared to the F-15, plus it needs more airspace than the F-15C. The optimum amount of airspace for the F-22 to practice its counter air mission is 150 NM by 100 NM, 500 feet AGL to 50,000 feet.

F-16 HARM SHOOTERS IN BOSNIA COMPARED TO F-4G

Senator KEMPTHORNE. General Eberhart, how have the F-16 HARM shooters in Bosnia compared with the previous performance of the F-4G's in Desert Storm.

General EBERHART. Both Bosnia and Desert Storm were successful SEAD campaigns. No aircraft were shot down by radar SAMs in Bosnia when SEAD forces were present. Likewise, no radar directed shoot down occurred in Desert Storm when the Wild Weasels were present. The Commander Allied Air Forces Southern Europe, NATO has stated, F-16 HTS with HARMs "are an integral part of a well integrated successful SEAD campaign."

F-16 HTS CAPABILITIES

Senator KEMPTHORNE. Is the Air Force still comfortable with the capability of the F-16 in the SEAD mission?

General EBERHART. Yes, the Air Force is comfortable and confident in the HTS equipped F-16's ability to accomplish the SEAD mission. F-16's were an integral part of the successful SEAD campaign in Bosnia's Operation Deliberate Force. No aircraft was shot down by radar SAM's when these SEAD forces were present. Additionally, the systems effectiveness has been enhanced with the integration of Version 5, which became operational March 1996. Further enhancements are contracted for future incorporation. What is now an effective system will be even better with these funded enhancements.

F-16 HTS VERSUS F-4G

Senator KEMPTHORNE. What work-arounds or loss of capability have resulted from the use of F-16's instead of the Wild Weasels? General EBERHART. F-16 SEAD tactics are employed to compensate for HTS pod limitations. Consequently, F-16's equipped with the Harm Targeting System are quite capable of accomplishing the SEAD mission. This is evidenced by the successful SEAD campaign in Bosnia's Operation Deliberate Force. While F-16 SEAD forces were present, no aircraft were lost to radar SAM'S. The newer, more capable/survivable F-16 Block 50's have doubled the number of "smart" HARM shooters over F-4G's. Additional capabilities include the ability to data-link specific target location information to other F-16 Block 50's through the use of Improved Data Modem (IDM). They are also able to receive targeting data from off-platform sources, such as Rivet Joint. Future funded improvements to the HTS pod will further enhance this effective platform.

QUESTIONS SUBMITTED BY SENATOR JOSEPH I. LIEBERMAN

F-22

Senator LIEBERMAN. I was pleased to note yesterday in General Fogleman's testimony before the committee that he stated the F-22 weight growth is no longer a major concern. For the record, would you describe the F-22 weight monitoring methodology the Air Force employs and the degree of confidence the Air Force has in its estimates?

General EBERHART. I'm glad you asked that question Senator. As you know, the F-22 program has requirements for effectiveness, but not weight. However, since weight impacts some aspects of effectiveness, particularly maneuverability and range, we track weight very closely. Based on the performance requirements for the aircraft, each Integrated Product Team (IPT) responsible for a major system, such as Airframe, Avionics and Utilities and Subsystems, were given weight budgets. Those weight budgets were further allocated to sub IPTS, such as Attack Avionics as a subset of the overall Avionics IPT. Every other week, the teams flow their design weights back up through the IPTs to get a total current estimate (CE) for F–22 weight. Those bi-weekly weight reviews are conducted by the Program Manager, who continues to aggressively manage weight. At the current estimate, we have over 2,500 lbs of margin before we impact any of the current maneuver requirements.

The F–22 design is being done using very sophisticated computer aided design (CAD/CAM) tools, and we have great confidence in their fidelity. We are beginning to weigh parts that have been manufactured for the first aircraft and comparing their actual weight to the predicted weight from the respective IPTS. Out of over 9,600 lbs of parts (about 30 percent of the aircraft), the actual weights are within 1 percent of the weight estimation. That demonstrated accuracy reinforces our confidence in the overall weight estimation for the aircraft. The F–22 program is on track, meeting every warfighter requirement.

Senator LIEBERMAN. I understand the Air Force has revised selected F–22 performance specifications. Can you explain the rationale behind those changes and the tradeoffs considered?

General EBERHART. After the Critical Design Review (CDR) in February of last year, the aircraft's estimated maneuver capability was very close to the requirement. There were two options available to us to regain margin on that requirement. One was to spend more money to increase the performance of the aircraft, and the other was to relax the maneuverability requirement. The warfighters and the engineers did a great deal of analysis to quantify how much money would be required to restore margin and to quantify the impact to the F–22 mission effectiveness if the requirement was lowered. After that analysis was complete, it was obvious that relaxing the maneuverability requirement had a negligible effect on overall mission effectiveness, gave us the margin we desired and provided the best cost/performance trade for the taxpayer. In fact, the F–22 will still maintain a significant maneuver advantage over its adversaries.

Because that requirement was one of our Key Performance Parameters, the F–22 program presented its cost/performance trade recommendations to the Joint Requirements Oversight Council (JROC). When the JROC reviewed the options, they agreed with the Air Force recommendation. The F–22 in its present configuration will provide the Nation a revolutionary capability that will allow total domination of any future adversary.

Application of cost/effectiveness tradeoffs such as the one illustrated here has allowed the F–22 program to maintain its required level of effectiveness while remaining affordable as part of the overall Air Force fighter modernization plan.

Senator LIEBERMAN. How does the concurrency in the F–22 program compare with previous fighter development programs such as the F–15, F–16 and F–18E/F?

General EBERHART. Numerous studies have shown that the F–22 program concurrency has been prudently balanced. Secretary Perry, in his September 1995 report to Congress on the F–22 program, stated ". . . the F–22 program contains a prudent balance between concurrency and risk based on historical precedent and sound engineering judgment." The report went on to say that DT&E was the most relevant metric for measuring program concurrency. The F–22 program will have only three production aircraft delivered at the end of DT&E.

At the behest of Congress the DOD conducted a study of F–22 concurrency. OSD convened the Defense Science Board (DSB), a panel including acquisition experts from around the country, to review the F–22 program. In their April 1995 review, the DSB determined ". . . there is no reason based upon risk/concurrency to introduce a schedule stretch [to the F–22 program] at this time." They also said that the ". . . F–22 program concurrency is consistent with and, in many ways, more conservative than previous fighter development programs [F–15, F–16 and F/A–18]." One of the studies cited by the DSB was a RAND study, dated November 1994. RAND found that major problems are uncovered in the first 10–20 percent of full scale system development test. Comparatively, the F–22 will have completed 27 percent of the total flight test program (some 1,400 flight test hours) before Low-Rate Initial Production (LRIP) begins.

The F–22 is an event-driven program that ensures key criteria are met as a prerequisite to production decisions. Needlessly stretching the F–22 EMD program will cause the taxpayer to pay a large bill. The DSB cites an estimated $8–10B increase in program cost if the pro ra remains at an initial production rate of four aircraft for 3 more years. The Program Office recently estimated an additional $2.6B of cost to the program if the low rate production schedule is adjusted to commit to 10 percent orless of the total production buy. The DOD believes the F–22 program is well managed and the level of concurrency in the program is optimal.

[Whereupon, at 11:10 a.m., the hearing was adjourned.]

DEPARTMENT OF DEFENSE AUTHORIZATION FOR APPROPRIATIONS FOR FISCAL YEAR 1997 AND THE FUTURE YEARS DEFENSE PROGRAM

FRIDAY, MARCH 29, 1996

U.S. SENATE,
SUBCOMMITTEE ON AIRLAND FORCES,
COMMITTEE ON ARMED SERVICES,
Washington, DC.

ARMY AND UNMANNED AERIAL VEHICLE (UAV) MODERNIZATION EFFORTS

The subcommittee met, pursuant to notice, at 9:02 a.m. in room SR–222, Russell Senate Office Building, Senator John Warner (chairman of the subcommittee) presiding.

Committee members present: Senators Thurmond, Warner, Coats, Levin, Lieberman, and Bryan.

Committee staff members present: Romie L. Brownlee, staff director; and Donald A. Deline, general counsel.

Professional staff members present: John R. Barnes, Lawrence J. Lanzillotta, and Stephen L. Madey, Jr.

Minority staff member present: Creighton Greene, professional staff member.

Staff assistants present: Shawn H. Edwards.

Committee members' assistants present: Judith A. Ansley and John H. Hoggard, assistants to Senator Warner; Richard F. Schwab, assistant to Senator Coats; John F. Luddy, II, assistant to Senator Inhofe; David A. Lewis, assistant to Senator Levin; Suzanne M. McKenna, and John P. Stevens, assistants to Senator Glenn; John F. Lilley, assistant to Senator Lieberman; and Mary Weaver Bennett, assistant to Senator Bryan.

OPENING STATEMENT OF SENATOR JOHN WARNER, CHAIRMAN

Senator WARNER. Good morning, everyone. Senator Levin and I welcome you before our subcommittee.

For those who may not know it, Senator Levin and I came to the Senate a number of years ago. In view of term limits, we do not discuss those number of years now, but simply greet everybody and say that we have worked as partners on many responsibilities here in the Committee on Armed Services, and I am pleased that he continues to serve here in the capacity as the Ranking Member of this committee.

(55)

Today, the Subcommittee on AirLand meets to hear testimony from two panels. The first panel will discuss Army modernization, and the second panel will provide us an update on our manned aerial vehicle—UAV—program.

It is always good to see you, gentlemen. We are looking forward to hearing your comments on the Army's fiscal year 1997 budget request and our remodernization efforts for the future. Although the complete details on the budget request are not yet available, we are somewhat concerned on several points as we review the budget request in its present form.

Speaking just for myself, the concern is that the Army's declining trend in procurement has not been reversed. This request represents 13 straight years of declining procurement budgets.

The decision to reduce end strength without regard to force requirements is also troubling. Force structure and end strength decisions should be based on strategy requirements and not the budget restrictions.

It seems that each year modernization is a bill-payer for other near-term problems, but that the promise to fix the problem in later years—of course, those later budgets have their own problems, and modernization again gets reduced. I fail to see how the budget provides for the future modernization in any meaningful way.

Decisions made now, gentlemen—and I have said this to each of the senior members of the military. The decision made now with respect to R&D and procurement will provide your successors—a decade hence, others will be here, and equipment that they will have at that time will be the direct result of the foundation that you have laid.

I am not here just in the nature of politics or anything else. It is just a grave concern of mine. The R&D and procurement budgets are declining at a rate where I am concerned now about the successor generations that will appear before this committee a decade hence.

Having said that, I will now turn to my distinguished colleague.

STATEMENT OF SENATOR CARL LEVIN

Senator LEVIN. Thank you, Mr. Chairman, and as you mentioned, we have been here together right from the beginning. For those who do not know it, we are some of the few who are trying to stay here this year. Most of our classmates have decided to open beer and bait shops. [Laughter.]

In any event, I want to again thank the Chairman for not only his courtesies but for the commitment that he brings to the issues of this committee, including the ones that are before us today.

I think we all understand the issue of readiness of our forces today, and nobody ever wants us to return to the hollow condition that our forces were in sometime back, but we also want to now focus, as the Chairman said, about avoiding a future condition where our forces are hollow, so we have to anticipate now what tomorrow's capability gaps are and try to fill those gaps with today's modernization, and our investments in modernization are going to determine, or at least help determine tomorrow's readiness, so that is why this hearing and these issues are so critical.

There are a number of problems in the modernization area. The Army has addressed a number of problems, too, that were identified last year, and we want to thank them for their efforts in that direction.

We are also going to be discussing some issues relative to the unmanned aerial vehicles, the UAV's. There is a linkage between these two subjects, between providing high quality intelligence and targeting information from the UAV's and the Army's efforts to digitize the battlefield. Both have the potential for helping to realize Admiral Owens' vision of dominant battlefield awareness.

So we will be hearing from our witnesses on UAV's, about the progress that the Department has made since last year in developing and fielding UAV systems, and I would note that The Predator UAV which is currently supporting our operations in Bosnia is the result of an advanced concept technology demonstration program, or ACTD.

This particular ACTD was identified as an issue late in the deliberations in the 1994 authorization act, and you, Mr. Chairman, and I on the United States Senate took action, now, what, 3 years ago, I guess, to get an amendment passed. It was our amendment—we are proud of it—to ensure that this program got off to an early, fast start.

So The Predator is performing well, and I was just handed a copy of the amendment that you and I introduced back on September 9, 1993, when Senator Nunn, for Senator Levin and Senator Warner, added funds for this particular unmanned reconnaissance aerial vehicle. I think it was $40 million that we added.

So this is something we have been working on, a lot of projects over the years, and this is one that we can be very proud of, I think. It is now functioning in Bosnia. That is the kind of thing you were mentioning, that we have to make decisions now for years down the road, and that is what the future readiness will be determined by.

So I want to thank you, Mr. Chairman, for, as I said, your efforts and your commitment to a whole host of programs, and an example we will ask our later witnesses about, The Predator.

Senator WARNER. Well, I thank you very much for those remarks, my distinguished friend and colleague, but I suppose one of the more vivid moments is when I went to Bosnia and saw it operate, and not only the technical ability of this system, but the basic simplicity of the infrastructure in Bosnia that was required. I mean, there it was, some tents, a dirt floor, a barn, and it was quickly put together and in an operational status.

In came the C–5's and put down the equipment, and she was operational and going, and a remarkable group of very, very bright individuals, technical people, servicing it, which brings me to one thing.

General Griffith, this morning there was a report about how the Governors in America are working with the CEO's on education, trying to instill at the lower grades of education the desire for people to follow a high tech career.

I think it would be very wise, as I look at the complexity of all the equipment today, and remark on your models here earlier, maybe the Department of Defense better wire into that program.

It possibly is in there right now, but I think it is just an excellent one to encourage young people to begin in the early stages of their education to prepare to have the option someday to go into the military and operate this extraordinary equipment.

Senator Coats, we are pleased to have you.

Senator COATS. Thank you, Mr. Chairman. I am pleased to be here. I echo the sentiments of my colleague from Michigan relative to your leadership.

Senator WARNER. Thank you.

Senator COATS. I do not have an opening statement. I look forward to the testimony.

Senator LEVIN. By the way, I was going to say along the line that you just mentioned, that we have a National Guard program which connects young people to these kinds of technologies that are in the Guard. That is called the Starbase program, and it has been a very successful program at incredibly modest cost.

Our young people are brought to Guard bases and actually touch and see and feel and use or at least watch this equipment being used, and it is a great introduction both to the military and to the advanced technologies that they would use in the private world as well as the military world, should they join it, and it is an example that the Chairman was talking about in terms of the Department of Defense connection to young people in these high technology areas.

Senator COATS. Mr. Chairman, we had a considerable discussion about that in the last authorization bill. I appreciate the Senator from Michigan opening that debate again, because I am sure we will have another discussion as we try to allocate scarce resources. He has been a champion in that program, and perhaps we can get some comment on it from our witnesses.

Senator WARNER. Mr. Secretary, this is your day, once a year.

STATEMENT OF GILBERT F. DECKER, ASSISTANT SECRETARY OF THE ARMY FOR RESEARCH, DEVELOPMENT AND ACQUISITION, ACCOMPANIED BY DR. FENNER MILTON, DEPUTY ASSISTANT SECRETARY OF THE ARMY FOR TECHNOLOGY

Mr. DECKER. I thank you, sir, very much.

Senator LEVIN. I thought you were going to tell us how much you look forward to this day. [Laughter.]

Mr. DECKER. I could probably dig a deep hole if I got too smart on that. [Laughter.]

In fact, as a comment on that, I had the pleasure of attending an honorary breakfast in honor of Congressman Montgomery the other day, and Bill Perry was the speaker, and, of course, Sonny Montgomery is a great man, but Bill Perry commented he had been over here like, three times in the week testifying, and he said, "I just cannot stay away from this place."

So we do look forward to it, and we thank you three gentlemen and other members of the staff and the subcommittee for this opportunity to testify on Army Research, Development and Acquisition budgets for fiscal year 1997 and the overall Army modernization program.

At the outset, I sincerely want to thank this committee for the help and guidance and strong devotion to maintaining an effective national defense, and the generous support of Army modernization that you did for us last year.

I have prepared a detailed written statement for the record, and copies have been provided in advance, and I offer that statement officially for the record at this time.

Senator WARNER. Without objection, the complete submission by all witnesses will be placed into the record.

Mr. DECKER. Thank you, sir.

America's Army is today the premier land force in the world. We continue to see an increasing role for the land forces. If you look at the 40-year period between 1950 and 1989, the Army participated in 10 deployments across the entire spectrum of peace and combat.

In the last 6 years since 1990, we have participated in 25 deployments across the spectrum of peace and combat. Our soldiers are prepared to go anywhere at any time to uphold the Nation's interest, and I believe our soldiers are once again proving this with their service in Bosnia.

The Army, soldiers on the ground, has been and will continue to be the force of choice in our military aspects of our national defense.

Again, this year, the Army, meaning fiscal year 1997 planning, the Army was faced with tough budget choices, as we all worked hard to balance readiness, quality of life, and modernization.

I am sure you realize, and certainly I know you do from your opening remarks, as well as we do, that severely constrained modernization resources have extended our fielding times, have delayed modernization of the total force, have delayed deploying the next generation of systems, and from a business standpoint have resulted in a number of inefficient programs.

Given this environment, where are we going in the future? In the broad sense, the Army set in motion a series of initiatives to arrive at the 21st Century with requisite capabilities, and called this Force XXI.

Force XXI is both a process and a product, designed to look at both the operational and institutional Army, leveraging technologies, information in particular, to enhance the capabilities of the quality force we have today.

Force XXI is America's evolving Army of the 21st Century, and it is a process of continuous learning and transformation.

The Army has been at this for about 5 years, with a very focused effort over the last 3. The Army warfighting experiments, and you will hear more about those from General Hartzog in a moment, are starting to show increased effectiveness with our new concepts.

We recognize, just as you said, sir, I recognize strongly, that today's modernization is tomorrow's readiness. To try to help ourselves, in addition to the kind of guidance and help we get from you, we are taking aggressive actions to further reduce our infrastructure. We are looking for efficiencies across the institutional Army, and with your continued help, we will continue to reform the acquisition process all the way from the program manager in the field to my office.

We hope to see significant savings from these painful efforts, and can program these savings into the modernization account.

Our Army today is the eighth largest Army in the world. Thank God, it is the first best due to quality people, superb training, and the best technology we can afford. We need to keep it that way.

Senator WARNER. It would be interesting if you could recount the other seven.

Mr. DECKER. I believe North Korea is certainly among those seven.

Senator WARNER. China.

Mr. DECKER. China, India, Russia still——

Senator WARNER. I interrupted you. You started with North Korea, and then I interjected China. Go ahead.

Mr. DECKER. I cannot recall. Maybe you can recall most of them. China, Russia still, India, Iraq is still larger than we are, that is four, Iran, the Army of Vietnam—I know I have them. I just cannot remember them off the top of my head.

Senator WARNER. We can put them into the record.

Mr. DECKER. We will get you list of what we think the top seven are. It is arguable whether we are eighth or ninth. Sometimes that eight is a little specious, but it is clear that we are no higher than eighth. That is in terms of numerical size.

[The information referred to follows:]

THE WORLD'S 10 LARGEST ARMIES

The International Institute for Strategic Studies (IISS) is an authoritative source of public information on military forces. The IISS publication *The Military Balance 1995/96* cites the following data (not including the United States Army):

Country	Size of Active Army
Peoples' Republic of China	2,200,000
North Korea	1,000,000
India	980,000
Russia	670,000
South Korea	520,000
Pakistan	520,000
Vietnam	500,000
Turkey	400,000
Iraq	350,000
Iran	345,000

Mr. DECKER. Today, our soldiers have the best war-fighting equipment in the world. The systems, when first fielded, were world-class, and at this instant in time, they still are, and there is a lot of life left in the platforms, and so our near-term strategy, if you look at the aggregate spending, is to leverage previous investments through technology insertion and upgrades.

Examples of that are the Longbow Apache, a marvelous weapons system, the mission equipment package is the upgrade, and some modifications, an upgrade to the air frame, and that is clearly still the very best attack helicopter in the world, not only by our own measurements, but I think it can be demonstrated that in the face of a lot of European economic pressures, both the Netherlands and the U.K. chose this over the French-German Eurocopter version.

We also in this year's budget request fund a limited but critical number of new weapons developments to compliment the technology upgrade programs. Some examples of that are the Sense and Destroy Armor (SADARM) seek and destroy Army munitions program, the Crusader advanced field artillery system, the Javelin antitank infantry missile, appliques for Brigade 21 for digitization of the battlefield, and Comanche, our number 1 development program.

We are striving to make the most efficient use of the dollars given us to modernize the Army. One of the aspects of that modernization which has always been there, but as we move forward in the spectrum of warfare we see we are raising the priorities extremely, and that is the individual soldier system.

I would like to emphasize that when you get back to basics, particularly in the kinds of deployments we are seeing now and for many, many years to come, once again, the soldier is the basic building block of the Army, and so we are investing heavily in the soldier, and with your permission, I would like to show you an example of our Soldier Systems Land Warrior program.

[The prepared statement of Mr. Decker follows:]

PREPARED STATEMENT BY HON. GILBERT F. DECKER, ASSISTANT SECRETARY OF THE ARMY FOR RESEARCH, DEVELOPMENT, AND ACQUISITION

INTRODUCTION

Mr. Chairman and Members of the Committee, thank you for the opportunity to appear before you to discuss the proposed fiscal year 1997 Research, Development and Acquisition (RDA) budget for the United States Army. It is our privilege to represent the Army leadership, the civilian and military members of the Army acquisition work force, and, most importantly, America's soldiers. Our brave men and women operate with great skill and precision the most technologically advanced weaponry on the face of this earth. Today's soldier is well-equipped. Tomorrow's soldier deserves no less.

America's Army is the premier land force in the world. Our well-trained, well-equipped, and ready force would not have been possible without the help and support from members of this committee. As representatives of the American people, you have strongly supported our programs and helped to guide them to fruition. The Army has been a careful steward of the resources provided, but our success would not have been possible without your advice and support.

It is imperative that we maintain the Army's technological advantage on the battlefield. Modernization is essential as we transition today's Army into a 21st century Army—Force XXI. Continuous modernization is one of the keys to dominance on the future battlefield and the key to readiness for unexpected challenges of the 21st century.

There is concern throughout the Army about the funding for modernization and long-term research and development. In fiscal year 1997, our RDA budget request totals $10.6 billion. Our procurement request is $6.4 billion, 16.3 percent of the Department of Defense (DOD) procurement budget request of $38.9 billion and 10.6 percent of the Army's total budget request of $60.1 billion. In fiscal year 1997, our Research, Development, Test and Evaluation (RDT&E) request of $4.3 billion totals 12.4 percent of DOD's RDT&E budget request of $34.7 billion and 7.2 percent of the Army's total budget request.

The fiscal year 1997 budget request will fund our highest priority programs. Our current strategy is to buy a limited number of new weapons, while extending the lives, improving the performance, and adding new capabilities to our existing systems. But ultimately, the Army will reach the point where additional technological improvements of today's systems will provide only marginal benefits. We must look now at new types of systems and capabilities for our 21st century force.

It is our belief that a stable investment in modernization will ensure the long-term readiness of the force. *Today's modernization program is tomorrow's readiness.* As we complete downsizing and restructuring the force, a renewed emphasis on the Army modernization account is essential. Our actions through the Future Years Defense Program (FYDP) will influence the readiness of the force for the next decade and beyond.

THE ARMY MODERNIZATION PLAN AND FORCE XXI

Throughout history, America's Army has been the force of choice to fight and win our nation's wars. This fact has not changed in the 1990's, and it will not change in the 21st century. As we approach the 21st century, the Army is transitioning from a "threat-based force" to a "capabilities-based force." Since 1989, the Army has seen a 300 percent increase in operational deployments. Missions other than traditional warfare have taken on new importance and have led to more soldiers being deployed on more varied types of missions than ever before. Whether we are doing disaster relief operations in Florida or Bangladesh, supporting democracy in Haiti, peacekeeping in Bosnia, or fighting drug traffickers in Colombia and Peru, all these missions have one thing in common. They require the presence of well-trained, well-led, and well-equipped soldiers on the ground.

There are numerous danger zones and the Army must provide potential solutions to the problems faced by our ground commanders and their troops. Because of the magnitude and urgency of the mine problem in Bosnia, for example, the Army has established a Countermine Task Force to accelerate the fielding of equipment to improve our capability to detect, avoid, clear, or neutralize landmines. The objectives is to move technologies from the laboratory to the soldier in Bosnia quickly. The Task Force is also establishing the strategy for future countermine technology efforts.

The changed world environment presents us with new and difficult challenges, the largest being the resource constrained environment in which we operate. Nevertheless, we cannot afford to take a time out from progress. The Army is redesigning itself to meet the new world order. With Force XXI, we are changing today's Army into a 21st century Army. Equipping Force XXI will be a tough challenge, but we have a plan. The Army modernization plan is a living, working document. It focuses our efforts to meet the challenges of the post-Cold War world and to maintain the capabilities necessary to protect our nation's interest and to achieve land force dominance over potential adversaries.

The smaller our Army becomes, the more modern and technologically overmatching it must be. If we do not dominate our enemies in the future as we do now, we may still win—but at the price of far more American casualties, and with the risk of a far longer campaign that will burden our resources and our citizens. The Army modernization strategy focuses our modernization efforts on five objectives where we must preserve our nation's technological overmatch. These five objectives: *Project and Sustain the Force; Protect the Force; Win the Information War; Conduct Precision Strike; and Dominate the Maneuver Battle.*

Project and Sustain the Force

Although we have a global mission, the Army is now largely based in the continental United States (CONUS). When called upon, we must project our power into trouble spots where often our forces can expect to be the first troops on the ground. The capability to deploy highly lethal combat forces rapidly and sustain them from bases both here at home and from our remaining bases overseas is fundamental to our success in any mission. The Army's strategic mobility is based on a critical triad of prepositioned equipment and supplies, strategic sealift, and strategic airlift.

Following are descriptions of systems and systems upgrades in development or in procurement that will help to ensure that we *Project and Sustain the Force.*

A key ingredient to many of our "project" initiatives is the modernization of our installations' information infrastructure. Much of that infrastructure contains World War II telephone lines, outdated telephone switches, and inadequate local area networks. Without upgrades, this outdated infrastructure will not support a power projection strategy which calls for the deployment of minimum support forces. Under this concept, the forward deployed force must have reliable communications with its home base installations. These installations must have a modern information infrastructure to handle the large amounts of data needed to ensure the life blood of the forward elements—a constant flow of personnel, goods, and services. The Army has synchronized various separate efforts into a cohesive program that we call Power Projection Command, Control, Communications, and Computers Infrastructure (PPC⁴I). This program will upgrade installation telephone lines and switches and install local area networks and global network gateways to facilitate transactions with the deployed force. The installation information infrastructure is critical to the exchange of data among the deployed force, stay-behind elements, and the industrial base for resupply, replacements, and repairs. This infrastructure is also vital to maintaining a high state of readiness prior to, deployment, preparation for deployment, and speedy return of the force.

Sustaining the power projection Army throughout the length of the mission will be enhanced by initiatives such as the Army's Total Distribution Program, which is designed to track the quantity, location, and condition of assets anywhere at any time and control the distribution of material within a theater of operations. Using primarily off-the-shelf commercial capabilities, this system will give us asset visibility throughout the force and its support system.

Tactical Wheeled Vehicles (TWV) are a critical element of the Army's operational effectiveness and are essential to projecting and sustaining the force. Today's modern, mobile Army doesn't run on its stomach; it runs on its trucks. Among our most important TWV programs is the Family of Medium Tactical Vehicles (FMTV). The Army is currently negotiating a contract modification to extend production under the current contractor. A family of diesel powered trucks in the 2½-ton and 5-ton payload capacity, built on a common chassis, FMTV will perform line haul, local haul, unit mobility, unit resupply and other missions in combat, combat support, and combat service support units. The Army approved full-rate production in August 1995. What you do not see in the budget submission is our 2½-ton truck Extended Service Program (ESP). We have an ongoing, multi-year contract that funds this program from the National Guard and Reserve equipment account. Through ESP, we take our old 2½-ton trucks, remanufacture them, and add state-of-the-art components. The improved vehicles meet current safety and emission standards and have improved mobility, reliability, and operability. After remanufacture and technology insertion, these vehicles are fielded to the Reserve components. The High Mobility Multipurpose Wheeled Vehicle (HMMWV), a Tri-Service program, is a diesel-powered, four-wheel drive tactical vehicle. In fiscal year 1997, the Army will purchase a HMMWV up-armored scout variant and a heavy variant. In fiscal year 1997, we intend to procure 1,126 vehicles.

In previous years, we made very painful decisions regarding our combat service support area. Several programs were decremented to pay higher priority bills, but the Army needs generators, trucks, and similar equipment. Our current fleet of 2½ ton trucks is older than the soldiers who drive them. We have got to fund these programs at a minimally acceptable level, which we have attempted to do in our fiscal year 1997 budget request.

Procurement of the Black Hawk helicopter will continue in fiscal year 1997 with a new 5 year contract for an additional 172 aircraft. These new UH–60Ls will go to "first to fight" units, and the "A" models they replace will be used for other priority needs such as Medical Evacuation (Medevac). Black Hawk procurement through fiscal year 2001 will bring the fleet to 1,622, almost 80 percent of the Army's requirement for 2,042 aircraft.

Force Provider (FP) is a soldier rest and refit facility for use in operations with limited or no supporting infrastructure such as our current peacekeeping mission in Bosnia. FP is a complete tent city with kitchens, showers, latrines, and laundries that is packaged in containers for ease of deployability. In fiscal year 1997, the Army will procure two FP modules, each to support 550 soldiers.

Protect the Force

Protecting our soldiers has always been important to us, but the lethality of modern weaponry and the availability of theater ballistic and cruise missiles to even third world nations causes us to reemphasize the protection of our forces. We need air defense, particularly defense against theater ballistic missiles, cruise missiles, and unmanned aerial vehicles (UAVs), to protect critical bases, ports, maneuver forces, and political targets/population centers. Realizing there is no 100 percent effective defense, we must maintain the capability for our soldiers to operate protected in a nuclear, chemical, or biological warfare environment. Finally, the potential for fratricide exists in any military operation. Accurate situational awareness is essential to reduce fratricide.

Following are descriptions of systems and systems upgrades now in development or in procurement that will help to ensure that we *Protect the Force.*

In the low altitude forward area air defense, the Stinger procurement request for fiscal year 1997 will provide for continued retrofit of this missile to the Block I configuration. This improvement will extend its life and help overcome some of the inherent deficiencies of the currently fielded Stinger, until the Army can move forward with Stinger Block II. RDT&E funds for Stinger Block I will provide continued, essential phased improvements to the software. The Army has also funded critical RDT&E efforts on the Stinger Block II program to continue developing technology for the 2.75" focal plane array seeker, the smallest seeker in the world.

In fiscal year 1997, funds will provide for the continued procurement of training devices for the Avenger system, and also for termination costs associated with the last year of its multi-year contract. Avenger is a surface-to-air missile/gun weapon system mounted on the HMMWV to counter hostile cruise missiles, UAVS, and fixed-wing aircraft and helicopters.

The proliferation of short range ballistic missiles in the world today poses a direct, immediate threat to many of our allies and to some U.S. forces deployed abroad in defense of our national interests. Over time, the proliferation of longer range missiles will pose a greater threat to the United States—both to our forces stationed here and to our civilian population. The Department of Defense (DOD) missile defense strategy first prevents and reduces the threat through nonproliferation and arms control regimes, then deters the threat with counter-proliferation activity and retaliatory forces. Missile defense is the final leg in this strategy. The most current threat analysis indicates that the short, theater range missile threat is here now. This threat analysis predicts that quantities of longer range missiles and third world missiles capable of striking the U.S. only grow or begin to appear over a longer period of time.

This understanding of threat timelines combined with the relatively large amounts of resources being applied to Ballistic Missile Defense (BMD) caused the Joint Requirement Oversight Council (JROC) and the Office of the Secretary Defense (OSD) to examine missile defense programs. BMD review results have not altered priorities. Theater Missile Defense (TMD) is still the highest priority—first with systems that defend against short-range missiles deployed now. Foremost among these is the Army's Patriot Advanced Capability 3, or PAC–3. Longer range TMD follows, and the risk assumed by delaying the Army's Theater High Altitude Area Defense (THAAD) was determined to be reasonable. The next priority is National Missile Defense (NMD), which would defend the U.S. against Inter-Continental Ballistic Missile (ICBM) attack.

Army efforts are key in all areas. We've already built and deployed more than 100 Patriot Guidance Enhanced Missiles (GEM) to improve PAC–2 performance by a factor of four over our capability in Operation Desert Storm. Three of our Patriot battalions are ready to fight with it now. We're also fielding the Joint Tactical Ground Station (JTAGS) data link that brings space based sensor data directly to our theaters and improves the accuracy of existing defenses.

The PAC–3 program provides even better enhancements with a whole new hit-to-kill lethality and broader area coverage. The BMD review added additional resources to PAC3 and the comparable Navy system, to compensate for delays they have both suffered and to make sure they could be fielded as soon as possible. Neither system is funding constrained. Patriot is fielded with U.S. forces and deployed in CONUS, Europe, Southwest Asia, and South Korea. There are extensive Patriot foreign sales and current foreign interest in the PAC–3 program, which will be fielded first to U.S. forces in fiscal year 1999.

The Medium Extended Air Defense System (MEADS, formerly the Corps SAM system) will defend ground maneuver forces against multiple and simultaneous attacks by short-range ballistic missiles, low radar cross-section cruise missiles, and other air-breathing threats. It provides immediate deployment of a minimum battle element for early entry operations with as few as two C–141 sorties; has mobility to move rapidly and protect maneuver forces during offensive and defensive operations conducted across large land masses; and uses distributed architecture and modular components for advanced survivability, employment flexibility, and firepower. It will also significantly reduce manpower and logistics requirements.

Last summer, senior military commanders, including the Chairman of the Joint Chiefs of Staff, the Army Chief of Staff and the Commander-in-Chief (CINC) of the Pacific Command all communicated to Congress their strong support for this program to counter maneuver force vulnerability to a growing missile threat. MEADS fills a critical need in both the Army and the U.S. Marine Corps (USMC).

We are not alone in this effort. We will soon sign a quadrilateral Memorandum of Understanding with our German, French, and Italian allies to cooperatively develop MEADS. The U.S. will provide 50 percent of the funding and receive 50 percent of the work for our industry. In October, the Army selected two U.S. contractors to proceed into the International Teaming and Project Definition and Validation phase of the program during which the concept will be finalized for full development and production. First Unit Equipped (FUE) is projected for fiscal year 2005.

Aerostats are tethered lighter-than-air platforms that carry sophisticated sensor packages to provide over-the-horizon surveillance and precision tracking for lower tier systems such as Patriot, MEADS, and Navy Standard Missile 2 (SM2). The Army Space and Strategic Defense Command (SSDC) has taken the DOD lead and formed a Joint Aerostat Project Management Office for Cruise Missile Defense in Huntsville, Alabama. Project management is headed by an Army colonel with Air Force and Navy deputies. The effort builds on this year's highly successful Mountain Top Experiment which also involved the Army, Air Force, and Navy.

This effort is similar to another highly successful acquisition the Army undertook in the eighties. concerned with a growing short-range missile threat, the Army then took the initiative and began to build on the highly capable Patriot Air Defense system for TBM defense. The result was a Patriot PAC–2 system able to fight TBM's in Operation Desert Storm. Without this 1980's effort by the Army, the Nation would not have had any TBM defenses in the Gulf War.

Today, there is similar concern over the cruise missile threat. This Aerostat effort parallels the work done in the 1980's to give Patriot a TBM capability, and will yield two Aerostat-based operational sensor units by fiscal year 2002, along with a residual capability for two Patriot battalions to be deployed with them and defeat over the horizon, low observable threats to our forces.

The BMD review validated THAAD as an essential part of our missile defense plans and determined it to be the most mature of our upper tier systems. Without it, near leak proof defense required to defend critical military assets and civilian populations, especially those inland, cannot be achieved. The program successfully completed a Milestone 1 Defense Acquisition Board (DAB) in 1992, is currently undergoing Demonstration/Validation (DEM/VAL) flight testing, and has JROC validated requirements. THAAD hardware and software was engineered to work together as a system from the very beginning. It has demonstrated overall system performance and maturity during extensive ground testing in hardware-in-the-loop facilities and during system testing at White Sands Missile Range in New Mexico. THAAD is a completely integrated hit-to-kill system including missiles, launchers, radars and battle management systems. The BMD review decided to delay THAAD because threat timelines are not as fast as once believed. It also emphasized keeping the User Operational Evaluation System (UOES) schedule for reacting to national need by 1998 with two radars, four launchers, two battle management systems and, by 1999, 40 UOES missiles. Our analysis currently indicates that THAAD will have an objective warfighting capability by fiscal year 2006.

The Army has been the Nation's NMD technical leader for nearly 40 years. The OSD BMD review decided to shift NMD efforts from a technology readiness program to a deployment readiness program. This program is comprised of a 3-year development phase after which acquisition could be accomplished quickly (within 3 years of a future deployment decision) if a threat warrants. Army efforts interface with existing and—planned CINC Battle Management/ Command, Control, and Communications (BMC3) and Integrated Tactical Warning and Attack Assessment (ITW/ AA) assets including the Defense Support Program (DSP), Early Warning Radars (EWRs), and the Space-Based Infrared System (SBIRS), when it becomes operational. When deployed, these NMD systems will detect, track, discriminate, and intercept threat targets in their midcourse phase of flight and will provide effective protection of all 50 States against quantitatively-limited threats. The Ground Based Interceptor (GBI) provides non-nuclear, hit-to-kill intercepts of strategic reentry vehicles at very long ranges. Although the detailed configuration is not yet final, the Army's approach consists of the Exoatmospheric Kill Vehicle (EKV) on a dedicated booster for which the Army recommends a very capable, commercial, low-maintenance solid rocket booster that a Ballistic Missile Defense Organization (BMDO) "Tiger Team" determined can be procured with acquisition reform techniques for no more cost than that incurred in retrofitting Minuteman missiles. The NMD Ground Based Radar (GBR) acquires, tracks, and discriminates strategic reentry vehicles in their midcourse phase of flight and performs engagement kill assessment. It leverages the investment in the TMD–GBR for THAAD using the same solid-state radar technology and large portions of common software.

The first EKV sensor flight test is scheduled for late fiscal year 1996 and intercept testing will begin in fiscal year 1998. The EKV on a surrogate booster, GBR, and BMC3 elements will be integrated in a systems test at the Kwajalein Missile Test Range in fiscal year 1999. The Army is an executing agent of the ground-based portions of the NMD program with BMDO funding and guidance.

In other areas of protecting the force, we will continue engineering efforts to lower the production cost of the Army's anti-fratricide system, the Battlefield Combat Identification System (BCIS), in fiscal year 1997 as well as consider promising alternatives being pursued by different allies. BCIS is a millimeter wave, ground-to-ground, point of engagement system that provides through the sight, day/night, all weather positive identification of BCIS equipped U.S., allied, and coalition platforms. Shooters query potential targets at ranges that can extend beyond five kilometers. Friendly platforms targeted by friendly shooters generate automatic electronic responses in less than a second. BCIS is resistant to electronic countermeasures, active exploitation, and deception. We are currently building 68 BCIS systems for Brigade Task Force XXI. There, BCIS will be tested as a stand alone system and as an input to the situational awareness of heavy forces to determine its value on the digital battlefield. In addition, BCIS will be evaluated along with four other systems in a four party exercise in 1997 (United States, United Kingdom, France, and Germany).

In fiscal year 1997, OSD will continue to improve the Joint Chemical Biological Defense Program. The Army, as executive agent of the program, has aggressively developed a management structure that serves to coordinate and integrate, Service RDA in this critical area. The Joint management structure is developing a program to eliminate duplication and provide the total force with improved chemical and biological protection in the future. Service participation in this process has been enthusiastic and highly constructive. The fiscal year 1997 budget request will continue procurement of protective masks; allow initial procurements of the Biological Integrated Detection System (BIDS) and protective shelter systems, a mobile medical treatment facility; and continue upgrades to the Nuclear, Biological, and Chemical (NBC) Reconnaissance System. Because of the continued emphasis on biological defense, the Army's first biological detection company will be activated in September 1996.

The soldier is our most precious asset. We continue to place great importance on enhancing the battlefield capabilities of the individual soldier. Soldier Modernization consists of the Warrior programs—Land Warrior, Crew Warrior, and Air Warrior; other support areas such as rations, organizational clothing, and individual equipment; and the Soldier Enhancement Program. Land Warrior is the Army's premier program for modernizing the dismounted soldier. It consists of an integrated and modular soldier fighting system that includes the soldier's computer, radios, Global Positioning System (GPS), heads-up display, modular weapon system, thermal weapon sight, video capture, improved ballistic protection, advanced load carrying equipment, laser rangefinder, and combat ID compatibility. Currently in Engineering and Manufacturing Development (EMD), Land Warrior has been combined with the Generation II Soldier Advanced Technology Demonstration at the direction of Congress. A single, consolidated system is scheduled for fielding in fiscal year 2000 and thereafter components will be upgraded through technology insertion. Other important areas of Soldier Modernization, including rations, organizational clothing, and equipment are in various stages of development or fielding in fiscal year 1997. The Soldier Enhancement Program fields individual soldier items in less than 36 months. This quick fix program provides the Army the ability to impact our short-term missions.

In the Information Age, protecting the information used on the digital battlefield is just as important as protecting our soldiers against the lethality of modern weapons. Having an adversary get into one of our data bases and manipulate or destroy the information in the system, will have a serious adverse affect on our forces and weapon systems. To protect our data networks and command and control systems, the Army has written Command and Control (C2) Protect Plans. These plans address the protection of information needed by our warfighting commanders at every level of command from the foxhole to the National Command Authorities. Their implementation will increase the Commanders' confidence in the integrity and confidentiality of the information processed and transmitted throughout the command and control infrastructure, and will help assure the Commanders that the communications networks will be available when needed. The implementation of the plans will also increase the awareness of attacks launched against Army Information Systems and help focus our reaction to these attacks. To implement the plans, we must purchase various security devices which prevent the exploitation of information through interception, minimize the hazards of processing and handling large volumes of highly classified printed cryptographic tapes and material, and resolve the problem of secure interfaces between strategic and tactical systems and links to commercial networks. Fiscal year 1997 development requirements have been identified, with limited prototype purchasing requested, and procurement funding planned in subsequent years.

Win the Information War

Information is power. On the battlefield, information is deadly power. A key factor in modern warfare is the ability to collect, process, disseminate, and use information about the enemy while preventing him from obtaining similar information about our forces. In short, we must destroy, disrupt, and control enemy information sources and distribution while ensuring our commanders get accurate and relevant data in time to use it. The goal is to provide Force XXI the operational advantages of information dominance. Targeting and incapacitating the information systems of adversaries, while protecting our own, will allow deep and simultaneous attacks and lead to overmatching force and decisive victory. Equipping our battlefield systems to transmit, receive, and display digital data, is fundamental to winning the information war.

Following are descriptions of systems and systems upgrades in development or in procurement that will help to ensure that we *Win the Information War*.

The Army's primary development system to ensure that our soldiers have the information advantage in the Information Age is the RAH–66 Comanche armed reconnaissance helicopter, currently in DEM/VAL. Last January, Comanche flew for the first time, a very successful flight. In fiscal year 1997, we will continue flight test of prototype number 1, complete manufacture of prototype number 2, and continue development of the mission equipment package and the TBOI engine. Comanche has the potential to make a major contribution to winning the information war, but it will also make significant contributions to the other four modernization objectives as well. During Operation Desert Storm, our ground commanders never got the near real-time battlefield information they needed to make the best tactical, timely decisions on the employment of battlefield forces. Comanche, if fielded, along with the Joint Surveillance and Target Radar System (Joint STARS) and UAVS, will help correct this most critical deficiency with greatly improved night/adverse weather reconnaissance and target acquisition, deep reconnaissance without detection, survivability, and deployability.

Let me briefly list the capabilities of this revolutionary helicopter under the remaining modernization objectives. (1) The Comanche's capabilities in extended range operations, low observability, target recognition, digitized communications, and armed reconnaissance as well as its ability to quickly respond to a "mission divert" makes it a superior vehicle for deep "precision strike" missions against time sensitive targets—especially targets so dangerous they must be confirmed killed or reengaged. (2) Comanche provides strategic agility to "project and sustain" (rapid inter/intra-theater deployability) with technical superiority that gives the maneuver commander a decisive force on the battlefield worldwide. Its self-deployment range of 1,260 nautical miles is sufficient to self-deploy from CONUS to Europe, Africa, and the Middle East, and it will require significantly less maintenance support than today's helicopters. (3) Comanche will "dominate maneuver" in its cavalry role by quality armed reconnaissance, developing the situation, providing security, maneuvering rapidly across the battlefield to the critical places and synchronizing other scout reconnaissance assets and weapon systems on the digitized battlefield. Designed for rapid rearm, refuel, and repair, the Comanche will increase the operational tempo. (4) The Comanche will reduce the potential for fratricide and "protect the force" through its advanced electro-optical sensors, aided target recognition and sensor/weapons integration. Its night/adverse weather air defense capabilities are unmatched as is its capability to conduct armed reconnaissance and provide early warnings in all conditions to include day/night/adverse weather. It is clear that Comanche is tailor-made for the new world order. Early Operational Capability (EOC) unit fielding is scheduled for fiscal year 2002 with six aircraft.

The Army Battle Command System (ABCS) is essential to realizing the Joint interoperability goal of the Command, Control, Communications, Computers, and Intelligence (C^4I) for the Warrior concept. Procurement of common hardware and control nodes for ABCS continues in fiscal year 1997. Under the ABCS umbrella, research and development (R&D) continues on the evolutionary acquisition of the Army Tactical Command and Control System (ATCCS) which is key to providing commanders in the Army's corps and divisions data to synchronize and direct their forces more effectively.

The ATCCS consists of interoperable automation systems supporting the five Battlefield Functional Areas (BFAs): Maneuver Control System (MCS) supporting the Maneuver BFA; Advanced Field Artillery Tactical Data System (AFATDS) supporting Fire Support; Forward Area Air Defense Command and Control (FAADC²) supporting Air Defense; All Source Analysis System (ASAS) supporting Intelligence/Electronic Warfare; and Combat Service Support Control System (CSSCS) supporting the Combat Service Support BFA. These systems assist the force commanders in pro i g information within the BFAS, planning and controlling operations, and exchanging information horizontally across the BFAS and vertically from battalion to Echelons Above Corps (EAC).

ASAS continues to be a good news story. The program is implementing Common Operating Environment (COE), Force XXI, and Modern Integrated Database (MIDB) additional requirements above and beyond the Operational Requirements Document. This has resulted in a restructure of functionality and performance. The program manager for Intelligence Fusion is accomplishing all of this with no additional funding. ASAS is deployed in Bosnia to support the U.S. Army Special Operations Command in Brindisi, Italy, the multinational brigade (Finnish, Russian, and American forces), 1st Armored Division, and V Corps.

AFATDS, the automated fire support command, control, and communications system will be the first totally automated fire support system and is interoperable with existing field artillery systems, the Airborne Target Handover System/Improved Data Module, other ABCS nodes, and selected allied fire support systems. AFATDS has been approved for full-rate production and fielding.

CSSCS is currently in EMD, with Low Rate Initial Production (LRIP) authority granted by the Army Systems Acquisition Review Council (ASARC) in February 1995. CSSCS is an active participant in Brigade Task Force XXI and other ongoing Army Warfighter Experiments (AWE) and is scheduled for an Initial operational Test and Evaluation (IOT&E), Phase II at Fort Hood, Texas, from September to November 1996. The MCS program will conduct a System Segment Acceptance Test (SSAT)/Customer Test (CT) in fiscal year 1996 and an IOT&E in fiscal year 1997.

All ATCCS systems will be provided to the 4th Infantry Division (4ID), designated as the Experimental Force (EXFOR) for Task Force XXI. In support of the lower echelon command and control and digitization of the battlefield, the Force XXI Battle Command Brigade and Below (FBCB2) Appliqué Program will equip and train a brigade size force during fiscal year 1997 for the AWE entitled Brigade Task Force XXI. Appliqué sets are being acquired for field exercises to provide command and control capabilities to platforms that either have no embedded command and control capabilities or where existing capabilities are inadequate to meet user needs.

The Army has adopted a technical architecture with open standards that will enable complete interoperability across all platforms on the battlefield. The Army is the first Service to do so. Our technical architecture is based on widely accepted commercial standards and the Defense Information Systems Agency's Technical Architecture for Information Management, and is composed of four elements: information processing, data transport, and information standards, as well as a human-computer interface framework. This architecture is applicable to all strategic, tactical, and sustaining base information, communications, and embedded C4I systems. By implementing these well-defined, widely-known, and consensus-based standards, the Army can leverage marketplace investments and assure a migration path into the future. The Army technical architecture has been selected as the baseline for a Joint technical architecture to be developed by OSD.

The Command and Control Vehicle (C2V) will enter LRIP in fiscal year 1997. FUE is planned for fiscal year 1999. The C2V will be a fully tracked, lightly armored vehicle that will ensure a mobile, responsive, and survivable command and control capability for armored forces. It is a battalion-through-corps-level command and control platform which supports operations on the move and integrates the ABCS components.

In support of higher level command and control, the Army Global Command and Control Sy e (AGCCS) will migrate from the current Worldwide Military Command and Control System support infrastructures to the AGCCS single Common Operating Environment (COE). Each of the ATCCS/ABCS tactical command and control systems will continue development and implementation of the COE software into their systems.

The CONUS-based power projection Army is dependent on military satellite communications to ensure the flow of critical command and control information to forces deployed anywhere in the world. To satisfy this critical command and control communications requirement, the Enhanced Manpack UHF Terminal (EMUT) program continues in procurement in fiscal year 1997. The EMUT provides single channel, Demand Assigned Multiple Access (DAMA), secure tactical UHF satellite communications to corps, divisions, and special operations forces to support command and control—during power projection and early entry operations. The need for this capability was shown to be critical during Operation Desert Shield/Desert Storm. It also satisfies the Joint Chiefs of Staff mandate to be DAMA and Advanced Narrowband Secure Voice capable, features which provide for more efficient and effective use of the limited UHF spectrum resources. operating in the UHF frequency band offers the warfighter capabilities for enroute communications/communications on the move, wider area earth coverage, and greater overhead foliage and adverse weather penetration, capabilities which are not possible in other frequency bands. The Army is the lead Service, responsible for the procurement of EMUTs for all Services and Agencies in order to meet the Joint Staff mandate to have Joint interoperability in DAMA and digital secure voice communications after fiscal year 1996.

In fiscal year 1997, as DOD Executive Agent for the Defense Satellite Communications System (DSCS), the Army will continue to modernize the current large fixed satellite ground terminals infrastructure. This modernization effort will improve ground terminal reliability to its original specification; reduce power consumption; and introduce semiautomation of manpower intensive functions (first introduced when DSCS terminals were installed in the late 1970s and early 1980s).

While this modernization was initiated in 1990 for sustainment purposes, it is now supporting the current Army downsizing and reduced funding. These gr terminals will continue to support the high operational availability required for CONUS-based power projection Army and other Service deployed forces. In addition, these modernized terminals will carry out their mission at lower operation and maintenance costs. The fiscal year 1997 R&D funds will complete the development of the medium data rate unit for the Universal Modem (UM) and procurement funds will initiate the UM acquisition. The UM will be the replacement for the 1980 deployed AN/USC–28 anti-jam modem that is installed in more than 100 DSCS locations and is becoming very difficult to maintain because of the unavailability of replacement parts. In addition, fiscal year 1997 R&D will complete the DSCS Integrated Management System (DIMS) development and start the effort for the replacement BATSON equipment that provides the anti-jam command link that is essential for commanding the DSCS satellites in all environments, including jamming. R&D funds will continue to support the Integrated Test Facility at Fort Monmouth, New Jersey, which is a critical element in support of the DSCS pr r and a major factor contributing to the Army's ability to participate in the development of the future DOD Space Architecture. Finally, fiscal year 1997 procurement funds will initiate hardware acquisition for the large fixed terminal family, the AN/GSC–52s, the last DSCS terminals to be modernized.

Currently, DSCS provides critical information transfer to our deployed warfighters at all echelons, as well as, high data rate secure information transfer in support of intelligence operations, electronic warfare, and smart weapons. As the Military-Strategic/Tactical Relay (MILSTAR) system comes on line (to support a CINC and his Division warfighters), the DSCS future mission will be the information super highway between the sustaining base (CONUS) and the deployed warfighter at EAC.

The MILSTAR system remains one of our most critical command and control programs for the deployed Army warfighter at Echelons Corps and Below. MILSTAR will provide a worldwide, secure, jam-resistant communications capability that is urgently needed to prosecute warfighting missions horizontally and vertically at Corps and Division levels for special users. The Air Force launched the first two MILSTAR I Development Flight Satellites in February 1994 and November 1995, and continues to develop the MILSTAR II satellite, an essential element of the Army's assured communications connectivity to our deployed warfighters. The Army's MILSTAR terminal program will acquire two types of mobile tactical terminals for Army and other Service needs. The Low Data Rate Man-portable Terminal Program awarded the full scale production contract in February 1996 for more than 300 terminals to meet Joint service needs. The medium data rate HMMWV-mounted terminal program awarded the LRIP contract in February 1996 and terminal deliveries are scheduled in phase with launch of the first MILSTAR II satellite in fiscal year 1999. Each of these two awards was made under the full provisions of our acquisition reform initiatives, resulting in savings of almost 60 percent when compared to the original budget estimates.

A key element of any digitization architecture is reliable and secure digital data links between fighting systems and commanders. The combat proven Single Channel Ground and Airborne Radio System (SINCGARS), with both voice and data channels, is an important link in any digitization scheme.

Conduct Precision Strike

The Force XXI commander must have rapidly deployable capability to conduct deep attacks against enemy maneuver formations, logistical centers, and command and control nodes. To successfully attack targets with precision at extended ranges requires the capability to see deep, to find designated high-payoff targets, and then transmit that information/intelligence in near-real time to firing units employing advanced weapons and munitions systems to destroy those targets. To accomplish this, the Army must have modern artillery, attack helicopters, missile systems with adequate range and firepower, effective munitions, and superb Reconnaissance, Surveillance, and Target Acquisition systems among which are included reconnaissance helicopters such as Comanche and a family of modern UAVS.

Following are descriptions of systems and systems upgrades in development or in procurement that are key to *Conduct Precision Strikes.*

Crusader, formerly the Advanced Field Artillery System (AFAS) and the Future Armored Resupply Vehicle (FARV), is currently in DEM/VAL. It is the Army's top priority, next generation ground combat system, providing leap-ahead indirect fire cannon and artillery resupply systems for armored forces.. Crusader will provide improved capabilities in range, rate-of-fire, time-on-target, accuracy, survivability, mobility, and ammunition handling speed with reduced manpower and logistics burdens. Crusader will use an advanced design armament system and is the "technology carrier" for other future armored systems—employing robotics, advanced fire control computing techniques, self-protection features, and signature control. FUE is scheduled for fiscal year 2005.

In fiscal year 1997, the Army Tactical Missile System (ATACMS) Block IA, the extended range version of the combat proven ATACMS Block I, will begin full-rate production. ATACMS Block I will end production this year with fielding completed in July 1997. Last February, the Army successfully fired the first production representative model of the Block IA missile. Launched from McGregor Range in Fort Bliss, Texas, the missile flew approximately 175 kilometers to a target site on White Sands Missile Range in New Mexico. The test was highly successful and met all planned objectives. Flight tests continue this spring leading to an LRIP decision in May.

In July 1995, the Army awarded the contract for the continued development of the ATACMS Block II missile. ATACMS Block II will provide the means to attack and destroy moving and stationary threat targets at long-ranges with high precision. In combat, the system delays and disrupts enemy forces in the deep battle, thereby interrupting threat force planning for operations in the close battle area. During fiscal year 1997, ATACMS Block II development continues with conduct of the critical design review, an engineering development test flight, and integration activities associated with the BAT, Brilliant Anti-Armor Submunition.

Continuing in EMD in fiscal year 1997, BAT completes contractor development testing in preparation for integrated flight tests with the Block II missile. The BAT, a self-guided submunition, uses both acoustic and infrared seekers to locate and attack moving armored combat vehicles without human interaction. BAT submunitions, carried deep into enemy territory by ATACMS Block II missiles and dispensed over areas of high-payoff targets, autonomously detect, attack, and destroy individual targets. The FUE date for ATACMS Block II with BAT is fiscal year 2001.

The BAT Pre-Planned Product Improvement (P³I) DEM/VAL continues in fiscal year 1997 with captive flight testing of the two competing multi-mode seeker concepts. The BAT P³I, through seeker and warhead improvements, adds cold sitting armor, heavy multiple launch rocket systems, and surface-to-surface missile transporter erector launchers to the BAT target set. ATACMS Block II and IIA are the delivery vehicles for BAT P³I. The extended range ATACMS Block IIA missile begins development in fiscal year 1998.

The ATACMS/BAT programs are currently undergoing a joint Army/industry initiative to reduce the overall cost. The President's budget request already incorporates initiatives from Phase I of the effort. These low risk initiatives resulted in a cost avoidance to the Army of $381 million. Higher risk initiatives in Phase II of the effort are still being evaluated. These initiatives include multiyear contracting and reinvestment strategies and have the potential to save $565 million for the Army through fiscal year 2008.

Sense and Destroy Armor (SADARM) continues in LRIP. A product improvement program is scheduled to begin in fiscal year 1997. The product-improved submunition is expected to yield a 30 percent increase in effectiveness. SADARM is a fire-and forget, sensor-fused submunition designed to detect and destroy armored vehicles, primarily self-propelled artillery. It is scheduled for fielding in fiscal year 1999.

The Extended Range Multiple Launch Rocket System (ERMLRS) is scheduled to begin LRIP in the fourth quarter of fiscal year 1996 with FUE scheduled for fiscal year 1998. The extended range rocket increases the range capability to 45(+) kilometers as compared to the current basic tactical rocket range of 30 kilometers. The program includes the addition of a low level wind measuring device on the M270 launcher to enhance accuracy and effectiveness, and incorporates a self-destruct fuse on the submunitions to increase safety for friendly maneuver forces.

The Army is also continuing development of the MLRS Improved Launcher Mechanical System (ILMS) and Improved Fire Control System (IFCS) in fiscal year 1997. These modifications have been linked to provide a one time major upgrade to all MLRS launchers starting in fiscal year 1998. These modifications include an embedded GPS, upgraded fire—control computer, improved launcher load module drive system, and improved built-in test equipment. These upgrades will increase crew/launcher survivability, reduce operation and sustainment costs, and mitigate component parts obsolescence.

Joint STARS is supported in fiscal year 1997 to complete the Limited Production of Medium and Light models of the Ground Station Modules (GSM) while continuing with P³I to migrate the system to a single Common Ground Station for use by all Services. The Joint STARS system has been a major contributor to the International Forces (IFOR) peacekeeping operation in Bosnia. Once again, the system has proven that its near-real time information collection capabilities play a critical role in total intelligence production and dissemination during peacetime and will provide the commanders superior targeting and battle management capabilities in future combat operations.

The fiscal year 1997 annual buy of additional Paladins will allow the Army to provide this howitzer to all cannon active component artillery battalions and also to begin fielding to the 14 National Guard battalions. The Paladin overcomes many operational limitations and outdated technology of the current M109 howitzer and provides longer range fires and substantially improved survivability through "shoot and scoot" techniques. This program is a true representation of government and industry cooperation.

Army forces require modern munitions and the assurance that munitions expended in a conflict can be replenished in a timely manner. Army forces also require a steady supply of training ammunition to ensure soldiers are constantly ready to answer when called on to support our nation. The fiscal year 1997 request fully resources the Army's requirements for training ammunition with a modest drawdown of war reserves, and continues an affordable build-up of modern munitions.

This nation requires a viable munitions industrial base to ensure ammunition supplies in peacetime and the capability to replenish ammunition stocks after a conflict. This industrial base is difficult to maintain in today's peacetime, resource constrained environment. The Army continues to work with industry to develop affordable and more efficient courses of action that provide for future needs.

The Army also requires an effective munitions logistics base to support operations in peace and war. The fiscal year 1997 request contains resources to support a necessary demilitarization program which frees storage for serviceable munitions while lping to reduce storage sites in support of the Base Realignment and Closure (BRAC) 1995 program.

Dominate the Maneuver Battle

Decisive operations require controlling vital land areas and the destruction of the enemy's land combat capability. The Army must always maintain a substantial overmatching capability in maneuver forces. It is in the maneuver battle that the risk to our soldiers is highest. Advanced weapon systems and technology will continue to proliferate around the world. To ensure swift, decisive victory with minimum casualties, the Army combined arms team must be able to outthink, outmaneuver, and outshoot its adversaries day or night, in any weather.

Following are descriptions of systems and systems upgrades in development or in procurement that will help to ensure that we Dominate the Maneuver Battle.

The Army is pursuing a technology insertion approach to modernization by integrating digital and advanced infrared sensors into Abrams tanks and Bradley Fighting Vehicles and modifying the AH–64 Apache helicopter to the Longbow configuration with a leap-ahead day/night/adverse weather target acquisition radar, fire-and-forget HELLFIRE missiles, and advanced digital processors and communications. These upgrades are all compatible and will allow these systems to exchange friendly and enemy position data directly from video display to video display. In addition, all can link with scout helicopters and artillery fire direction centers, and transmit data directly to C2V and to ABCS components. This powerful linkage of combat systems allows the commander to provide a common view of the battle to all elements, speeds-up the tempo of maneuver, and reduces the potential for fratricide. It allows us to "dominate the maneuver battle" by dominating the information battle.

Javelin provides our soldiers a man-portable, highly lethal system against conventional or reactive armor threat. It features fire-and-forget technology with a range in excess of 2,000 meters in adverse weather, day or night, and weighs less than 50 pounds. The Army, in cooperation with its Joint Venture partners (Texas Instruments/Lockheed-Martin), continues an aggressive cost reduction program that will significantly reduce the total cost of the Javelin program by an estimated $1.4 billion. Savings will be achieved by reducing Javelin production from 14 to 11 years, taking the savings, and reinvesting them into the program. The program begins its full-rate multi-year production contract in fiscal year 1997. A recent program budget decision to provide additional procurement money from fiscal year 1999–01 will accelerate production duration from 11 to 8 years which should result in additional savings.

The Improved Target Acquisition System (ITAS) for the TOW (Tube-Launched, Optically-Tracked, Wire-Guided) missile will complete EMD and enter LRIP late in fiscal year 1996. Because of funding constraints, fiscal year 1997 procurement funding has been combined with fiscal year 1998 funding to maximize production efficiencies. ITAS will improve the target detection, recognition, and engagement capability of the HMMWV mounted and ground launched TOW missile by incorporating a Second Generation Forward Looking Infrared (FLIR) capability, a laser range finder, and aided target tracking features. This program is the pathfinder for Second Generation FLIR systems and is the foundation for the IBAS (Improved Bradley Acquisition System). The high degree of commonality among Second Generation FLIR systems provides a strong production base and reduced logistics costs.

We continue to upgrade older M1 tanks to the M1A2 configuration. To date, more than 130 M1s have completed the upgrade proccss, and we have fielded 85 to operational units. We also are continuing the Bradley A3 upgrade program, and are working to bring this system on line more quickly. Longbow Apache continues in production in fiscal year 1997. Currently, the Army is negotiating a 5 year multi-year contract as recommended by Congress. Once fielded, Longbow Apache's all weather target acquisition system will provide first-ever long-range detection and automated classification, prioritization, and target hand-over for the modernized Apache team and the other combat and command and control systems linked to it. For the first time ever, a coordinated, rapid fire, precision strike capability will be available to the maneuver force commander on a 24-hour basis in day/night/adverse weather conditions. Longbow HELLFIRE will continue in LRIP in fiscal year 1997. The Army, in coordination with its Joint Venture partners (Lockheed- Martin/Westinghouse), has in-place an aggressive cost reduction plan that will reduce the production program from 10 to 8 years while reducing the total procurement cost by a projected $860 million. The addition of the fire-and-forget Longbow HELLFIRE to our missile inventory will significantly enhance the survivability of our Apache helicopter fleet and provide the battlefield commander flexibility across a wide-range of mission scenarios.

The Grizzly, formerly the Breacher, program will continue in EMD in fiscal year 1997. Efforts will focus on design refinement and prototype modifications. The system is based on the M1 Abrams chassis and is equipped with a full-width mine clearing blade and a power-driven excavating arm to support maneuver force mobility through minefields, rubble, tank ditches, wire, and other obstructions. The Army currently has no system with these capabilities. Its importance cannot be overstated because the Grizzly will provide the combined arms team with an integrated, counter- mine and counter-obstacle capability in a single, survivable vehicle.

In fiscal year 1997, the Line-of-Sight Antitank (LOSAT) program remains in the technology demonstration phase to continue to mature the Kinetic Energy Missile (KEM) and Advanced Fire Control System. Numerous studies and analyses have suggested that the KEM's overwhelming lethality can help satisfy the critical anti-armor needs of our early entry forces.

The Army is committed to a Follow-on to TOW (FOTT) program, formerly called Advanced Missile System-Heavy (AMSH), to address TOW stockpile depletion and provide the force increased range, survivability, and lethality to overmatch current, emerging, and postulated threats. Results from the Army's Anti-Armor Requirements and Resource Analysis clearly demonstrate that the FOTT missile gives the ground-based early entry forces and TOW-equipped Bradleys greatly improved lethality while making the entire force more survivable. The Army continues to fund critical efforts leading toward an engineering and manufacturing start in fiscal year 1998. Requested funding in fiscal year 1997 will support modeling, information flow to potential bidders and Government test facilities as an opportunity for potential bidders to demonstrate the technical merits of their proposed hardware concepts.

Although the Army has no plans for continued TOW missile production, funding has been requested in fiscal year 1997 to continue repairs to the missiles for increased effectiveness in cold weather; provide for support for deliveries of missiles procured in fiscal year 1995; and initiate production line shutdown.

The Multi-Purpose Individual Munition/Short Range Assault Weapon (MPIM/SRAW) is the dismounted soldier's lightweight, shoulder-fired weapon for short-range/urban terrain combat. This weapon will have the capability to accurately fire at targets up to 500 meters distance, from enclosures or in a prone position, and thereby increase survivability. The robust warhead has the capability to defeat modern armored personnel carriers and incapacitate personnel in reinforced masonry buildings and inside bunkers. The Army and the USMC are partners in this cooperative development program which has reduced development and procurement costs. The Army's MPIM/SRAW program uses the same launcher and flight module as the USMC's Predator anti-tank program. This cooperative efforts will reduce development and procurement costs for both Services. Fiscal year 1997 funding continues EMD for the MPIM/SRAW program.

BATTLEFIELD DIGITIZATION

The creation of the digitized battlefield is critical to the Army's efforts to maintain a modern, but smaller, force capable of decisive victory—Army XXI. In order to field

Army XXI, we must employ digital information technology across the battlefield at all levels. Digital information systems provide the capability for a geometric increase in the amount of information gathered and the speed with which that information can be analyzed, tailored, and provided to the warfighters at appropriate levels of command.

Simply moving information around the battlefield is not the answer. The ultimate objective must be improved situational awareness to ensure integrated operations through all echelons within the Army and at both the Joint and Combined levels of warfare. Clearly, when a commander can rapidly see where his forces are, what condition they are in, make decisions and issue orders; he can concentrate combat power at the time and place on the battlefield to dominate the maneuver battle.

The Army has made significant progress over the last year towards developing and fielding a digitized experimental force, the EXFOR! An Army Digitization Master Plan guides the Army Digitization Office's efforts to provide information technology to redesign the Army by the year 2000. During the last year, the Army has conducted two key experiments with digital information systems: one with mechanized troops at Fort Knox, Kentucky, and one with light infantry at both Fort Drum, New York, and the Joint Readiness Training Center at Fort Polk, Louisiana. We gained great insights into the value of digitization for enhancing mission planning, decision making, execution, and increasing tempo on the battlefield. The Army has developed and approved the Army technical architecture, which is "building code" for Army command and control systems. As mentioned earlier, the Army's technical architecture is being used as a start point for development of a DOD/Joint technical architecture. This will greatly enhance integration among the Services.

At the brigade and below level, we are experimenting with an appliqué to bring digitization quickly into the Army. The prototype appliqué sets are currently being installed on EXFOR systems at Fort Hood, Texas, in preparation for the kickoff of the brigade level AWE. The appliqué, along with programs to upgrade digital systems on the M1A2 Abrams Main Battle Tank and the M2A3 Bradley Fighting Vehicle to an open architecture, will lead to a seamless digital communications architecture from the tactical to the strategic level and set the stage for a successful development of Army XXI.

Emerging systems such as Joint STARS, Comanche, and Crusader will enhance the digital systems as they are fielded. They will be brought on line under the rules of the architectures in place and be more cost effective as a result. The future battlefield will link the force at every level and across the globe. Space and sea information will be gathered and analyzed with the ground force information and tailored for every level of operations from the corps commander to the squad leader. Commanders will be able to "see" the logistical status of their units in real time. Digitization will speed the tempo of the battle and increase lethality and survivability of all friendly formations.

ARMY SCIENCE AND TECHNOLOGY STRATEGY

To ensure that the Army science and technology (S&T) program is consistent with National Security, Defense, and U.S. Army requirements, the *Army Science and Technology Master Plan* (ASTMP) is prepared annually. This strategic plan for the S&T program is based on the Army leadership's vision of the future Army, as constrained by realistic funding limits. It serves as "top down" guidance from the Headquarters, Department of the Army, to all Army S&T organizations, and it provides a vital link from the Defense S&T Strategy and Defense Technology Area Plan to the Army major commands, major subordinate commands, and laboratories. We are vigorously supporting the five S&T management principles articulated in DOD's S&T Strategy:

1. Transition technology to address warfighting needs;
2. Reduce cost;
3. Strengthen the commercial-military industrial base;
4. Promote basic research; and
5. Assure quality.

The Army S&T vision is to:

• Provide demonstrations of affordable weapons system concepts that meet the warfighter needs by being responsive to diverse, new-era threats and the requirement for force projection.
• Provide a world-class network of Government and private S&T capabilities that can maintain land warfare technology superiority, exploit rapid advances in information technology, and provide the Army with a smart buyer capability.

- Encourage reduced cost to the material acquisition process through the early retirement of technical risk and requirement uncertainty and through support for acquisition reform.

The Army's S&T program is designed to provide the technology to support the Army's vision for the future, Force XXI, and to provide opportunities to reduce casualties across the spectrum of possible conflict.

The *Army S&T Agenda* to support this vision is to:

- Comply with the Defense S&T Strategy and Army Force XXI vision.
- Conduct "world-class," relevant research.
- Strengthen the requirements process through:
  - System of systems demos
  - Advanced Technology Demonstrations (ATDS) and Advanced Concept Technology Demonstrations (ACTDS)
  - Synchronization of S&T with Training and Doctrine Command (TRADOC) AWEs and DOD Joint Warfighting Experiments (JWES)
  - The Advanced Concepts and Technology II (ACT II) program.
- Provide affordable options with a focus on system upgrades.
- Improve technology transition—the coupling of S&T to development programs.
- Improve technology transfer and "spin on" by forming partnerships with academia and industry.
- Stabilize S&T priorities and funding.
- Improve program execution and oversight.
- Attract, develop, and retain quality scientists and engineers.
- Downsize the infrastructure.

RESOURCING THE STRATEGY

The Army strives to maintain stable funding for the Army's 6.1, 6.2, and 6.3 programs, consistent with the long-term nature of basic and applied research. However, because we must protect readiness and the quality of life of today's force the fiscal year 1997 budget request is 2.2 percent lower (4.4 percent lower considering inflation) than the fiscal year 1996 request and 8.3 percent lower (10.3 percent lower considering inflation) than the fiscal year 1996 appropriation. Today's modernization investment decisions will determine the legacy we leave future commanders and their troops and will determine the readiness of Force XXI to deal with agrarian, industrial, and/or Information-Age enemies in the future.

In the *basic research* category (6.1), the Army maintains a strong peer-reviewed scientific base through which the underpinnings of land warfare technology can be further developed. Peer reviewers include many of this nation's leading scientists and engineers from the National Academy of Sciences, National Academy of Engineering, Institute of Medicine, and the Army Science Board. In addition to conducting in-house research, Army scientists monitor developments in academia and industry and evaluate the many proposals received for 6.1 funds.

The *applied research* category (6.2) focuses on specific military needs and develops the concepts and components to enable a variety of weapons system applications. We are vigorously pursuing the following three high priority technologies cited in the Defense S&T Strategy: information technology; modeling and simulation; and sensors.

The final S&T program funding category—advanced technology development (6.3)—provides the path for the rapid insertion of new technologies into Army systems, be they new systems or product improvements. In the 6.3 category, components are integrated and experimental systems are demonstrated to prove the feasibility and military utility of the approach selected. It is the 6.3 program that funds our ATDs and ACTDS. In recent years the Army has increased its commitment to system of systems demonstrations which seek to identify the lowest cost approach to accomplish a particular mission. These programs have central oversight and often include a number of separate ATDS. With supplementary OSD funding for leave behind equipment, many of these have now been converted into ACTDS.

Advanced Technology Demonstrations (ATDS)

ATDs are characterized by the following: large-scale both in resources and complexity; the operator/user involved from planning to final documentation; tested in a real and/or synthetic operational environment; finite schedule, typically 5 years or less; cost, schedule, and objective performance baselined in an ATD Plan approved by the Deputy Assistant Secretary for Research and Technology; and exit criteria agreed upon by the warfighter and ATD manager at program inception before the technology in question will transition to development. Active participation by the user, as well as the developer, is required throughout the demonstration. A simulation plan and at least one demonstration at a TRADOC Battle Lab is required. This enables the user to develop more informed requirements and the materiel developer to reduce risk prior to the initiation of full-scale system or upgrade development. ATDs seek to demonstrate the potential for enhanced military operational capability and/or cost effectiveness. ATDs are developing and demonstrating critical technologies ranging from digitization for the dismounted warrior to integrated survivability for future rotorcraft and armored vehicles.

Since the Army first approved ATD programs in fiscal year 1990, we will have completed a total of 19 by the end of fiscal year 1996 and transitioned a variety of technologies into development or other Army uses. Examples range from the first soldier based communications capability now being manifest in the Land Warrior EMD program, to the technology underpinning distributed interactive simulation, to our first ever capability to remotely detect mine fields and clear off route mines. Additionally, many of our ATDs have helped the Army enlarge its dominant battlespace knowledge through better sensor-to-shooter linkages, target recognition, and sensor fusion.

Advanced Concept Technology Demonstrations (ACTDS)

ACTDs are jointly planned by the warfighter and acquisition communities. They allow operational forces to experiment in the field and in simulation with new technology and concepts to determine potential improvements in doctrine, training, leadership, organizations, tactics and warfighting concepts. A CINC sponsor is required. Following successful demonstration with the sponsor, the capability is rapidly prototyped and left for up to 2 years with the CINC, thus giving him an interim, stay-behind capability pending formal acquisition decision. The Army has four approved ACTDS:

1. The *Precision/Rapid Counter*—Multiple Rocket Launcher ACTD is developing and demonstrating a system-of-systems concept that integrates surveillance, target acquisition, command, control, communications, weapons delivery, and combat assessment functions for counter battery operations against a mobile threat that can hide in caves. Successful experiments have already been conducted at Fort Hood using the Army's Integration and Evaluation Center near Fort Belvoir, Virginia, to coordinate the combination of simulation and live exercise. Later this year there will be a demonstration in Korea of a much improved counterfire capability against simulated enemy long-range, multiple rocket artillery operating from heavily fortified and protected positions in mountainous terrain. Emerging technologies will be integrated with advanced concepts and doctrine to ensure timely and responsive target acquisition and streamlined command and control to destroy enemy multiple rocket launchers swiftly, thereby r   g our troops in South Korea.

2. The *Rapid Force Projection Initiative (RFPI) ACTD* is demonstrating technologies, concepts, and tactics to permit our lift-constrained early entry forces to defeat heavier forces without compromising their deployability. RFPI employs a "Hunter/Stand-off Killer" approach which relies on forward deployed sensors connected to lightweight, precision, indirect fire weapon systems to attack an enemy armored force beyond direct fire range. Several stand-off killers will be evaluated, including the High Mobility Artillery Rocket System (HIMARS) and guidance for the MLRS, guided mortar rounds, smart mines, and the Enhanced Fiber-optic Guided Missile (EFOG–M). Simulations by TRADOC and Government contractors have shown high potential for the RFPI approach to improving the survivability, lethality, and deployability of our "first to fight" forces. A major field exercise to validate the hunter/stand-off killer concept for light forces is scheduled for fiscal year 1998.

3. The *Joint Countermine ACTD* is a joint effort by the Army, USMC, and Navy to demonstrate improved technology, concepts, doctrine, tactics, and organizations to counter the mine threat from the sea, across the beach, and inland. The Army has the lead for the detection and neutralization of the landmine threat. The emphasis is on remote detection and neutralization, both by vehicle mounted and dismounted approaches.

4. The *Joint Combat Identification ACTD* is an Army lead, all-service effort to demonstrate a joint, integrated air-to-ground and ground-to-ground combat identification ability. The ACTD will quantify the contributions of identification techniques and improved battlefield situation awareness to reduce fratricide and increase combat effectiveness. Specific technologies included in the ACTD are: a BCIS pod for fixed wing and rotary wing aircraft for point-of-engagement friend identification; enhanced forward air controller capability with integrated BCIS and Situation Awareness Data Link (SADL); modified SINCGARS System Improvement Program (SIP) radios that will provide automatic target location query for friend identifica-

tion; and situation awareness data from the digitized battlefield delivered to the gunner's sight.

SCIENCE AND TECHNOLOGY OBJECTIVES

To better focus our scarce S&T resources on the customer's highest priority needs, the Army has established a set of 200 Science and Technology Objectives (STO). Each STO states a specific, measurable, major technology advancement to be achieved by a specific fiscal year. It must be consistent with the funding available in the current year budget and the Program Objective Memorandum (POM). only major, measurable, and foreseeable objectives are designated as STOs. Not every worthwhile, funded technology program is cited as a STO because the Army must reserve some program flexibility for the laboratory or Research, Development and Engineering Center (RDEC) director to seize opportunities within his or her organization, based upon the organization's local talents and resources.

As is the case with ACTDs and ATDS, STOs are used by the Army S&T community to focus the program, practice management by objectives, and provide feedback to our scientists and engineers regarding their productivity and customer satisfaction. STOs are reviewed and approved annually.

TECHNOLOGY TRANSFER

The Army continuously monitors new developments in the commercial sector looking for military applications. This "spin-on" of technology is of growing importance to the Army S&T program—not only from the domestic R&D programs but also from development overseas. The Army has two commercially focused programs to leverage technology for application to Army platforms: the National Automotive Center and the National Rotorcraft Technology Center. Both of these centers involve a small in-house staff monitoring contractual R&D efforts.

Because of our tight resources, it is important that we work with other Government research agencies such as the Defense Advanced Research Projects Agency (DARPA) to fully leverage our research and development (R&D) efforts. To this end, we have a number of efforts in conjunction with DARPA to meet real warfighting needs. These include:

— Advanced seeker technology;
— Infrared Focal Plane Arrays;
— Aerostats (missile defense);
— Battlefield Awareness and Data Dissemination ACTD, which will be jointly tested in the Task Force XXI Brigade;
— Counter Sniper;
— Advanced sensors such as synthetic radar mapping;
— Small arms protection for the individual warfighter; and
— Helmet mounted displays.

Other Army initiatives strengthening technology transfer include:

• *Cooperative R&D:* It is Army policy to actively market technology that can benefit the public and private sectors as long as the technology clearly has applicability to Army needs, and to respond quickly to requests for technical assistance. The mechanisms for accomplishing this are Cooperative R&D Agreements (CRDAs), the Construction Productivity Advanced Research (CPAR) program, Patent Licensing Agreements (PLAs), and technical outreach programs. The cumulative Army totals from 1988 to 1996 are 690 CRDAS, 71 CPAR agreements, and 55 PLAS. Of these 816 agreements, 487 were still active as of 1 March 1996. The Army has more cooperative agreements than all the remainder of DOD combined.

• *SBIR Programs:* The Small Business Innovation Research (SBIR) Program was established in 1982 by Congress. The Army is a key participant in this DOD-wide program to stimulate technology innovation in small businesses to meet Federal R&D needs. The fiscal year 1995 Army funding for this program, which has had some remarkable successes, was $90 million, which includes $4.6 million for the Small Business Technology Transfer (STTR) program. Our estimated fiscal year 1996 program is $86 million, including $6 million for STTR.

• *University Research Centers:* The policy is to further Army basic research objectives by leveraging research programs in our world-class academic institutions. To accomplish this, the Army Research Office in Research Triangle Park, North Carolina, sponsors research through the Army Center of Excellence Program and through the Defense University Research Initiative. Through these programs the Army focuses active research participation with more than 20 American universities.

● *Advanced Concepts and Technology II (ACT II) program:* The ACT II program, begun by Congress in fiscal year 1994, continues to fund competitively selected proposals from industry to demonstrate promising technology, prototypes, and nondevelopmental items of keen interest to all the TRADOC Battle Labs. The program provides seed money (a maximum of $1.5 million) for 1 year, proof-of-principle demonstrations of relatively mature/high-payoff concepts proposed by non-Army sources. In 1994, ACT II funded a total of 28 projects, and in 1995 we supported an additional 35 efforts. We expect to initiate another 24 new starts in 1996 for evaluation by the TRADOC Battle Labs.

PROJECT RELIANCE

In November 1991, all three Service Acquisition Executives directed full implementation of Project Reliance in their respective Services. In November 1995, Dr. Anita K. Jones, the Director of Defense Research and Engineering, joined the Services and Defense Agencies in the Reliance process. She formed the Reliance Executive Committee to strengthen Reliance's role in the DOD strategic planning process and continue to improve Service/Agency S&T coordination. Implementation of Defense S&T Reliance also responds to (and provides inputs for) a number of important management functions and planning processes including the budget planning process and—development of technology investment plans through the Defense Technology Area Plan, and updates of the Defense S&T Strategy.

The goals of Defense S&T Reliance are to:

● Enhance S&T;
● Ensure critical mass of resources to develop "worldclass" products;
● Reduce redundant capabilities and eliminate unwarranted duplication;
● Gain efficiency through collocation and consolidation of in-house work, where appropriate; and
● Preserve the Services' mission-essential, Title 10 capabilities.

Managing technology development is a dynamic process, and the S&T activities of the Services and Agencies are not islands unto themselves. The notion of "leveraging" is based on a simple fact: The Services' individual S&T accounts cannot fund all the R&D activities that any one Service needs.

INFRASTRUCTURE

Laboratories and RDECs are the key organizations responsible for technical leadership, scientific advancement, and support for the acquisition process. Working at a diversified set of physical resources, ranging from solid-state physics laboratories to outdoor experimental ranges, these personnel conduct research, develop technology, act as "smart buyers," and provide systems engineering support to fielded systems for the total Army.

The Army is consolidating laboratory and R&D center facilities, eliminating aging and technologically obsolete facilities, and leveraging relevant facilities of contractors and the other military services. From fiscal year 1989 to fiscal year 1999 the Army will close seven sites out of 31 labs and RDECs through BRAC decisions and reduce our in-house lab/center by 28 percent. our in-house facility investments are focusing on those unique capabilities that truly must be owned by the Army itself.

Converting the Army Research Laboratory to an open, federated laboratory system is a major initiative that has caught the imagination and strong support of Government, industry, and university researchers and leaders. The Army awarded three cooperative agreements in January 1996, establishing Federated Laboratories: Advanced Sensors, Advanced Displays, and Telecommunications. Partners include Lockheed Sanders, Rockwell International Corporation, and Bell Communications. Besides these industrial partners, each consortium as a minimum consists of at least two academic institutions, one of which is an Historically Black College or University or Minority Institution. The partnerships will focus on basic research using facilities that already exist in the Government, in industry, and in universities. The Army Research Laboratory is in the process of developing the definitive plans to be collaboratively executed over the next 12 months. Following the lead of the Senate Authorization Committee, the Army will await clear evidence of success with these partnerships before proposing to expand this initiative. Meanwhile, the Army need for software and simulation technology will be pursued through more traditional means.

Highly motivated, competent, well-trained people are essential to the success of the Army S&T strategy. Keeping the in-house work force technically competent in a rapidly changing environment is a high priority objective for the future. The Reinvention Laboratory initiative allows revised procurement rules and personnel initiatives which will assist in meeting the challenge. Allowing Army scientists and engineers to perform more research at the bench has long been recognized as the number one recruitment and retention factor. Letting them share that bench with the best in class from industry and academia via the open, federated laboratory initiative will clearly strengthen the smaller Army laboratory system of the future.

ACQUISITION REFORM

Acquisition reform is absolutely critical to our modernization program and the future readiness of the force. In our resource constrained environment, we must acquire our weapon systems and equipment, supplies, and services far more efficiently than in the past. Each year, the Army places more than $32 billion on contract. By creating efficiencies within our own operation, we will provide badly needed savings to reinvest in modernization and other high priority needs.

The Army is making steady progress. We have been working hard to get as much of acquisition streamlining reform and better business processes into the procurement and acquisition system from all fronts as quickly as possible. Much has been accomplished, including the elimination of military specifications, the adoption of commercial and performance standards, and reduced internal management. We are reaching the point where this needs to be viewed as continuous process improvement rather than radical reform. We need to constantly improve and streamline the acquisition system.

The Army S&T program is contributing in several ways. Our ACTDs will contribute by getting small quantities of new equipment quickly to our operational forces for a 2-year period, directly providing a limited go-to-war capability. S&T support of our AWEs is helping the Army evaluate nondevelopmental and commercial technology solutions. Finally, closer coupling with the Program Executive Officer (PEO) organizations and more robust risk reduction within the S&T domain is permitting a combined Milestone I and II for selected programs with a transition directly from S&T to EMD. The elimination of DEM/VAL phase results in significant savings in time and cost.

Comanche is a model program for acquisition reform initiatives. We have eliminated all non-essential military specifications and streamlined the test plans. The Army decided to build only two early flight test models, formerly called the DEM/VAL phase, and immediately proceed, using the same two early flight models, to EMD. Essentially, we combine DEM/VAL and EMD into one phase. With success there, we will buy six pre-production models. These will go to our troops in the field as Early Operational Capability (EOC) systems. Upon completion of that evaluation, we will do a limited IOT&E and move right into LRIP. The cost savings are significant.

How can we do this? There are two reasons. One, entrepreneurial management in the Army and industry knows that we don't need to create a superfluous trail of paperwork and associated expense. Second, modern, simulation-based computer-aided design techniques. This allows the entire aircraft to be designed right down to the last nut and bolt and tested through simulation. Then, when the Army releases the build to parts the first time, the rework and scrap rate is minimal. The first helicopter in the air is very close to the final production model.

We have identified substantial savings as the result of acquisition reforms applied to missile systems. The Army conducted an intense cost reduction study before entering production on the Javelin. We used all of the streamlining methods, including an Integrated Product Team. The net result was a savings over the number of missiles we plan to buy of $1.4 billion or one-third the initial cost of this program. similar savings are being realized in the Longbow HELLFIRE and ATACMS/BAT programs. As I mentioned earlier, we also have realized remarkable savings in our ground terminals for the MILSTAR satellites.

We have also significantly streamlined acquisition operations. The Army Materiel Command (AMC) has reduced the time it takes to award a contract by 29 percent and the time it takes to deliver a product by 38 percent. We are aggressively expanding the use of credit cards with a goal that they be used for 80 percent of all purchases under $2,500.

The Congress has assisted us considerably in these endeavors, notably by passage of the Federal Acquisition Streamlining Act of 1994 and the Federal Acquisition Reform Act of 1995, enacted as part of the National Defense Authorization Act for fiscal year 1996.

In terms of process, we are doing our very best to energize, educate, and solicit "buy in" from our acquisition entities in the field. The managers and their staffs in the field are where the action really happens, and we are empowering our work force to practice acquisition reform initiatives. one of our primary vehicles is the Army Roadshow series. There has been highly active involvement by all senior leaders in the Army. With Roadshow IV, we traveled to 10 sites throughout the United States with three-day seminar/workshops to train our personnel on performance specifications and best value source selection. We also trained with industry. Roadshow V began in March at the Army Missile Command in Huntsville, Alabama. This is the first of 13 sessions planned in 1996. This series has been so successful that our sister Services have adopted the Roadshow format and content.

The Army is presently reengineering our Acquisition corps, both military and civilian. our vision is to develop a small, premier professional corps of acquisition leaders, willing to serve where needed, and committed to developing, integrating, acquiring, and fielding systems critical to decisive victory for the 21st century. Congress has provided a tool to help accomplish this goal. The Acquisition Work Force Personnel Demonstration Program in Section 4308 of last year's Defense Authorization Act provides the authority to suspend p rs l laws and regulations governing the acquisition work force that may impede our acquisition mission and to replace them with reengineered processes of our own design. This authority will prove immensely valuable in instituting a cultural change and will allow us to evaluate improvements in personnel policy designed to enhance the quality, professionalism, and effectiveness of our acquisition work force.

To the extent that we can eliminate superfluous, defense-unique processes and standards in our acquisition, we will truly be able to buy more from the total industrial base of the country, not just from defense-unique industry. This has huge potential advantages. One, technology in most areas is now led by commercial industry, not by the Government. This is particularly true in electronic components, computer architecture, information systems and software, telecommunications, and automotive technology, all of which are critical in every Army system. Two, we can leverage off the R&D base of commercial industry and buy items already developed, thereby devoting more of our RDT&E dollars to unique defense technologies. We are already well along in these endeavors.

Secretary of Defense Perry has highlighted the success of the Army's acquisition reform efforts on the Secure Mobile Anti-Jam Reliable Tactical-Terminal (SMART–T). By introducing competition during development; reform initiatives such as reduced data requirements and failure free warranty; Jointness; and stable funding; the program cost was reduced from an early estimate of $790 million to a fiscal year 1996 contract award for less than $250 million. Another acquisition streamlining success is the Near Term Digital Radio (NTDR), which we are currently testing. The recent contract provided radios for test and experimentation at one-quarter the cost of other digital radios. What is of great interest here is the radio's open architecture, which allows us the flexibility to insert new information technology as it becomes available.

There are many other examples. Our Special Forces in Bosnia were in need of light cold weather clothing. In the interest of time, we went strictly commercial off-the-shelf. In less than 6 weeks, 1,200 sets of four layers of clothing were delivered to Fort Bragg, North Carolina, at a cost of $187 per set. This represented a 64 percent savings over a 1994 market survey on the cost of lighter cold weather clothing. In addition, these sets were 16 percent lighter with 45 percent less bulk than the Army's existing extended cold weather clothing system.

CONCLUSION

As we complete the drawdown of our armed forces, we are devoting a larger share of our limited defense resources to readiness and quality of life programs for our men and women in uniform. Money for modernization is tight. Our concern is for the future readiness of the force. Today's modernization is tomorrow's readiness.

As we look to the turn of the century, we must increase our investment in modernization, and the Army's current plan does as we go from $10.6 billion in fiscal year 1997, to over $12 billion in fiscal year 1999, and nearly $15 billion in fiscal year 2001. It is our solemn responsibility to ensuring that our men and women are well-equipped and have the decisive advantage they need to deter or win decisively in future conflicts. Today's soldier is well-equipped. Tomorrow's soldier deserves no less.

With your support, we will continue to provide our soldiers with world-class equipment. Thank you for your attention this morning, and thank you for helping to keep America's Army the premier land force in the world.

Mr. DECKER. Colonel Meadows, Project Manager for (PM) Soldier, will narrate the demonstration.

Colonel MEADOWS. Good morning, sir. I am Bill Meadows, project manager for Soldier, and among the responsibilities that I have for

Soldier is the Land Warrior. The Land Warrior is a system of systems. It is a system that is modular. It is tailorable, and it is the system that links the individual soldier on the battlefield into the digital battlefield. It is what gives him his way to be a major player on the battlefield. He becomes a weapons system in this configuration.

He has a tactical overmatch in several areas. First of all, this is the first time the individual soldier has the capability to talk with his individual squad members, with his fellow squad members. In the past, he has been able to use hand and arm signals, but that is it. He also has the capability to see at night, or in daytime, with either a thermal imager or through an eye square device, where he can see through any kind of obscurance, whether it be rain, fog, smoke, or whatever.

He also has the capability, with this weapon, because of his imaging capability, being pumped up to a heads up display to be able to see around objects, to be able to detect an enemy, acquire that enemy, and engage that enemy without endangering himself.

So what we see here is a soldier that has greatly overmatch capabilities. What I would like to do at this point is introduce to you this particular soldier. This is Private First Class (PFC) John Taylor. He is assigned right now to the Training and Doctrine Command (TRADOC) systems manager's office at Fort Benning, Georgia. He is enroute to the 375th Regiment. I would like to let him talk to you about some of the capabilities of the system.

PFC TAYLOR. Good morning. My name is PFC Taylor. I am currently equipped with technology that represents a requirement for the Land Warrior system, wearing the improved helmet with the camera material that provides equal protection and is a Kevlar helmet, that has 15-percent reduction in weight.

The helmet also has a flip down mounted helmet display device that will allow soldiers to view digital map information, troop locations, imagery from sites, or, in the daylight, video camera. I can also send and receive messages. The weapon I carry——

Senator WARNER. Before you get there, the transmission is built into—in other words, the sending and receiving, where is that equipment?

PFC TAYLOR. I have it on my back.

Senator WARNER. Can you swing around so we can see it?

Colonel MEADOWS. He has two radios at this point. One is a soldier radio, and then he has also a Single Channel Ground and Airborne Radio System (SINCGARS) capability built right into the back of the pack. These are personal computer multi-cartridge input adapter (PCMCIA) card-sized components which are totally interchangeable. They are standard components. They are commercial items, and when technology changes, we will be able to change that technology out so that we do not have a system that is not up to the current technologies.

Senator COATS. What is the weight of that package?

Colonel MEADOWS. The whole package is designed to be no greater than the load that is on the current squad leader, which is right now defined at about 75 pounds, and our soldiers in certain situations—as PFC Taylor indicated earlier this week, he normally carries around 119 pounds. This system is designed to be 75 pounds.

Senator WARNER. That is the entire system, weapon and all, including the round-out of ammo?

Colonel MEADOWS. That is correct.

Sir, just, if I may, to make it plain, the one radio that he said was the squad radio lets him talk horizontally to his fellow squad members. The second radio——

Senator WARNER. That is the line-of-sight communication?

Colonel MEADOWS. Yes, sir.

Senator WARNER. So maybe 100 yards plus?

Colonel MEADOWS. 1.3 kilometers.

Mr. DECKER. You normally will not have an individual soldier that far away from the squad leader, but it has that capability.

Senator WARNER. But that is line-of-sight.

Mr. DECKER. Essentially.

Colonel MEADOWS. The second radio that he has allows him to talk to his higher headquarters, to his platoon leader and platoon sergeant, the optimal, what we are seeking, is about a 6 kilometer range.

Senator WARNER. Again, line of site transmission?

Colonel MEADOWS. Yes.

Senator WARNER. What sort of jamming capabilities is that susceptible to? In other words, if the enemy would be put a jamming situation into the battlefield——

Senator COATS. Senator, that SINCGARS radio is made in Fort Wayne, Indiana. [Laughter.]

It is absolutely the best technology you can get. It cannot be jammed. [Laughter.]

Senator WARNER. Despite the comments of my distinguished colleague——

General HARTZOG. To answer your question directly, at the squad level, at the shorter ranges they are susceptible to some local jamming, but it is not as tactically important as the higher level radios. They use satellites and other non line-of-sight means, which I will talk to you about and demonstrate to you.

Senator LEVIN. That picture that you are taking does not, then, go to a satellite? That has got to go to a headquarters within 6 kilometers, is that right?

General HARTZOG. No, sir. It is a line of sight from him to his platoon leader.

Now, if it goes from the platoon leader or company commander over SINCGARS to a higher headquarters, it goes into a more complex system, and it does go—it could go through satellites, and I will give you a demonstration of that, if you will.

PFC TAYLOR. The weapon I am carrying, gentlemen, is the modular weapons system. This weapon was designed to mount various types of weapons and sights, depending upon the mission.

Today, it is equipped with a daylight camera, the thermal weapons sight, the laser range finder, PAC–4 Bravo laser aiming light. The daylight camera was designed to allow the soldier to send a still video picture back to his leadership from the battlefield. The thermal weapons sight was designed to allow the soldier to engage targets day or night, in any weather condition.

The range of the thermal weapons sight far exceeds that of the maximum effective range of the weapon. What you are seeing on the wall is Mr. Paul's hand print.

Everything this system does enhances the soldier's capability, and allows him to complete his mission more effectively, and it allows him to save troops' lives, because he is a more enhanced soldier. However, it does not take away the fact that he does not know how to Land Navigation, or those soldier skills that he is taught in basic training, he still has to know those skills, and even if it is totally broke down, the soldier would still be able to function as we have in the past.

In my present combat ensemble I am the Land Warrior.

Senator WARNER. How long did it take you to train to use all of that diverse equipment? You went into the Army and went to basic training, and then at what point did you begin to learn the specifics of some of these pieces?

PFC TAYLOR. Sir, I was prior service National Guard, and when I came back on Active duty the next month, I was interviewed for this position, which was approximately a year ago, and I had about 4 or 5 days to learn this equipment when I got to the office and briefed the Secretary of the Army as well as other general officers.

Senator WARNER. Well then, you were unusual. Let us take the average man or woman coming out of high school. What would you think the period of time would be?

General HARTZOG. Sir, I think I can probably better answer that. We think that this whole ensemble, we will be able to get up to speed in in about 7 days.

Senator WARNER. He or she?

General HARTZOG. He or she. Now, how you use that in the context of bigger operations is a different issue. He can use his equipment within about 7 days of training, but he could be a scout, or he could be a forward observer, and what he sends back to his higher headquarters and how it is used we are in the middle of experimentation on, and I cannot quite tell you how long it would take him to conglomerate holistically to key up an entire unit, but I will talk to that if you would like in a moment.

Senator WARNER. What has been your experience, private, in terms of the educational base that an individual must possess, in your judgment, to acquire knowledge of this.

PFC TAYLOR. In my best opinion, sir, it would be at least high school level.

Senator WARNER. A minimum of a high school level? I cannot see this clearly. Is that some protective armor you have on?

Colonel MEADOWS. Yes, sir. If I could just give you a little bit of information about it, what he also has on is soft light armor. This is protective armor. It is also of Kevlar material. It will give him fragmentation protection. We also have an upgraded plate that will give him 5.56 mm ammunition protection also.

He has—in the back side he will have with this frame—this is a tubular frame. It is hollow on the outside. Therefore, all the wiring and so forth is within this. Once again, the components are very small. They are credit card size personal computer multicards, standard format. The Global Positioning System (GPS) is located here. He has antennas here, located and protected so he cannot damage those when he goes into the brush, and what he has here, he is outfitted as a squad leader, so he has SINCGARS, which will give him a greater range.

Senator WARNER. What is this down here?

Colonel MEADOWS. This is his pack, his normal pack.

Senator WARNER. Which he also at the same time would be carrying?

Colonel MEADOWS. He would be carrying this. You will see there are four buttons that pop right into the system, and they will pop right into his—four, and then he can just pop these right off. This pack would be for when he is going out on a mission for being in the field for a full mission.

He can pop off either side of the sustainment pouches, and then have just the center pouch and the lower pouch. The lower pouch would then have his additional ammunition, and that would allow him to be very mobile and be very light, and he would not be carrying all of this, and he would be able to move in this configuration, because you see, this is hinged.

It also has a torsion bar suspension at the bottom that allows him to adjust the weight of this pouch or this pack on the back to put more of the weight from the hips up to the shoulder. We have got a very flexible system here for soldiers, so if you go in the field——

Senator WARNER. What is this one right here?

PFC TAYLOR. This is the computer module.

Colonel MEADOWS. We do not have a biodetector on this. This is one of the technology enhancements that we expect to integrate into the system once we have some of this, once we can get this man portable, so we can integrate it into the system.

Senator WARNER. The basic weapon——

Colonel MEADOWS. The basic weapon is a modular weapons system. It is an M–16.

Senator WARNER. What iteration of the 16? We have gone through a number of iterations of the 16.

Colonel MEADOWS. This is the A–2.

Senator WARNER. Now, how many troops are equipped with this?

Colonel MEADOWS. Right now, sir, this is an Engineering and Manufacturing Development (EMD) program. It is in advanced development. What we plan to do is to put a squad of these soldiers—I am sorry, a squad of this equipment on soldiers for early experimentation in November of this year. We will have our production decision in 1999, and we will field the first unit in the year 2000.

Senator WARNER. The unit with this equipment would be integrated at what, the battalion level?

Colonel MEADOWS. What we are going to do, the first unit equipped will be a battalion, but what we are going to do is to field to the contingency corps. A division will be fielded in the system.

Senator COATS. Do we have a cost associated with this whole package yet?

Colonel MEADOWS. What we are looking at is a production—what we are looking for as a unit production cost for this system is $35,000 for the target cost.

Senator LEVIN. What does that include, the $35,000?

Colonel MEADOWS. That includes——

Senator LEVIN. Is that the whole headquarters part?

Colonel MEADOWS. It includes everything here, what the Army is doing.

Senator LEVIN. Just on the individual soldier. That does not include the equipment back at headquarters.

Colonel MEADOWS. No. This is just the individual pieces. What the Army is doing is something that I think is very smart, and that is, it is modularly putting these pieces of equipment into the field as they become available, so that we do not have to wait until every single piece of this is available, so we can get some of those capabilities.

This thermal weapons sight that you see here is already in production, and the Army will start fielding those items already. Some of these systems, some of these pieces are already in ongoing programs, and they will be in the field.

What we are going to do, though, is we are going to integrate those so that this soldier goes to the field as an integrated unit, as a system, as opposed to going to the field as a soldier that has to integrate himself, those components that we give him periodically.

General HARTZOG. Sir, let me help out on this one. This is a product of experimentation. We invented little pieces of it in a laboratory much as we have always done, and then we put those pieces in the field and let a soldier figure out whether they were good or bad, which is always our best laboratory.

As an example, just this last year, in one of the experiments, we took a version of this that had the camera, that was mounted on the helmet and had the optical system here that saw whatever the soldier was seeing in the camera, and had the two radios, and had a sending unit, or a keyboard, and that allowed him to punch buttons and send those messages that he saw, or the images that he saw to a higher headquarters.

We put those in the 10th Mountain Division, 35 sets of them, took them to the Joint Readiness Training Center, tested them in the cold and the wet and the snow under battlefield conditions, and found that there was a problem with this particular piece of the ensemble, so we have cured that problem and we will have another version of 100 of these that will go into the Fourth Infantry Division, the experimental force, in June of this year, and they will be using them for 8 months of training and in another experiment in March of 1997.

So as soon as the good pieces come out of this, we proliferate it, and put it back into the experimentation and let the soldiers fix it, and then, as he said, the optimal solution of what it will turn out to be will come in a couple of years.

It turned out the camera was too heavy to be in the helmet. We thought it was a great idea, but it is better on the weapon

Senator WARNER. A question to the panel. This committee has tried through the years to foster exchange of information with our allies and foster joint Research and Development (R&D) projects. Any of this equipment as a result of such initiatives by the United States? In other words, the derivation of any of this equipment from innovations in our allied forces?

General HARTZOG. Sir, right now we are quite a bit in front of our allies. The allies are extremely interested in this. There are Canadian systems, and there is a German system. There is a French system and a Canadian system. They are all looking at what we are doing.

Senator WARNER. We are looking at what they are doing?

General HARTZOG. We are absolutely looking at what they are doing, sir. They have some components that we are looking at to see whether or not we can use those to enhance our system also. We are certainly looking at interoperability. We are looking at standard architectures, and making sure that we will be able to talk when we get our systems into a situation where we are working with our allies.

Senator WARNER. That is very important, because time and time again this committee has discovered lack of interoperability with our allies on the battle front.

Senator COATS. Mr. Chairman, that is a very interesting point. I had the opportunity to go down to TRADOC and the Joint Warfare Training Center at Fort Monroe about a month ago.

Senator WARNER. Would you get the State, please? [Laughter.]

Senator COATS. That is Virginia. Fort Monroe, Virginia, yes, sir. [Laughter.]

A question arose there as to the interoperability with our allies, and one of our major considerations is that most of our allies do not have the resources to begin to absorb and incorporate all of the equipment that we have, and so one of the real challenges, I think, is the fact that we are doing more and more joint efforts with our allies, and yet we may find ourselves on the battlefield with very sophisticated equipment with our troops, but the people on your flank may not have that, and that is a real challenge from a funding standpoint, from a training standpoint and development standpoint.

Senator WARNER. Also, tactical. If you are on a joint front and you are able to move—given this is a force multiplier of some magnitude, am I not correct, gentlemen, that this enables the Army to have a lesser number of standing troops if it gets into full production?

General HARTZOG. Yes, it does, sir.

Senator WARNER. If you are drawn up in a line like, in my modest experience over in Korea, we had different divisions on each flank, and when we moved they were supposed to go with us. If they cannot move with the same speed and agility that our forces can, you do have a tactical problem, as the Senator points out.

General HARTZOG. Sir, you are absolutely correct, and that is one of our concerns. I visited Germany, France, and eight different places, some of which are in the Pacific, Korea, Thailand and India, Japan, and all of the different places that might be in some of this business. Each of them are doing some small piece of it. No one is doing a composite, holistic version of it, so in the course of doing our experiments over the last year, as we looked at joint interoperability with the other U.S. service forces, Army, Navy, Air Force, Marines, as well as interoperability with those places that I just talked to, we came to several basic conclusions.

One, us having the equipment is imperative to the future of our force, but we need to retain a frequency modulation radio capability within this so that you can fall back on that for interoperability, or in some cases use that as a conduit to pass some of this information, and we have done that throughout.

I do not believe we should seek a median level here just for interoperability. I think you can have this and ensure the interoperability as long as you do not discard the radio as a basic means of voice communication.

The second thing to that point that we found in the experimentation is that generally what we are trying to do is to take the information that is routine in our business, where are you, where am I, where is the ammunition, where is the food, and take that out of conscious mental effort by leaders and put it into digital electronic routine cans, so that you can go get it when you need it, and you do not have to be absorbed with the production of it all the time.

For 10 years at the National Training Center, our tapes that we have had for battalion level commanders indicate that 48 percent of all of the traffic that was passed out there was, I am here, where are you, where am I, position location things, so the GPS takes that immediately out of the conscious realm and puts it into the digital realm, and it is there if you need it. If you do not need it, you do not deal with it.

But nobody likes to have a tech mount order scrolled across his screen and read it that way. All our tests say that all of the commanders at all levels, all the leaders at all levels want the order to be issued into their ear by someone totally engaged in the same conflict, and so we have kept the FM nets in all of that. That enhances our potential for interoperability.

Now, the issue of interoperability within our own joint service is a different one, and if I may, I will show you a demonstration of that a little bit later.

Senator WARNER. Gentlemen, are there further questions for the soldier?

Senator LEVIN. I had a couple of them on that last point. Those FM nets, there is also sort of a fallback in case the technology just gets totally bolluxed up for us in some situation, I take it.

One of the problems here is the jamming issue, and another thing is that there could be, I take it, the more you rely on this tremendous technology, which is very exciting, I visited the training center, too, to see it, that you have the potential of failure.

If you have a failure in your picture, and your picture is going backyand forth to your headquarters, for instance, you have to allow that unit to be able to operate without this technology. You need a safety net, a fallback of some kind, I take it.

General HARTZOG. Sir, there are three levels to that. One is that we hope that the thing works. We are spending a lot of time and effort at all levels to make it as good as it can be. None of it is infallible. All of it breaks down and has any number of times during the testing.

The second level is redundancy within the systems, which, I will show you about the higher level business, and the third is, as you stated, a fallback.

Now, the fallback is not an additional system, because most of the digits travel on other phone lines, or FM modulated lines, so the SINCGARS and secure package switch radios are the backs upon which all of this travels, and it is either pick up a microphone and talk in it, or press a key and the digit is sent on the same line, so it is not an additional cost, or an additional effort to do that. It is just a conscious decision to retain both capabilities.

Senator LEVIN. The other question has to do with what a soldier is getting in that eye piece. Is he going to have an option as to what comes in there? Will he be able to, for instance, get a picture that his buddy is picking up 100 yards down the line, or could he get a different picture, or is that going to be controlled by headquarters?

General HARTZOG. Sir, there are two answers to that. Right now, with the state of the art of this particular system, he sees what comes out of his camera with overprints on the heads-up display that he intends to put in it with his computer keyboard.

Now, he has some preprinted things, like today and in the past we have had a little format that we use when you report on seeing an enemy. It is just a discipline system. It is called a Size, Activity, Location, Unit, Time, Equipment report. You look at what is there, how many of them it is, is it traveling, et cetera.

But unfortunately, that is a product of how good your training is, and it is much like the childhood chairs game, where you put a message in one end, and by the time it gets to the other, it is somewhat garbled, occasionally.

Today, one of the formats that he has is that he can overprint over his television camera in the format, and a lot of that format is filled in automatically. Where am I comes directly from his GPS and is printed there. Where is the target that I am looking at? Again, a GPS estimate, and a laser, and it is printed there from the laser site.

Then he punches a button, and that whole message goes forward to his platoon leader or company commander. So that is the state of the art right now. Right now, that one picture is what he sees as a picture, and it is also what can be transmitted.

Eventually, I suppose, we will get to the point where we can exchange picture transmissions, but this particular set does not have that.

Senator LEVIN. My last question has to do with the laser interoperability, which is a crucial question, but also then raises a question, what about our potential adversaries having access to this. To what extent does this control the commercialization?

Mr. DECKER. I can give you the best intelligence estimates that we have at this time. A lot of this is on open market. A lot of the components are on open market, but the system is not.

We think that at this level, at the tactical level it is probably not necessary to engage in the security of the transmission, the electronic security of it. At higher levels, at battalion, brigade, and division level, we are still engaged in the same sort of scramble of technology that you have today in phones and radio nets.

Senator LEVIN. I was not talking about scrambling signals. I was talking about the availability of the equipment itself. Can Iraq buy this equipment?

Mr. DECKER. Let me make a point. I think General Hartzog touched on it. If you take any individual module of the system, we dealt heavily on commercial technology. That is one of the things we are trying to do in acquisition reform, and so the two major contractors involved in the system are Motorola, which is very heavy in the commercial RF world, and Hughes.

These individual modules are not magic. The technology of the radios—there is some miniaturization involved, but the fundamental technology of both radios that he has in this particular configuration, the fundamental GPS receiver you can buy for $200 from Trumble Navigation, or any number of people, the computer (486 computer from Intel) are all commercial items. So there is no magic, no black magic like stealth technology, or something, at the technology level.

The system configuration, the systems integration to make it all play together, is what this system is all about. So the system as a whole is the thing you would not want to sell. But any one of these items is certainly available on the open market.

Colonel MEADOWS. We certainly have a path to some additional technology insertions that we are looking at out in the future that will be significant increases to this system, but what we are doing right now, we are putting a system out there that will be interoperable with the digital battlefield in the year 2000. Upgrades are in the tech base right now, and are being worked on in a separate program.

General HARTZOG. I would like to make one more comment on the thought that came up about interoperability and what happens if the system crashes. Let us just take this configuration. He is the squad leader. The individual soldier does not have that squad radio that goes up to the platoon.

That is SINCGARS. Now, it is a miniature SINCGARS, but it is a SINCGARS. If something failed in the rest of his digital system, he picks up his little microphone, or the microphone is up by his lip there, and he talks on the voice mode of that radio, which is what he has to do today, so that is inherently built in.

If the SINCGARS radio today fails, he has got no radio communication with his platoon leader, so there is an inherent overlay of the old way of doing it built in here. You just revert to voice mode from the squad and platoon level, so you have not made these people any more vulnerable than they are today, and in fact you may have a little bit of increase in the reduced vulnerability.

Senator WARNER. I guess we had better proceed on, Mr. Secretary.

Senator COATS. If I could just ask two very brief questions. I know we are testing how long PFC Taylor can stand there with 75 pounds on his back, and maybe that is part of the exercise here, but just two really quick questions, and one point.

SINCGARS radios do not fail, so you do not have to worry about that. [Laughter.]

Senator COATS. Two quick points. One at $35,000 a copy, are we looking to equip the entire—is Force XXI equipping the entire combat Army forces here, or are we looking at specialized units, or has that decision not been made?

Mr. DECKER. Sir, the decision has not been made, but where we are right now, we know that we will not equip every soldier like this to start with, regardless of how many units are involved. We know that it will be primarily a leader's tool, a scout's tool, and a forward observer's tool. That is a very small number out of the total number, but the decision of how many divisions and the affordability and the efficacy of doing that, I think we need to finish this year's testing to determine.

Senator COATS. Clearly, at that cost there are going to be some trade-offs here and some tough decisions, and this is going to be competing against some unglamorous stuff like tanks and trucks, and Humvees, and tents, and boots, and everything else. It is fun to fund the gee-whiz stuff, but I hope we can have a thorough discussion about how it impacts the nonglamorous, basic stuff.

My second question is, is there a concern that you are going to get to the point where there is too much information for the individual soldier, platoon leader, platoon sergeant to process effectively so that in the confusion and chaos and battle we do not have so much information flowing into the decision-making point that everybody is worried about their computer and laptop and where they are while the enemy is—you understand what I am saying.

There is a problem, or a potential problem, here of just overwhelming the soldier with information.

General HARTZOG. Sir, you are absolutely correct. We are, and have been, and will be concerned about it.

Now, what we have found in the four exercises we have done this year, the four major troop tests, is at every level you have the potential of blacking out the screen.

I mean, you have the potential of overloading leaders at every echelon. At division commander's level you can take his screen and turn it black with overprinted information, if you so desire, but the solution to it is threefold.

One is to understand what kind of information you want to process and allow to go to each of the levels, and while everyone has access to it at each level, to the whole kit, what you want to send to each level is only that which is required usually at that level, and then it is a training issue to teach each level, where they can go to pull things that they might need that are not in their normal conscious sphere.

We have made a pretty good bit of progress with that, and I will demonstrate the battalion level business in just a moment, and show you what kind of information is culled out.

The theory is, at each level you try to pick out those things that are key and essential for that particular level. That does not mean they cannot go into the electronic can and pull out other things if needed, but it is stored there in the electronic can, and you do not have to go to it. It is not forced into your consciousness.

So it is both a disciplined push and an educated pull system.

Now, having said all of that, the closer you get to the moment when you fix the bayonet and get into personal contact, the more you tend to rely on voice transmission, and we think that is about right.

Most of this digitization is going to be of most use in planning, in the approach march, and in movement to contact, and at the instant of combat we do not want someone, I do not think, to be punching buttons on an individual keyboard.

I think I want them talking in a modern, new radio that they do not have to push to talk, like this whisper mike, and I want them using this camera to see better around the corner if they are fighting in a city, or to see longer and more enhanced at night, like you saw here, and enhance, or use those kinds of the enhancements, those part of the enhancements, but the information transfer at the moment of combat is going to be voice to ear, in my judgment. That is what we are learning.

Senator COATS. Thank you.

Senator WARNER. Thank you. Soldier, we salute you, a job well done. I think you are going to have a tough time explaining to your bunk mates the pictures out of this thing. [Laughter.]

Mr. DECKER. Thank you, sir. I would like, with your permission, then, to turn it over to General Hartzog, and he will spend a few minutes bringing together where we are in our total Force XXI program.

General HARTZOG. Thank you, Mr. Chairman. I am Commander of the Training and Doctrine Command based at Fort Monroe, Virginia, sir.

About 3 years ago, my predecessor, General Franks, had the privilege of appearing in front of your committee and told you at the time that he was looking into the 21st Century and was going to try to pull together a way to move information better.

Now, as his successor, my job is to do two things. I run the schoolhouses for the Army, and second, I have the mission of preparing the Army for the future to be the architect of what the future force in totality is to look like—that is, organization, doctrine, equipment, kinds of units, unit training, leader training, quality of people—and today I would like to do three things in a very short period of time here. If you will allow me to use three charts and one small demonstration, I would like to summarize the Army's blueprint for change into the future, Force XXI, where we are today.

What we have learned about it in the last year, we are way past Chart D. We bent a lot of metal, and a lot of things have worked, some have not, and I would like to share with you where that is.

Finally, I think that we need to look at how we are going to take this into the future for the next few years, and I will do that.

Now, with your permission, sir——

Senator WARNER. Before you go into that, I would say we all want to acknowledge the contributions of one of you predecessors, General Max Thurman, whose vision laid the foundation for this very hearing we have today.

General HARTZOG. Yes, sir. I had the privilege of being one of his pall-bearers, sir.

I would like to change this just a little bit, if I may, sir, since we have just looked at the individual soldier and the information that he can garner and move. Perhaps it would be useful to look at a small demonstration of what happens at battalion level and what kind of information can be available there, so if I may, I would like to put a laptop computer just in front of you there, and talk to that organization.

Senator Warner, if you recall, in 1989 we spent a day in a TOC together in Panama, chasing our friend there, and the characteristics——

Senator WARNER. He might have been your friend, but he was not mine. [Laughter.]

General HARTZOG. What you saw there was time after time during the course of that evening General Thurman and I and others put out different frag orders, and the way we did it was, we had paper maps on the wall and acetate overlays, and people running in and out.

Senator WARNER. I remember it as if it were yesterday, and you were then the——

General HARTZOG. I was the J–3, the operations officer. I am the one that you lurked behind there, sir, that was working on the maps and what-not.

Senator WARNER. I remember, you allowed me to come right into the command center.

General HARTZOG. Yes, sir, but as a point of reference, what you saw then in 1989 was, as we put an order together, all of those 100 people in the outer room there frantically ran around to organize the information, put it onto a little machine called a jelly roll, which is a chemical reprinting facility, crushed out about 18 or 19 orders, the liaison officers that slept out by the latrine, if you recall, in the hall, roused up, came in, and we issued and order and an overlay to each one, and they went off in the night, into the city, into the fire fights and rain and what-not, and they generally would get those orders to where they were supposed to go, sometimes on time, and sometimes just after the attack occurred.

Well, it is now 6 years later, and what I want to demonstrate to you is what you would have seen in that bunker if you had walked into it today and we had the same conditions.

It is called a Sigma Star of information devices, and the chart that Colonel Kobbe has laid on the table there shows five nodes in that star. One of them is a device that brings together intelligence information The acronym is irrelevant, but it draws into a computer all of the inputs from flying devices, national sources, and sources of intelligence above that level, whatever it is.

It also draws in all of the reports from the levels below issued by front line officers and scouts such as the one that you saw right here, squad leaders. It synthesizes them, analyzes them, and prints them as an intelligence point of view.

There are similar systems in each headquarters now that in a computer gather all of the data that is available about indirect fire that is targeting by artillery, air, and Navy, all of the data that is available about air operations, where the friendly air is flying, what the air corridors are, and the fourth has to do with logistics, both personnel and supply, and so all of those things are available, and they are continuously updated as information automatically comes in.

Then there is a horizontal integrating program called MCS Phoenix. That is at the center. That is a television screen that is the analogy to that map that you so graciously signed that night in 1989, that had the six acetate overlays on it that was an attempt to put all that information together.

Now, in 1989, it took about 4 hours for us to put together an order, issue it to the field, and if we were lucky, it got to the people that needed it 2 hours later.

Now, if you recall, we had subordinate commanders all over the country, 50 miles away, General Cisneros at the commandant's—at the Nunciatura, General Downing, and others.

If you walked in there today and you needed to issue a frag order, here is what you would do. You would in the first place have on you screen a map of the area. That is a 1 over 50 map. That would be on the MCS Phoenix screen. On it, you would punch a button, a single button, and put the operational boundaries that you were working on, and then you would punch another button and bring up the friendly, the location of friendly forces.

Now, that is the Seventh Division, and in your parlance from the night in 1989, that is the 82nd Airborne Division, where they were, the Seventh Division, where they were, their battalion headquarters, the forces at the Nunciatura, and all of the other things you recall.

Now, you need to know where the enemy is on the battlefield, and ASAS provides that with a punch button. It shows you the synthesis of all the National air-breathing and lower echelon reports.

If an incoming enemy rocket, or an incoming enemy aircraft happens to be flying in your area when you punch that button, it will also come up on the screen, and you punch another button if you want to know about the obstacles, things that are very important to us today in Bosnia, you bring those locations up.

Then if you want the indirect fire data and the targeting that comes out of the air tactical order or the fire order, you bring that up, and if you want to know the status, the logistics status of your units, you can punch one button and bring that up.

Now you have the overlay that took us 4 hours to produce, produced in about 2 minutes of discussion here today.

These are real pulls off of the machines, so you are seeing what would occur in that command post.

Now, if you wanted to send that to your subordinate commanders, the J–3 or the S–3, in this case, me, who always thinks that he knows as much about the issue as anyone, you would draft an op order, or a fragmentary order, two or three lines to send out.

But as General Thurman always said, "You are not in charge, I am, and so I will approve that", and occasionally he was out in a Humvee somewhere. Well, today he would have that laptop, and we would send that information out to him, and I would say, "Boss, do you think that is about right?", and as he always did, he said, "Yeah, it's about right, but here are the changes."

He would say, "I don't want to go up the right side, I want to go up the left", and he would take his John Madden light pen, as he just does there, and he would draw the circle around the one that he wanted to move, and show me the direction in which he wanted it to go, and today we would both be looking at the same map across an electronic bridge as he was doing that.

Then he would say, "Now, get it right, Billy, write the right words at the bottom of the page", and I would redo the words at the bottom of the page as they are being done there, and then I would have an entire frag order.

Then, instead of calling in the sleepy LNO's out of the outside area there, and issuing them a jelly roll produced paper product, you punch one button and send it to however many subordinate headquarters you have.

Now, that is 6 years' worth of effort, actually about 2 years' worth of effort, and that is where we are today. You have that star of capabilities in each of your battalion, brigade, and division headquarters. What we not done is, we have not put an entire division on the ground. We have put a brigade on the ground to see what an infantry brigade will do with that kind of technology.

The next steps in the process are to put a full mechanized brigade on the ground—and I will tell you in a moment about that process—with that kind of technology and link up the individual soldier and the applique in the tanks and the applique in the helicopters together to make sure that the backbones and the appliques work.

That is where we are today, sir, and that is what you would see today if we were in that same little bunker.

Senator WARNER. Let me make a note for the record that the Chairman of the committee, Senator Nunn, was with me on that trip, and this is astonishing.

General HARTZOG. Sir, I think in the order of time I will just omit the charts here and just make about three points off of them. You have the charts in front of you and can study them.

The point is that we are not insensitive to the threat. You have heard a lot of people talk about capabilities-based Army because we do not have the precision with the threat that we have had before, but I will just explain this first one that you have in front of you that looks like this.

This one just says that right now the threat upon which we base our force structure is the threat of two simultaneous MRCs with some lesser conflicts and security assistance and special operations.

We do not know exactly what the threat will be in the next 10 years, but we think it will be a mixture of major regional conflicts and lesser regional conflicts, and a lot of the smaller operations, security assistance and special ops, and the best that our intelligence community tells us is that a resurgent peer competitor will not come along before about 2010 to 2015.

If that is about correct, our challenge is to go from today's Army——

Senator WARNER. Wait a minute. That is not withstanding—excuse me, you said a peer competitor?

General HARTZOG. Yes, sir.

Senator WARNER. Notwithstanding the seven nations with armies larger than ours?

General HARTZOG. That is correct, sir, and I put them in the potential for major regional conflicts or lesser regional conflicts, but we are where we are today, and where we need to go for sure is to have Army XXI—that is, the Force XX1 in place logically before we get out in the near peer competitor business, and we need to remain balanced in terms of doctrine, force mix, modern equipment, leader and unit training, and quality people, and we remain balanced throughout this transition period.

Now, the way we are doing that is described in here. Let me not bog you in this at the moment. Let me just go to a second chart quickly and tell you that the process that we have had going on for the last 2 years has been to conduct four major exercises or advanced warfighting experiments with troops on the ground, aircraft in the air, and in some cases 20,000 people involved.

We did this with scrutiny. We tried some new ideas, we tried some new equipment, we assessed what that was all about, so this is on the ground experimentation in theater missile defense, division command and control. What you just saw came out of this experimentation. Heavy task force operations and light infantry brigade operations, we went across the spectrum.

At the same time, we thought that we needed to do some constructive analysis, and so we ran hundreds of computer runs at division level against scenarios in the upper end of the MRC spectrum like Northeast Asia, defense of Korea, like a resurgent Southwest Asia, Desert Storm-like operation, like meeting engagements in Europe, or operations like the Bosnia operation.

We came up with a division design for experimentation, not the end product but a division design to put into the experimental force, which is the Fourth Infantry Division at Fort Hood, Texas, and they are reforming into that division design today.

With the insights that came out of this, and with those two things together, we felt that we needed to relook, given digitization, given new equipment, given what we learned there, how would we fight in the future? Would it be different from the way that we fight today?

Would it be a deep, a close, and a rear? Would there be linear boundaries, or would the boundaries look circular like the ones you just saw on that diagram? Would we have to be more flexible, would we have to go to places simultaneously on the battlefield?

So we had a series of seminars, 2 or 3 days apiece, throughout the last year with all of the commandants of the different branches and all of the active division commanders involved, and we have the product of these three things today going into the Fourth Infantry Division at Fort Hood.

Our plan is to take this composite 21st Century unit and have it in place with all of the equipment, and all of the lessons, and all of the tactics, techniques and procedures by June of this year.

We think it is important that they train with all of these things for about 8 months so that when they go to operate with these new techniques and procedures, we are not just seeing how well they are trained, but we are seeing a new unit that is fully trained in whatever the new ideas are, and they are substantial.

For instance, I just picked up a stack this morning, but there are 60 new manuals on how to operate a force in a digitized environment. It makes a big difference. It moves at a different pace. It works at different levels. We train it in different ways.

Always in the past we have books and books and books. There are 591 manuals and books on this single CD-ROM disk. There are another 17 how-to books about training on this single CD-ROM. These two things together are everything that you need to put together a training schedule for a battalion, or a brigade, or a division.

So it is not just digitization, and it is not just new organizations or new equipment, it is also new ways of training folks, and a lot of this is done over a television set now. We just trained a battalion in the Sinai Desert completely by distance learning on television, and it worked very well.

Senator WARNER. General, there is always the old adage, the Army is always preparing to fight yesterday's battle. I remember also General Thurman, out of your presence, referring to you as the best set of brains he knew. That is yet to be proved—[Laughter.]

General HARTZOG. He frequently overstated things. [Laughter.]

Senator WARNER. Can you assure the committee today the Army is not fighting yesterday's battle, but really is looking to the future?

General HARTZOG. Sir, I can assure you that the Force XXI is so very different that the concern is not that we are preparing for yesterday's battle, but that we are standing on the right mountaintop in the future, seeing the right future.

Now, we all stood on the mountaintop and looked out in the 21st Century, an we saw things like information being far more important, all kinds of equipment looking different, an amorphous threat across a wide spectrum of different potential adversaries, but I am not sure that we are on the right mountaintop, or that it was not a cloudy day.

None of us are omniscient, and so it probably is going to be more of a tool kit into which you can reach and pull out what you need, rather than something that is optimized for a specific threat.

I feel very good about where we are. I can also tell you we do not have all the answers, but we probably will by about a year from now have most of the brigade-level answers, and we probably need to continue to fund the experimentation until we get to those.

Senator WARNER. I think by necessity you have to put into your equation the likelihood that one or more nations will try and build a standing army to where it not only in manpower but in technology would be a peer to the United States Army.

General HARTZOG. Yes, sir, I think so. Our best estimate is that may not be in the next 10 to 15 years, but history tells us that is likely to occur.

Senator WARNER. Thank you.

[The prepared statement of General Hartzog follows:]

PREPARED STATEMENT BY GEN. WILLIAM W. HARTZOG, U.S. ARMY, COMMANDING
GENERAL, TRAINING AND DOCTRINE COMMAND

Mr. Chairman and Members of the Committee, thank you for the opportunity to appear before you and discuss the future of your Army. As Commander of the United States Army Training and Doctrine Command, I have two major responsibilities. First, I run the schoolhouse for our Army a schoolhouse which trains more than 545,000 students annually either in resident or correspondence training. Many of these students are members of our sister services and friends abroad. Second, I have the lead for developing the requirements for the Army of the future—developing warfighting concepts, designing Army organizations, developing equipment requirements, and developing complementary training strategies and training support packages. It is a great time to be in our Army and I again appreciate the opportunity to represent the great men and women who serve proudly in America's Army.

For the United States Army, the decade of the 1990's has been, and will continue to be, one of change. We see change not only in terms of increased operations around the globe, but also in the manner in which we conduct operations. Force XXI is the Army's effort to harness that change and move into the 21st century while remaining the most capable land combat force in the world.

We work from a strong base. Today's Army is clearly the best in the world. But it was built in response to a well-defined threat. The Army of today was organized, equipped, and trained to oppose our superpower opponent, the Soviet Union, on a European battlefield. Our warfighting doctrine, as codified in FM 100-5, *Operations*, was modified in 1993 to accommodate our revised position in the international community, but still today we are conducting operations with the Big Five—the Abrams main battle tank, the Bradley fighting vehicle, the Apache attack helicopter, the Blackhawk utility helicopter, and the Patriot air defense missile—the five major systems developed in the late 1970s. While modifications and up-grades to the entire force are continuous, modernization is one of the keys to dominance on the future battlefield and the key to readiness for the unexpected challenges that will face us.

To get us to the end of the decade, the Army modernization strategy includes horizontal technology integration (HTI). When technologies are identified as providing a significant capabilities improvement, we incorporate them into the force through a mixture of individual system improvements, horizontally integrating these technologies in with other systems while limiting new acquisitions. Although this strategy accepts some risk, it greatly reduces the costs of modernization by taking advantage of previously fielded systems. To manage limited modernization resources, the Army has extended system fielding times of new systems while upgrading existing systems to maintain the capability of the total force, while waiting deployment of the next generation of systems.

With that awareness, the Army has taken steps to move beyond today and tomorrow and leap into the 21st century and all of its unknowns. For the past 3 years we have been on a march into the 21st century. In response to the rapidly changing environments, international and national, the Army has undergone a transformation. Our Army has a plan, a plan which includes our joint partners. We have developed a vision of the future and written it down in TRADOC Pamphlet 525-5, *A Concept for the Evolution of Full-Dimensional Operations for the Strategic Army of the Early 21st Century*. It is how we envision Army operations in the future. Force XXI is our bridge to the future, our Army's campaign plan to provide focus for the modernization and growth of the force into the 21st century.

The Force XXI campaign plan is a descriptive process that includes the framework for achieving modernization objectives. The Training and Doctrine Command's charge is to plan, develop, and achieve Force XXI fielding decisions for the operational force by the end of the century.

The Army is redesigning the operational force by way of a series of experiments and analysis of warfighting and training concepts, ideas, and technology in the Training and Doctrine Command's battlefield laboratories culminating in a series of advanced warfighting experiments. Many of the experiments will be enabled by an experimental force, the EXFOR, which is in place at Fort Hood, Texas. Experimentation is being done to enable us to make informed investment decisions. To date, and as a result of aggressive advanced warfighting experimentation, we are incorporating 97 "good ideas" into a brigade-sized advanced warfighting experiment. That comprises approximately 87 new systems for the EXFOR heavy units and 37 new systems for the EXFOR light units, systems which range in complexity and cost.

Central to our experimentation is digitization. Digitization is the Army term for providing computers to individual soldiers as well as installing them in tactical vehicles. Experimentation is providing the foundation upon which to gauge the relative value of the Army's proposed investments to build the Army of the early 21st century—including but not limited to our investment in modernization of new equipment. A very important complementary investment is the investment in training and leader development.

Three key ideas have emerged from our experiments. First is the importance of information, second is a new way to conduct Army operations, and the third is the importance of sustaining the link to our sister services.

Information is far more important than it has ever been and may well dominate how we organize in the future. Internetted information systems can provide common situational awareness across the battlefield and may well redefine command and staff processes and methods. We will be able to know almost everything about the enemy and our own forces before conflict and during conflict. Therefore, we anticipate that control of information may be the objective of conflict itself.

Important, therefore, is the research, development and acquisition of capabilities which will leverage information technology to fully advantage our quality soldiers and leaders on the battlefield. Additionally, we need to have modern technologies to train and educate them wherever they may be assigned or deployed, making a seamless linkage between our schoolhouses and the units and soldiers around the world. The Army plans to use advanced technologies as a force multiplier and create a deployable force capable of meeting the Nation's needs at home and abroad—an Army that is perhaps smaller, but more lethal, survivable, and versatile.

The second major insight from our advanced warfighting experiments is that information technologies will change how we conduct Army operations. We have constructed a new operational concept for the force of the early 21st century. A major change is the way we visualize the battlefield. We know that our future force will operate in an expanded battlespace. We will have to attain success across the width, depth, height, and electromagnetic dimensions as well as the human dimension. Also, Force XXI operations will be non-linear—devoid of rigid organization of unit or function—decentralized and simultaneous. Operations will be characterized by faster tempo, precision, and a common view of the battlefield enabled by the bow wave of information technologies.

Another major change is the way we conduct operations. The patterns are more simultaneous than they are sequential. They are project the force, protect the force, gain information dominance, shape the battlespace, conduct decisive operations, and sustain the force. Significant change is found in the patterns of gaining information dominance, shaping the battlespace, and conducting decisive operations. This new operational concept is supported by the Army's modernization objectives.

Finally, the lessons from our advanced warfighting experiments reinforce the importance of continuing the strong partnership between the Army and our sister services. We recognize that future military operations will be not only "joint", but also require the Army to operate as part of a multinational or interagency team as well. Therefore, we not only train with our joint, multinational, and interagency partners, the Army includes them as key participants or observers in our advanced warfighting experiments.

The Army constantly upgrades and changes the way it fights in order to maintain battlefield superiority over all potential adversaries and to achieve complementary capabilities with other services and nations. Previously, we determined requirements based on deficiencies identified in comparison with our major threat, the Soviet Union and the Warsaw Pact. In that manner, and for that reason, we developed what we called "The Big Five" some 15 years ago. They represented capability driven by threat. Perceived threat, rather than cost or consideration, determined need to a great extent.

Today's requirements are determined differently. We now determine requirements more holistically based on desired capabilities. Those are driven by warfighting concepts focused on the future and tempered by experimentation. No requirement is determined in isolation. Senior leaders make requirements decisions based on an understanding of all potential requirements, cost, and impact on the operational force. We do not expect performance at any cost.

Recent deployments (25 since 1990) and our advanced warfighting experiments over the last 3 years have reinforced a lesson important to our Army in the early 21st century—we must have balanced change across the Army. We must balance today's readiness with modernization for tomorrow—today's modernization is tomorrow's readiness. The fiscal year 1997 budget reflects the Army's minimum requirement for modernization. Further reductions in modernization would put the Army's long term readiness at risk. I assure you that the Army is a good steward of these resources and is aggressively assessing innovative ways to gain efficiencies by re-engineering and recapitalizing.

But modernization is more than just upgrading or buying new equipment. Transitioning the Army to the early 21st century requires balanced modernization—a balanced investment—across the other Army imperatives—doctrine, training, leader development, force mix, and what we do for our quality men and women—not just new equipment. This balanced investment across all the Army imperatives is being informed by the advanced warfighting experiments conducted by the battle laboratories in the Training and Doctrine Command. In March 1997 we will conduct a brigade-level advanced warfighting experiment at the National Training Center (Task Force XXI) and follow that up with a division-level exercise.

A challenge facing our Army is how to buy and field things that work and add value to the soldier based on what we are learning specifically from our Force XXI advanced warfighting experiments. So, the Army is developing a two part strategy. First, an investment in Fiscal Year 1997 in some key Force XXI enablers which must be in place early on as the foundation for balanced modernization at the end of the decade and into the early 21st century. These key enablers include research and development of doctrine, unit and leader training strategies and technologies, and information and other technologies designed specifically for the individual soldier. Second, an annual investment in doctrine, unit and leader training, and technologies targeted as proven "good ideas" resulting specifically from our Force XXI advanced warfighting experiments. If we already had all the answers now we would not be doing the experiments.

There is a clear correlation between today's technology and tomorrow's application of it. The Army must maintain a balance across the Army imperatives—doctrine, organization, materiel development, training, leader development, and quality people.

Modernization is not a cheap process. But neither is the alternative. To quote Creighton Abrams, "People are not in the Army, they are the Army. Every effort must be made towards insuring that our men and women receive the finest care and the best leadership that is humanly possible."

CHANGING THE OPERATIONAL ARMY

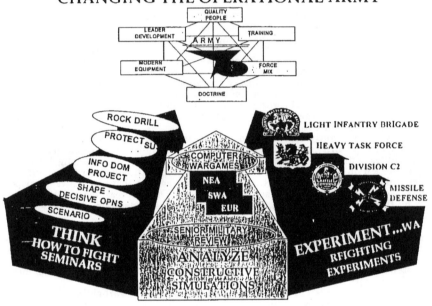

CHANGING REQUIREMENTS PROCESS

· INTEGRATED CONCEPT TEAMS TRANSITIONING TO
  INTEGRATED PRODUCT TEAMS

· HOLISTIC ANALYTIC UNDERPINNINGS USING
  MULTIPLE OPERATIONAL SCENARIOS

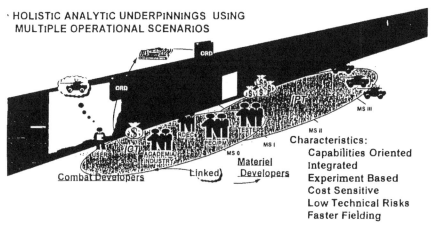

Characteristics:
Capabilities Oriented
Integrated
Experiment Based
Cost Sensitive
Low Technical Risks
Faster Fielding

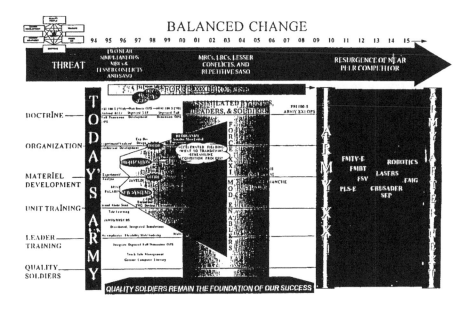

BALANCED CHANGE

QUALITY SOLDIERS REMAIN THE FOUNDATION OF OUR SUCCESS

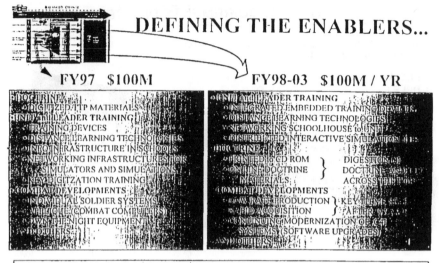

DEFINING THE ENABLERS...

FY97 $100M   FY98-03 $100M / YR

BUY AND FIELD THINGS THAT WORK AND ADD VALUE TO THE SOLDIER

Senator WARNER. Senator Levin.

Senator LEVIN. Just a couple of questions. I would emphasize here what has been mentioned briefly, and that is the emphasis which should be given to overload and to failure in this whole communications revolution which you are so brilliantly integrating in the Army. I see that as a problem out there as well.

We are trying to reduce information to useful information in real time and in a form that somebody in the heat of battle can use. It seems to me it is going to be probably a greater challenge than putting together the information or having access to the information.

I can see pictures coming into a headquarters from 50 different directions at once and being unable to integrate it and make it useful, so I think we are going to have to spend a hell of a lot of time on overload issue and on the crash issue, the fallback issue, and the safety net kinds of issues.

This is awfully exciting stuff. I have seen an earlier version of it, and it is magnificent. You are going exactly in the right direction. I just want to kind of put up some cautionary flags, and you are more aware of them than I am. I just want to make sure that we put adequate emphasis on them.

Second, which of the equipment that we have seen this morning, these technologies, everything from the laptop to the soldier who was here, is currently in use in Bosnia in some form or another?

General HARTZOG. Sir, we have bits and pieces of all of this, because we are not trying to go to an optimal solution and not spin off anything that we have learned. We are trying to find the good things and move them. As an example, the television camera that you saw on the soldier here today we began using operationally in Haiti, and it produced pictures that could be sent back, so that is functioning in Bosnia.

A personal keyboard, not exactly the one you saw today, but one like it, is used in the artillery units today in Bosnia. That sends digital information back and forth.

The ASAS portion of the Sigma Star, that is, the different elements that you just saw demonstrated on the laptop, the intelligence part of it is in use in Bosnia.

The centerpiece, the horizontal integrator, the MCS Phoenix, an earlier version of that software is in use in Bosnia, and, of course, the laptops are proliferating.

STATEMENT OF GEN. RONALD H. GRIFFITH, USA, VICE CHIEF OF STAFF

General GRIFFITH. Just to pick up on that, sir, the FLIR technology you saw—the demonstrated capabilities of, the FLIR technology—we have on our tanks and Bradleys. That is the First Armored Division. The tanks and Bradleys have that FLIR technology. We had that in the desert, and they can engage long-range. The night vision capability is there.

So a lot of the technology that you saw on the soldier is not only with soldiers but it is on systems, weapons systems.

Senator WARNER. Let me just interrupt. For purposes of procedure, Secretary Decker, had you any further opening statements you wish to make?

Mr. DECKER. No, sir. I am sorry. We can go right into Q and A. We are finished.

Senator WARNER. General Griffith, did you have some opening statements?

General GRIFFITH. Sir, I have no opening statement. I just would like to respond to a couple of points you made, sir, earlier.

Number 1, sir, you mentioned in your opening——

Senator WARNER. So in other words, the committee can now just proceed to question the entire panel?

Mr. DECKER. Yes, sir.

Senator WARNER. We will proceed accordingly, but you wished to make a couple of comments.

General GRIFFITH. I would just like to respond, sir, to a couple of points that you made. Number 1, you mentioned the technology overmatch that we enjoy today, and the need to ensure that the soldiers 20 years from now enjoy that same technology overmatch.

We are very committed to that, sir, because, as I am sure most of you are aware, the technology overmatch advantage we enjoyed in Panama and later in Desert Storm was for the most part the vision of the leadership of the Army back in the seventies, and most specifically General Creighton Abrams, but I can tell you the modernization commitment is one that we take very seriously.

The other thing, sir, is the concern over interoperability in a joint context; you mentioned Admiral Owens. I think that he has been a real leader in ensuring that the forces of the future are able to fight in a joint context.

I can tell you the JROC, which I have the responsibility to participate in as the Vice Chief of the Army, is focused absolutely on that need, and I would tell you also that the JROC is seriously concerned about our ability to operate with allies in a combined coalition context.

So the things you mentioned that are of concern, I will tell you we take very seriously, and while we have not solved the problems, they are very much a part of our attention.

Senator WARNER. At some point, Mr. Secretary, if you could give the current status of the Department of the Army with respect to land mines, and then, General Hartzog, the current status of such training and future planning as is in place today, subject to, I presume, a final decision within the Department as to the use or nonuse of this weapon.

Mr. DECKER. I will give an overview.

Senator COATS. Mr. Chairman, could I interrupt for just a moment? I have a commitment at 10:30, and I tell you what, after all of this sophisticated presentation, I have some very unglamorous questions about trucks and jeeps. He will probably reach in his pocket and pull out a truck.

Mr. DECKER. You make some real good trucks in Indiana, too. [Laughter.]

Senator COATS. I will submit those for the record.

Mr. DECKER. We will be happy to get you answers to the questions you submit.

Senator COATS. Mr. Chairman, I want to tell you that this is a very, very important and helpful presentation here. I wish all our colleagues were here.

Senator WARNER. Would you care to also put in questions on force level, because for the committee as a whole, that is a responsibility that you have as Chairman.

Senator COATS. Yes, and how that will deal with force levels.

Mr. DECKER. Yes. Thank you very much for coming, sir.

Senator WARNER. If you would just complete the land mine question, then I will turn to my colleagues here, and then I will have a wrap-up question for you.

Mr. DECKER. There are two dimensions to the mine issue, one is countermine, the other is use of mines.

Senator WARNER. I beg your pardon?

Mr. DECKER. Countermine and use of mines. We are very heavily and intensely involved, and have had several technology-based programs, and some of these programs have actually gone into implementation on the countermine piece. That is certainly critical in Bosnia or any other place we will go similar to Bosnia.

Senator WARNER. What is the status of the policy decision of the President and the SECDEF down and Chief of Staff of the Army and Secretary of the Army as to the use of mines?

Mr. DECKER. Let me ask either the Vice or General Hartzog to handle that. They really deal with those more along the operational channels.

Senator WARNER. General Griffith.

General GRIFFITH. Sir, Congress passed a law to have a moratorium on their use, and we understand the restriction, I would say, sir, from a soldier's perspective.

Senator WARNER. So in other words the moratorium is in place, while presumably the JCS is in consultation with the President. It is at that level ,is it not?

General GRIFFITH. Consultation is correct, sir, but the moratorium does not take effect until January 1999.

Senator WARNER. So at the level you are in sort of a stand-down both in operational deployments around the world, as well as, perhaps, even planning and training on that weapons system, is that correct?

General GRIFFITH. That is correct, sir.

Senator WARNER. Are you utilizing them at all in Bosnia, as a protective measure for your forces?

General GRIFFITH. None of the restricted mines are being used in Bosnia. There are mines that are not restricted.

Senator WARNER. Differentiate between a restricted and a non-restricted.

General GRIFFITH. Yes, sir. An example is a Claymore mine, which a soldier can use to protect a position. Quite frankly, sir, I am not sure that we are using the Claymores, but that would not be a restricted capability because that is command-detonated. You put it out. If you do not use it, you pull it back in and disarm it and use it for the next operation.

Those are not restricted, sir. We are not using obviously, any of the restricted mines, and we do not envision any need for them in that context.

Senator WARNER. So at the moment, it is stand-down across the board in our military forces, and most particularly the Army.

General GRIFFITH. Not exactly, we are assessing how best to implement the law. I would say there is a commitment to do the research and development that is needed to look at nonlethal anti-personnel capabilities. We have traditionally had lethal mines, and so there is a commitment to look at that. I am not sure what the outcome will be.

Senator WARNER. What is an example of nonlethal?

General GRIFFITH. A stunning sort of device, sir, or a device that disables an individual but does not cripple or maim an individual. Quite frankly, sir, at this point it is all theoretical, but it could be some sort of system that could disable an individual for 24 or 36 or 48 hours, but not a system that would kill or maim.

Senator WARNER. Are we in a stand-down on the training mode with the use of this system?

General HARTZOG. Sir, we are in a stand-down in most of the training mode with the exception of detection, clearing, and protection. All of those are going ahead. That is, the countermine piece.

Senator WARNER. Are we putting an added emphasis, given the problem throughout the world, on the countermeasures?

Mr. DECKER. Yes, sir, big time.

Senator WARNER. You might just sketch what that involves today.

Mr. DECKER. In terms of the training, General Hartzog can speak to that, and I will speak on the R&D side.

General HARTZOG. Sir, in mine training we have done intensified mine awareness classes to describe the different kinds of mines we are finding in Bosnia, which are unique and relatively broad. We have done that by video teleconferences over the training network business to all units that are headed there and to the professional development classes up through the advanced course level.

We have done hand-outs. We have generated an engineer contingency book that describes all of the different mines as they are being identified. That comes back to us electronically, so we update that frequently.

We have produced three different small laminated mine infocards for soldiers to carry, and that have been updated, and we have a 3-day course by mobile training team in Italy for all units as they come into the theater, so the training system has been relatively robust.

We also sent forward a number of pieces of equipment to use to try to determine the best ones. We sent the Panther system, which is a remote-controlled M–60 tank with a blade that you can put out in front of you, blade and rollers, and just brute force run without anyone on it.

We sent Point Man, which is an explosive ordnance demolition robot vehicle. We have tried World War II technology and the miniflails that were used at Normandy, which seemed to work very well, because some of the mines are of the same type and same makeup.

We have a remote controlled 5-ton truck with a thermal detection system on the front of it that can be driven from behind.

We have a number of field-expedient countermine systems like electronic coils mounted on vehicles to detonate mines.

We use the Barrett rifle to explode mines that are identified, and we have a number of different protection kits, thermal blankets and Kevlar helmets that have been sent forward.

So we have a number of different systems involved, and a goodly bit of mine training going on.

Senator WARNER. I would say to my colleagues here I will come back with other questions, but please proceed.

Senator LEVIN. Thank you, Mr. Chairman.

First, Secretary Decker, let me ask you about the overall budget numbers and how that relates to modernization. We adopted a number for the top line last year for 1997 which is $13 billion higher than the President's actual budget submission for 1997. In addition, the Army was asked for an add-on list. I think it is called a 1 to N list, is that right?

Mr. DECKER. Yes, sir.

Senator LEVIN. That list adds up to about $7 billion.

Mr. DECKER. Yes, sir.

Senator LEVIN. The problem we are going to face is that in the outyears the relationship between the budget resolution, last year's budget resolution for the outyears and the President's budget reverses, so that the President has more spending in the outyears than does the budget resolution and less spending in the near term.

So the real question, Secretary Perry and others have said that we should give priority to accelerating programs which are already planned, rather than new starts, so we do not create a large tail at the very time when our funding is going to be constrained.

I am wondering whether or not you can comment on these issues and tell us how does that fit with your 1 to N list, because we do not see any reductions on that list in the outyears. In fact, we see tails created in the outyears on that 1 to N list.

You have a CH–47 cargo helicopter replacement which adds big bucks. We do not see any things which fit what the realities are going to look like. Instead, we see new starts instead of accelerated starts on your list.

How does that all fit together?

Mr. DECKER. I think on the list, particularly if you group it by categories of capability like combat service support, which includes items like some of the unglamorous items that Senator Coats and I referred to, such as trucks and tactically quiet generators and things, and if you look at aviation programs that you mentioned—there is a great number of things on that list where we would propose, to accelerate the procurement parts of our modernization.

Senator LEVIN. Was that list developed consistent with Secretary Perry's priority to accelerate?

Mr. DECKER. I think it was, sir. We are looking at where we can try to do things if we had the resources to do it now, to accelerate procurement and fielding of items that are virtually finished, or are in development and are already in production at slower rates than we desire.

So I believe there is a substantial part of that list in the procurement accounts that we could accelerate at more efficient rates.

Senator LEVIN. That would also require that there be some items on that list that would result in savings in the outyears.

Mr. DECKER. Yes, sir.

Senator LEVIN. Are there such items?

Mr. DECKER. Yes, sir. I will give you an example of what is in the President's budget that we looked at hard for ourselves that is not on the 1 to N kind of list, where we made the decision in the basic budget submission to buy out all of our modernized SINCGARS radios early so we would get the entire fleet equipped. That was stretched out over several years.

The budget proposal you have in the core budget, we buy those out early and that saves in two ways. We get a better deal from the contractor if we offer the whole contract up at once, and substantial savings because he can produce at a more efficient rate. He can commit to buy all the parts at once, and do all those sorts of things.

Second, the year that we would have had tails on buying out the remaining SINCGARS goes to zero, and those funds that would be in there can be put some place else.

So there are quite a few items that we have in the 1 to N list that do procure early, and we buy out early, so if that happens you would see some changes in the tails of those items as they now exist in the Future Years Defense Plan (FYDP).

Senator LEVIN. Last year, the committee sponsored an initiative to provide armor tiles for part of the Bradley Fighting Vehicle force. The Army apparently liked the idea, but I do not know that there is any funding to complete that program. Do you know whether there is in this budget request, and if not, why not?

Mr. DECKER. I do not believe there is any in the core budget. That is a fairly high item on our 1 to N list, but in the core budget we had just run out of money.

Senator LEVIN. Can you give us a report on the vehicle leasing program for the record?

Mr. DECKER. Yes, sir, I will. We are getting ready to submit a report to you that was requested on one of the documents. I have just reviewed the draft of that report the other day, and we will give you a response for the record.

[The information referred to follows:]

Noncombat Vehicle Leasing Program

The Army completed a study regarding the lease of the Commercial Utility Cargo Vehicle (CUCV). Under the terms offered by General Motors, leasing of CUCVs is not cost effective at this time. However, the Army has recently commissioned a study, which is just getting underway, on leasing heavy line haul tractors and medium trucks for specified Army and Reserve units.

Senator LEVIN. You are also going to report to us on the valuation of the leasing option, and in addition the possibility of looking at other portions of the vehicle fleet for leasing.

Mr. DECKER. We not only looked just at the commercial utility cargo vehicle (CUCV) commercial trucks, we looked at the entire concept of leasing noncombat vehicles, and you will be getting that report in the near future. Anyway, we will certainly make it a part of the record of this testimony.

Senator LEVIN. Are you going to continue to upgrade the existing fleet of tanks?

Mr. DECKER. Well, a 1,000-some odd is the objective. You are talking about up to the M1A2 configuration.

Senator LEVIN. Yes.

Mr. DECKER. The number of total ones we will upgrade in the estimated force mix has not changed. It is 1,079.

Senator LEVIN. There has been no change in your plans relative to that program.

Mr. DECKER. When you say plan, you mean rate or total quantity?

Senator LEVIN. Both.

Mr. DECKER. Total quantity is still 1,079. We have stabilized the rate at approximately 120 per year, and are planning to do that in a multiyear. We are virtually in agreement in negotiations with the contractor and the pricing and everything to do that, and it fits the budget numbers you have been submitted. We would like to accelerate that program, too, but I think we will do well with a multiyear that is envisioned in the core budget we have submitted.

Senator LEVIN. Is there any truth to the suggestion the Army would have a 15-year production break in tank upgrades or modernization?

Mr. DECKER. I am not sure how to read that. I mean, when we finish producing the 1,079th tank, we need to have a plan someplace of where we go from there. If we do not have a plan there could be a break. I do not know where the number 15 came from, sir.

Senator LEVIN. Are you looking at a new development effort for a future tank in lieu of continuing the upgrade?

Mr. DECKER. Yes, sir. There are several studies ongoing right now, some internal studies and the Army Science Board is looking intensively about where thou goest in future armor.

Senator LEVIN. That is not going to affect your plans for the upgrade program?

Mr. DECKER. Not likely, sir. These things would be the things we do beyond tank 1,079.

Senator LEVIN. Recently, Secretary White sent a memo to all the service Secretaries directing them to implement privatization and outsourcing initiatives, and to use the savings to invest in modernization. That is a big issue in terms of funding modernization. Are you familiar with that memo?

Mr. DECKER. Yes, sir.

Senator LEVIN. Do you fully support and intend to implement that memorandum?

Mr. DECKER. Yes, sir, a great deal. I am not copping out on you, but I am an acquisition guy, and the way the responsibilities are assigned within the Army, some of that is out of my lane, but I do support and encourage privatization—as long as we do our data correctly, and make sure that our numbers are right. We would do that in business and I believe we will see in many cases that privatization and outsourcing pays by dividend. I am a great believer in privatization, even in many nontraditional areas.

General GRIFFITH. Sir, I sit on that task force, and I can tell you we do see opportunities to help ourselves in the outyears through privatization. Obviously, you have to make sure that as you move in that direction you protect core capabilities within the force, and we would obviously not move without taking those into consideration.

The second thing, of course, is that there are a lot of enablers that would be required from the Congress if we are going to move privatization down the road where there are big dollars.

Senator LEVIN. You intend though, General, to fully implement the White memorandum on privatization?

General GRIFFITH. Sir, I am very familiar with the initiative, and I sit on that task force. I am not familiar with the specific memorandum or the details of that.

Senator LEVIN. We will get it to you.

Mr. DECKER. I would like to echo—and this is not intended to be challenging or anything else. There are some barriers that make it very difficult. We can do the right business decision much faster and easier in many of these areas if some of the regulatory and legal things——

Senator LEVIN. We will work on those barriers, but in the meantime, where there are no barriers——

Mr. DECKER. I push personally every chance I can—we run into a few internal barriers, too, sir.

Senator LEVIN. Thank you.

Senator WARNER. We are pleased to be joined by the Chairman of the committee, Senator Thurmond, who has a very distinguished Army background, but in the 18 years I have served with him, I have never seen him once show that bias. [Laughter.]

Senator WARNER. Do you have a comment or two you would like to make, Mr. Chairman?

Chairman THURMOND. Mr. Chairman, I am not going to make any talk. I just want to commend you and the members of the subcommittee for the fine job you are doing.

Senator WARNER. Thank you, Mr. Chairman.

Chairman THURMOND. I have just had the pleasure of seeing this new soldier with all of this equipment on him. It is just miraculous what has been done, the progress we are making, and we have got to keep on. We have got to give them the best we can possibly give them. These soldiers are offering their lives for their country, and we must give them the best equipment that money can buy, and I will do everything I can to see that they are properly provided for, and thank you, gentlemen, for coming this morning.

Senator WARNER. Mr. Chairman, did you notice any difference in that equipment than the equipment you wore when you went in on D-Day? [Laughter.]

Chairman THURMOND. All of the difference in the world. [Laughter.]

When I was a second lieutenant, or even when I did go in on D-Day with the 82nd Airborne Division, all of the difference in the world. I am very proud of what we have done and the progress we have made.

I congratulate all of you people in the Army for the great job you are doing.

Senator WARNER. Thank you, Mr. Chairman.

Senator Lieberman.

Senator LIEBERMAN. Thank you, Mr. Chairman.

Mr. Decker, and General Hartzog, and General Griffith, thanks for your testimony. I regret that I was not able to be here at the outset, but I also ran into the soldier of the future—I did not run directly into him. [Laughter.]

That was fortunate for me, but I had a good tour of what is on him. I wanted to ask a couple of questions in that regard.

One of the battles we have had here in the legislature and the Congress over the last couple of years has to do with the dual-use technology budget of the Pentagon, and I must say this has particularly been in the House side.

Senator Smith of New Hampshire has been the co-Chair of the relevant subcommittee and has really been a good advocate for these programs.

But one of the questions that comes to my mind as I see this miraculous application of modern technology to the capability of the soldier in combat is the extent to which—I do not know whether you can point to particular items we have seen today, but the extent to which the modernization of the Army depends on some of the dual-use technology investments the Pentagon is making, or am I on the wrong track?

Are you basically picking up most of this stuff off the shelf because it is out there being developed in the private sector already?

Mr. DECKER. I think it is a combination of both, in reviewing the explicit dual-use initiatives that get funded as such with Dr. Kaminski and Dr. Jones and my colleagues in the other two services and our entire staffs.

I think last year certainly at Senator Smith's subcommittee on technology, that was a subject of high interest, and I believe I am reflecting correctly what Dr. Kaminski testified and we concurred in is that if you go back to the first year that the explicit dual-use funding came out and the proposal to put it in, it got off to a rocky start. It was not focused, and I believe like many new initiatives it did not jell the way it should.

He has made a hard commitment, and we back him fully to get the program focused. To the extent we do any explicit dual-use initiatives, they will have an outcome, and it will be a militarily relevant outcome and it is being pushed very hard to the degree a substantial part of the budgets for the advanced technology program and those kinds of dual-use initiatives are being given to the services to actually execute and implement.

So I think we will see some good use come out of it, and we need it. It is kind of a pump priming to kind of get the thinking going to get used to using stuff developed on the commercial standards.

The second part of your question, are we finding things off the shelf. Well, through the really intensive acquisition reform efforts that we are pushing to streamline the whole acquisition system, to eliminate military specs and develop specific requirements for the system, we are finding that the commercial technology is better than anything we can sponsor in-house anyway, and we are literally drawing off the shelf components and subsystems to integrate into our system wherever we can. I have numerous examples of that.

We are finding the quality is better and the prices are cheaper, so it is a dual thrust, and I know the latter one is working, and I believe this year we will see some real good results out of the explicit dual-use programs, because the military relevancy test is really being pushed now.

Senator LIEBERMAN. I appreciate that answer and you make an important point, which is that the explicit dual-use technology program is relatively young, so that we will just begin——

Mr. DECKER. Well, it is in its third year, depending on how its funded this year. The first year was ragged. It was better last year, and I think we are honed down now to where the real focus and review on military relevancy is being applied.

Senator LIEBERMAN. Let me ask either of the Generals whether, as you look forward both to Army XXI and to what you call in one of the charts the Army after the next, how important the dual-use technology programs are to your quest for continually modernizing the Army?

Mr. DECKER. You know what I would like to do. I think they are important, but to give you more than a qualitative judgment, I would like to ask Dr. Milton, the Deputy Assistant to me for Research and Technology, and is responsible for our entire Science and Technology (S&T) base program.

Senator WARNER. Would you kindly stand and identify yourself, please?

Dr. MILTON. I am Fenner Milton, chief scientist in the Army Secretariat. S&T has tried to look at spin-on in particular, and we have established, of course, two centers to deal with our major platforms in particular, the National Automotive Center, and the National Rotorcraft Technology Center, so they have been the focus of the work we have done, but we have cooperated with Defense Advanced Research Projects Agency (DARPA) and OSD in what was formerly called the TRP program to make sure that the topics that we had cognizance over would lead to military relevant solutions as a part of those programs, and we are looking forward to continuing those efforts.

Senator LIEBERMAN. General Hartzog, did you want to add anything to that?

General HARTZOG. Yes. From the second part, the Secretary mentioned about the sub rosa dual use business, we find, particularly in the digitization, that software produces and morphs and changes so rapidly that our best sources are in the civilian market, and the development is self-generating.

As an example,when you saw the 21st Century Land Warrior, we had a small problem here with the software involved in the keyboard, the sending unit, and when we looked to other manufacturers there were literally a squad of people there ready with similar products, because there were any number of parallel utilities in business and industry, and we did not have to do a new start, and we could make a rapid switch.

That is very important in the experimentation, because all good ideas are not, and all things do not work as we have seen them to do, but it is far more robust than it was a year or two ago in alternatives because of the multiplicity of the utility of the things.

Senator LIEBERMAN. Let me ask a different kind of question.

As I looked at the soldier of the future, which goes to the durability of this equipment, maybe because I am not a child of the computer age, and I am trying to catch up with my kids, I treat the laptop we have with a kind of tenderness—and of course I watch my 8-year-old daughter, and she jams everything and does not worry about it. Of course, it just works beautifully for her.

Here is my question. When that soldier has to hit the mud in combat, is that stuff going to hold up?

Mr. DECKER. I think so. There will be some breakage, but I would submit this. I mean, that is pretty tightly designed.

You saw the section on the backpack that contains the radios. Just below that there is a card-based 486 computer. It is pretty heavily mounted in there, that 486-chip, and the card is a commercial item. It is pretty rugged, and it is encased in the load bearing comonent of the backpack, so it is not going to get wet, or whatever, inside that case on the backpack.

So unless you hit it with a hammer, or he falls backwards on a rock, he can fall in the mud and he will get up, and it will still be working, so I think with 90, 95-percent reliability under something other than the most severe kind of jar, or deliberately putting it underwater for hours on end or something, it will do just fine.

Senator WARNER. If the Senator will yield on that, you might also mention temperature differentials. I mean, in Korea we experienced minus 25, 30, and in the desert you have got up over 100.

Mr. DECKER. 120 degrees F. You are absolutely, right, sir.

The way we have approached that——

Senator WARNER. I do not think we can take our laptops into that sort of temperature differential.

Mr. DECKER. No, but let me give you a specific example, and it relates to something I was going to comment along with Senator Lieberman's line. Our approach in the past to try to deal with that is to have a military spec, and its envelope was the extreme of the extremes, and so you would automatically put out the mil spec, and I have worked the temperature spec in industry many times, and all electronic equipment in the old mil spec had to operate from minus 50 Centigrade to 100 degrees Centigrade. That is the boiling temperature of water. Maybe it was 120, but some huge, high temperature.

Now, that is a ridiculous specification. There is probably one out of a jillion times in any operation that it would ever be that cold or that hot, and so what you need to do is decide, is this equipment itself going to actually have to go to the cold weather mountain troops, and simultaneously the same item go to the troops that will go into the desert or the tropics.

When you finally get down to that you will find that like minus 30 degrees Centigrade on the low end and maybe 90 degrees Centigrade on the high end, covers 95 percent of that envelope, even in the mountaintop in Korea.

I was stationed there after the war, and you are right, it is colder than hell there in the winter, but when you do that, you then find, because of what I have just said, commercial companies have designed it go——

Senator WARNER. I think you have the record tight on that.

Gentlemen, are there other questions here? We intervened on you.

Senator LIEBERMAN. Thank you, Mr. Chairman.

If my eyes do not deceive me, and I know it is a stealthy helicopter, I do believe one of those is the Comanche.

Mr. DECKER. Yes, sir. It is hard to see it, is it not? [Laughter.]

Senator LIEBERMAN. I wanted to ask you for a brief report. I notice in your statement, your prepared statement, that you talked about the Comanche. But give us a status report, if you will, on how we are doing on the development of the Comanche.

Mr. DECKER. Yes, sir. We restructured the program after the reduction from prior years to the 1996 budget, if you remember. You gentlemen helped us some with the 1996 budget. That restructured program profile, is designed for two prototype models which are almost as good as the manufacturing models that will lead to the acquisition of six user-operation evaluation systems which will be used with the troops for a year or two. Then we will go to operational tests and go to production. That program layout is on schedule and on budget and the first machine has had its hover flight test. It continues its envelope expansion flight test next month, is on the mark in every single parameter, technical performance, cost, and schedule, and it is an executable program, and it is in excellent shape, and that is an auditable statement.

Senator LIEBERMAN. Obviously an important program. I was struck and pleased by your statement: The Army's primary development system to ensure that our soldiers have the information advantage in the information age is the RAH–66.

Mr. DECKER. Yes, sir.

Senator LIEBERMAN. Last year, as you recall, we upped the funds for the program by 100 million from what the administration requested to accelerate delivery. If we again decided to increase funding for the Comanche do you think the program can use those funds effectively, which is to say to continue to move up the initial operational capability?

Mr. DECKER. The answer is yes, but I would like to perhaps refer back to a statement that Senator Levin had, where he commented that perhaps if we had lots of plus-ups in 1997 we would create some big tails downstream that would move things in, and I said no, there is a number of advanced procurements that will eliminate tails that are at the procurement stage. We only have two significant new—we have some smaller ones—two big-time significant new programs in the Army, and one is the Crusader advanced field artillery, because we desperately need to get back to number one in field artillery in the world, and Comanche.

If we accelerate, we could certainly accelerate and field Comanche 2 to 3 years earlier, but it means getting into the production monies 2 to 3 years earlier, and that does create a tail. We have debates within the Army. I would personally like to see that, but it takes up-front investment money. In keeping with General Hartzog's comments about trying to envision when we want to make sure we get everything fielded and even the new systems fielded to be ahead of the potential peer threat, the Army leaders feel that the '05 time frame for first fielded production meets that kind of pressure.

From a pure business viewpoint, when you look at 20-year life-cycle costs and the inflations that go with it and all the other costs of maintaining the older fleet longer, if you had the up-front money and you could field it a couple of years early you see substantial savings over its life cycle, because that is earlier of a better, more capable, less expensive machine to operate. So you have those kind of debates.

Senator LIEBERMAN. I hope we will take a look at that this time around.

Mr. DECKER. It is still our number one program, but in terms of the scheduling against the threat and the concepts, we have lots of debates on that. Not withstanding the program is in good shape and executable the way it is. It is not a stretch out. You are not going to have a basket case on your hands. I personally would like to accelerate it because we will see the efficiencies of operations support costs as I said earlier, even if the threat is not quite there yet.

Senator LIEBERMAN. Thank you.

Thanks, Mr. Chairman.

Senator WARNER. Well, thank you, Senator. Senator Levin, as I understand, you are about to wrap up. I am just going to ask a couple of quick questions. This is fascinating here. This is one of the better charts. I have not had full time to analyze it, but I see this area out here which you must plan for, and that is a peer resurgence, and that means you have got to maintain an industrial base, which brings me, Mr. Secretary, to the question about the arms programs.

Will the Army be able to execute? In other words, the ammunition situation. I know you have put in these various plants around the country to stand by to produce ammunition. Let me just put it very carefully, then. It is the ARMS program.

Mr. DECKER. Right. I am familiar with it.

Senator WARNER. Two ammunition plants are now being maintained at zero cost to the taxpayer, four more are approaching zero cost. ARMS seems to be an excellent alternative to the layaway facilities that could be critical in a time of war, and it seems to be an excellent defense conversion program. Yet there is evidence the Army does not support the program.

Mr. DECKER. ARMS has probably been one of the very few defense conversion programs that has had a positive payoff. It was initially funded at perhaps too high a rate first year as a start-up program, and there was a rescission of half that money, as you recall. But the remaining monies have been quite effective, to my surprise, to be honest. Defense conversion is a very hard thing, if you have been in the defense industry, to learn how to do things commercially. But the objective of a defense conversion program are both social and military objectives, and I think you need both.

The ARMS successes so far and the plants you have referred to have achieved both, in that we have companies that have come in and are manufacturing things there that can use that kind of manufacturing capacity. We get a payback from that. It takes about 3 or 4 years after they start up till we start seeing the payback, and then it reduces the cost of just maintaining that capacity in standby.

Senator WARNER. Mr. Secretary, you will want to consult with some of your staff, but if you will note, much of what Congress did in this area is now on the Army recision list, and that is of concern. So I am going to ask if you would go back and analyze that question, the rescision list, and be prepared that the Congress is going to continue to push in the direction as we have done in earlier years.

Mr. DECKER. Yes, sir. I would like to comment on it being on the rescision list that we are not immune, nor do we not understand this committee and others' interest in the program.

Senator WARNER. The action of putting it on the rescision list, to me is in conflict with your opening statement that it is one of the most successful programs that you have experienced. So I would suggest at this point you might want to deal with it for the record, unless you want to press on. It is your choice.

Mr. DECKER. I will do both.

Senator WARNER. All right.

Mr. DECKER. But I think it is important here while we are face-to-face to understand we got pressured for some huge rescissions that we would rather have not taken, partially for the Bosnia issue and partially from other programs that were mandated on high, and we just ran out of room, sir. Something had to give, or we are going to have to wreck some other programs. But we will give you some record statements on that, as well.

[The information referred to follows:]

ARMAMENT RETOOLING AND MANUFACTURING SUPPORT INITIATIVE

The Armament Retooling and Manufacturing Support (ARMS) progrwn benefits the Army by reusing idle ammunition industrial capacity at 16 active and inactive facilities through commercialization. Our objective is to reduce operating costs at the six active facilities and maintenance costs at the ten inactive facilities. This helps to ensure preservation of the Armies industrial readiness by minimizing facility maintenance costs, retaining critical job skills, lowering operating overhead cost, and thus, decreasing unit costs. The Congress provided $200 million in fiscal year 1993. The Army used these resources to develop strategic reuse plans at all 16 facilities and marketing plans at 11 participating facilities. We also provided financial incentives (building and equipment modifications) to attract commercial tenants at these facilities. As you mentioned, the Army is now maintaining two plants at zero cost and four more are approaching zero cost. However, the program must compete for funding within Army priorities, such as readiness, modernization, and bills for current operations. This forces us to make tough choices. Placing ARMS on the rescission list was not an easy one. Doing so should not be considered evidence of lack of confidence in or commitment to the program.

Senator WARNER. I do not want to open up the Bosnian question, because I think the enormity of the expenditure by the American taxpayer with the incremental increase of the land forces is going to be a tough bill to pay in the years to come. That bill is approaching what now, General Griffith?

General GRIFFITH. Sir, the costs to the Army this year, sir, are running, as I recall, about 1.7 billion overall for the Army.

Senator WARNER. Let us talk about your procurement, General Griffith. The Joint Chiefs of Staff indicated a $60 billion level shortfall, and I wish to commend all members of the uniform for their absolute straightforward candor on this under Goldwater-Nichols. That was the intention of that law. To that extent, certainly fulfilling the guidance that Congress gave. But I am concerned about the projections for future years and what modernization requirements that you have in mind will not be met. Can you equip your forces in the years to come so that your successor a decade hence can give the same favorable report that you have given today?

General GRIFFITH. Sir, as you point out, the goal was established by our chairman, and quite frankly I was part of the deliberative body that gave him that number, the JROC. It is one that we feel is a goal that is needed to adequately resource the force of the future. That is overall. That is all forces, sir, all services. We believe that we would like to see that brought back to the 1998 time frame. That is a matter of the record. Of course, as you well know, we do not achieve that level of commitment until, I believe, 2001 in the current budget. So there is going to be slippage in programs that we need, but it is important to set the goal.

For the Army, sir, as indicated by Senator Coats, some of the things that we are most concerned about are the less glamorous things, like the truck fleet of the United States Army. I think it is well known that the trucks out in the force in many cases are older than the soldiers who are driving them. That is very important to us in the combat service support context, and is a major requirement for the United States Army.

So if we do not achieve those levels, certainly, the ability to modernize our combat support and service support elements of the force will be jeopardized.

The Force XXI initiatives that General Hartzog has talked about are important to us as we move into the next century, and those would not be resourced to the level that we believe they should be resourced. Of course, the Reserve Components are also critical to us. I do not think the United States Army has ever been more dependent on our Reserve component forces, the National Guard and the Army Reserve, than we are today. They are committed all around the world, to include Bosnia. So we have a compelling need to modernize our Reserve Components.

We are doing a lot in that context. Artillery: We are very dependent now on the Army National Guard for artillery support and air defense capabilities. We certainly want to ensure that as we rely on the Reserve Component forces that we provide them modern artillery systems. We are giving the Paladin to more National Guard Units starting in fiscal year 1998.

Those are the types of things, sir, that would not be resourced to the levels we need until we achieve the stated level of commitment.

Senator WARNER. Mr. Secretary, General Griffith, General Hartzog, this has been a superb hearing, and I hope your Department of the Army salutes you well for this hearing today. You have presented an excellent case. The concern that we all have is the amount of dollars needed to maintain the same momentum that you have underway. So we will now proceed to a second panel, unless there are further comments by you, Mr. Secretary, or either of your general officers.

Mr. DECKER. No, sir, except thank you very much.

Senator WARNER. Thank you. We will take a 3-minute stretch and start the second panel. [Recess.]

The subcommittee will come to order, and we have a subject which is of great interest to me and many, many other Senators. Mr. Levin and I wanted to make certain that we had an opportunity for some open testimony on this subject, and we welcome you, Admiral. You are here in your purple hat, is that correct?

Admiral STRONG. Correct, sir.

Senator WARNER. Mr. Heber. That is interesting, because when I was in the Department we had a fellow named Dave Heber. Do you know him?

Mr. HEBER. Yes.

Senator WARNER. Any relation?

Mr. HEBER. None.

Senator WARNER. It was a different spelling, was it not? He was an absolutely remarkable person.

Mr. HEBER. It goes with the name. [Laughter.]

Senator WARNER. That is a good attitude to take.

I know of no more interesting things than some of the projects that you gentlemen are working on. So let us proceed.

You and I had an occasion to meet at one time, Admiral, is that correct?

Admiral STRONG. Yes, Senator. I remember when you were Secretary I was one of the people in the gallery in San Diego. We were looking at the LAMP system out there, and had a chance to shake your hand and say hello.

Senator WARNER. What was your specific job out there?

Admiral STRONG. Well, I was working in the program at that time, and was out there working with the operators to see how the system was going and the integration aboard ship.

Senator WARNER. What ship was that? You say the Gallery?

Admiral STRONG. No, I was in the gallery.

Senator WARNER. All right. Proceed.

STATEMENT OF CHARLES HEBER, DIRECTOR, HIGH ALTITUDE ENDURANCE/UNMANNED AERIAL VEHICLE ADVANCE RESEARCH PROJECTS AGENCY

Mr. HEBER. I will start off describing the HAE/UAV program, the high altitude program, and the Admiral Strong will conclude with the tactical program.

Senator WARNER. Give us a little overview of the structure and the like.

Mr. HEBER. Sure. I will try to do that in my comments, and if I have not answered, feel free to ask questions afterward.

First of all, Mr. Chairman, thank you for inviting me here today. With your permission I will provide a written statement for the record, and I will briefly summarize my comments today. If I may, I would also like to point out the models that are sitting directly in front of you. On your left is the Tier II Plus or Global Hawk, and on your right is the Tier III Minus, or Dark Star. I might just mention that today's hearing just happens to be a tremendous coincidence, given that about an hour and a half ago the Tier III Minus Dark Star completed its maiden flight. It was a flight that lasted 20 minutes. We did beat the Wright brothers old record of 51 seconds, so we are pretty proud of that fact.

Senator WARNER. That is interesting. ·

Mr. HEBER. It is an amazing coincidence.

Senator WARNER. She is on the ground now?

Mr. HEBER. She landed safely. I do not have any final reports.

Senator WARNER. Why do you not give us a little discussion of the envelope she flew?

Mr. HEBER. It was a very benign envelope. Basically she took off from Edwards Air Force Base at 9:25 a.m. The plan that we hoped to follow was a short climb to about 2500 feet, not much more than that. This is, again, the maiden flight so we are not taking any chances.

The intent was to really check out the links of the communication system and make sure we maintain command and control with the air vehicle at all times, and basically the maneuver was one of just flying a straight leg, doing a very, very careful bank turn. I am sure it was a tremendously large radius. We did not want to upset the aerodynamics of the aircraft in any way, shape, or form. Completing the turn and flew a return leg parallel with the runway in the opposite direction from its takeoff, and if everything went according to plan it came right back around again and landed some 20 minutes after takeoff. So it is a relatively simple flight for the first one.

Senator WARNER. How is she powered?

Mr. HEBER. The aircraft is powered by a single turbojet engine. It is a bizjet engine. It is really a commercial engine. But the aircraft itself, as I will get into in my comments here, is a fully automatic aircraft. Once it reaches the top of the runway it is fully hands-off operation, and it flies basically a preprogrammed course, and lands all by itself, as well.

Senator WARNER. In your testimony, please address what other Nations are doing in this area.

Mr. HEBER. Yes, sir. I will add that to my testimony.

Senator WARNER. Thank you very much.

Senator, welcome. Would you like to have an opening statement?

Senator BRYAN. Mr. Chairman, thank you. Let me forebear. I am here more about this concept. Being from Nevada and Nellis Air Force Base, I am very much interested in this.

Mr. HEBER. I was invited to provide you with a description and a status of the high altitude or HAV/UAV program. The HAE system is an advanced airborne reconnaissance system comprised of two complementary air platforms, the two that I just pointed out, the Tier II Plus Global Hawk, and a Tier III Minus Dark Star, and a common mission ground control station that provides command and control and data receipt functions for both of the aircraft.

Senator WARNER. I think it would be helpful at some point in your testimony to sort of front it and say what is in inventory today, what is operational, and then take us into the next generation.

Mr. HEBER. Currently, what these systems are intended to do is basically an adjunct to the missions currently being performed predominantly by the U–2 aircraft. These are intended to be theater controlled assets much like the U–2. They are high altitude systems much like the U–2, and certainly a portion, at least, of their concepts of operation will mirror that of the U–2, as well.

In addition, particularly the Tier III Minus system, because of its stealthy characteristics, will have a penetrating capability much akin to the SR–71. So the types of missions that you could think of for that kind of a vehicle would also be performed by the Tier III Minus, a totally different type of vehicle, but similar type of mission capability.

Does that answer the question?

Senator WARNER. Yes.

Senator BRYAN. Mr. Chairman, could you yield just for 1 second? Mr. Heber, is what you are saying that currently there are no UAV's in the inventory that are operational?

Mr. HEBER. There are currently no UAV's that are designed to perform the specific mission of these two aircraft.

Senator WARNER. High altitude is above what?

Mr. HEBER. The Tier III Minus is capable of altitudes up to 50,000 feet. The Global Hawk flies up to 65,000 feet.

Senator BRYAN. I thank the chair.

Senator WARNER. Now, high altitude is one category we will discuss. We also will talk about low level, correct Admiral?

Mr. HEBER. That is right, and Admiral Strong will be talking about those after I am finished.

Senator WARNER. So you are talking about the next generation, primarily?

Mr. HEBER. Exactly. These are next generation theater level airborne reconnaissance systems.

Senator WARNER. You might tell us how soon these will be operational and what is the time line for the phase out of those things we have in inventory.

Mr. HEBER. I will go through that in my testimony today.

Senator WARNER. All right.

Mr. HEBER. The HAE system is currently under development by the Defense Advanced Research Projects Agency who I represent, or DARPA, for the Defense Airborne Reconnaissance Office, or

DARO. That is General Israel's organization. The HAE system addresses several service needs that are currently validated by the JROC of the JCS. The HAE system is specified, each of these two aircraft, is specified to have a unit fly-away price of no more than $10 million per copy. Specifically what the $10 million applies to is everything that is resident within the air vehicle itself. That includes all the comm systems, all the payloads, as well as the aircraft itself.

The Global Hawk vehicle is optimized for supporting low to moderate threat long-endurance surveillance missions in which range, endurance, and persistent coverage are paramount. The Dark Star vehicle features an incorporation of low observables, as is obvious from its shape, and is tailored for missions in which ensured survivable coverage is more important than range and endurance, and as I get into the descriptions of the air vehicles further on in my testimony you will see that there are substantial differences between the performance levels of these two systems.

This dual approach provides what we believe is a flexible and cost-effective mix of platforms, and in fact the Chairman of the Joint Chief of Staff is on record as strongly recommending that we pursue both the Global Hawk and the Dark Star systems to achieve this mix.

The Global Hawk being developed by an industry team being led by Teledyne Ryan Aeronautical and E-Systems is considered the workhorse of the mix. It is a conventionally designed aircraft, as you can see. It is a wing/body/tail configuration capable of operating, as I said, up to 65,000 foot altitude with up to 42 hours of endurance, a pretty substantial capability in terms of endurance. Its overall size is comparable to a U–2 at about half the weight.

The Dark Star, being developed by Boeing Military Aircraft, is a more conventional design—I am sorry, being developed by Lockheed Martin Skunk Works and Boeing Military Aircraft—is a more unconventional design, and as mentioned is optimized for stealth for survivability. It has a gross weight of about a third of the Global Hawk system, and can operate at just over 45,000 feet for about—somewhere between 8 and 12 hours. So it is substantially less endurance capability than the Global Hawk.

The common ground segment, which is being developed by E-systems, provides control and data receipt functions for both aircraft in a transportable system housed in two ruggedized shelters. Both air vehicle systems are being developed to support the collection of high resolution radar and optical imagery at high collection rates, up to 1600 square nautical miles per hour, and over the course of a standard mission for the Global Hawk system, which we call out as about 24 hours for a standard mission within a particular area of interest, that translates to about 40,000 square nautical miles per day of area coverage capability.

The common ground station that is being developed will disseminate the imagery products from the two air vehicles to existing exploitation systems. We are not developing a new exploitation capability within the HAE program. Rather, we are going to use the existing exploitation systems that exist within the services today.

The HAE system is taking advantage of a number of unique acquisition practices in order to achieve an affordable system solution. First of all, cost is the single requirement for both of these aircraft. The contractors are being driven to a $10 million unit fly-away price requirement, and all other system attributes, including performance, are traded off against this requirement.

Second, the HAE program is one of the Department's Advanced Concept Technology Demonstration programs, or ACDT's, and as such takes advantage of early user involvement in the program to ensure that user needs and desires are being addressed up front. Our prime customer and user is the United States Atlantic Command—USACOM—working closely with the service components. In later phases of the program these users will be directly involved in operational demonstration and evaluation of HAE capabilities.

Thirdly, DARPA is executing the program, both of these two developments, using section 845 agreements authority. This allows us tremendous flexibility in how we develop and acquire these systems, and provides a mechanism for ensuring that we can achieve that $10 million unit fly-away price goal.

Finally, we are executing the program within an integrated product environment, an IPD environment, which has created the unique atmosphere between Government and industry that promotes teamwork and trust and provides complete visibility in the program progress; again, another key feature in trying to achieve that $10 million price.

Both the Global Hawk and Dark Star developments are in Phase II of a four-phased program. Phase I was the concept definition phase, completed over a year ago. Phase II, the current phase, is focused on developing, fabricating, and flight testing both systems. During phase II, two Global Hawks and four Dark Star vehicles and one common ground station will be built and tested. This phase is currently expected to run through December of 1997, about 18 to 20 months from now.

Phase III will focus on operational demonstration and user evaluation of the two systems, through field demonstration and military exercises. During this phase, eight additional air vehicles in a mix to be determined, it could be either all Dark Stars, all Global Hawks, or some mix of the two, will be built, and two more common ground stations will be fabricated. Phase III is expected to run through December 1999. The completion of phase III will support a decision to enter into production of additional HAE systems in phase IV and beyond.

As I indicated up front in talking about the maiden flight of the Dark Star, the program is obviously entering a very, very exciting period in its development. Contrary to what you will read in my formal testimony, the Dark Star has now flown. The fabrication of air vehicles number three and four, in addition to the two Dark Star air vehicles that we have currently completed fabrication on, will be initiated once we get a couple of flights of air vehicle number one under our belt. I anticipate that those air vehicles will begin fabrication probably within the next month or two.

The Global Hawk program entered development almost a year after the Dark Star, so understandably it is not quite as far along. Design of the Global Hawk, though, is nearly complete, and fabrication and software development has already begun. The first flight of the Global Hawk is currently projected for the second quarter of next fiscal year, 1997.

Following the completion of Phase II in December of 1997, and shortly after the initiation of Phase III, DARPA is scheduled to transfer management of the program to the Air Force. Six months ago the Air Force established a Systems Program Office, or SPO, at the Aeronautical Systems Command at Wright Patterson Air Force Base. Planning for the transition, as well as transition to production at the end of Phase III, has already begun. The Deputy Under Secretary of Defense for Advanced Technology, Mr. Jack Bachkosky, has initiated the process for working out the transition of ACTD programs into production, and is leading the discussions currently ongoing regarding the HAE transition.

The HAE system differs in many ways from the tactical UAV systems which will be described shortly by Admiral Strong. These differences involve both technical and operational considerations. The HAE's are theater level assets in order to be controlled predominantly by the Joint Task Force commander. The tactical UAE's will come under the control of lower echelons. The HAE's provide broad area surveillance over wide sections of the battlefield, while the tactical UAE's will provide much more focused coverage.

Senator WARNER. Let us stop on that broad area.

Is this photographic? ELINT? What is the mix, within the bounds of classification that you can share with us?

Mr. HEBER. Sure. The Global Hawk system is designed to carry a synthetic aperture radar and an electro-optic IR sensor, as well. At the unclassified level, the 40,000 square nautical miles per day of area coverage rate that I quoted was attributable to the synthetic aperture radar, and that is in operation in a wide area collection mode at 3 foot ground resolution.

Senator WARNER. What about all-weather capabilities and so forth?

Mr. HEBER. Well, the SAR is an X-band system, so it is an all weather system.

Senator WARNER. So it is both photographic and ELINT, correct?

Mr. HEBER. Correct, although the data that it sends to the ground is all digital. It is digital images, both radar and EOIR. The Dark Star system, on the other hand, the can carry only one of the payloads at a time. It can carry either the SAR or the EO. In compatibility with its stealth characteristics it is an LPI system and has an A–12 heritage, built by Westinghouse.

Senator WARNER. Are the systems interchangeable, they can bring it back, put the other one in, and send it up again?

Mr. HEBER. On the Dark Star you can either swap out the SAR or swap out the EO system within hours, right.

The SAR and the EO system have similar performance capability in terms of both collection rate and image quality as the Global Hawk system does.

Senator WARNER. What other countries are active in this area, and are some of them participating in these programs?

Mr. HEBER. Right now there is no direct participation with any foreign Governments on either of these two programs; however, we have had a lot of interest expressed from the UK, and we have had also most recently interest expressed by the Israelis, and in particular they are looking at the Global Hawk system as a popular platform of opportunity for handling their unique boost phase intercept problem against theater ballistic missiles.

Senator WARNER. Is there reason to believe that we could sell these units to certain countries that are our allies?

Mr. HEBER. It is something we are just beginning to explore.

Senator WARNER. Is any other country this far advanced or further advanced in this technology?

Mr. HEBER. No, sir.

Senator WARNER. Were are we to the nearest competitor, so to speak?

Mr. HEBER. I would say right now—and Terry, you might want to chime in here—probably the closest competitor that I am aware of in terms of an operational capability for this type of system is the Israelis. They have a number of different designs that are in various stages of development, some of which are just simple extensions of existing air vehicles where they would basically add more wingspan to the air vehicle to take it up to higher altitudes and give it more endurance.

There is a study on paper that they have completed that targets again the boost phase intercept problem that they are most concerned with, but that particular design is purely a paper design at this point.

In terms of lesser capable moderate altitude systems along the same line there are also some configurations in some other countries in Europe, but none of them even come close to the capability of these two systems.

Senator WARNER. Now, in terms of their operational status and what assets we have now, how do those curves dovetail?

Mr. HEBER. I missed the point.

Senator WARNER. Well, we have got certain collection devices now. Will they be able to last until these come into the inventory?

Mr. HEBER. Yes. As a matter of fact, as you are probably aware, the U-2 is currently in an upgrade program for the ASAR's and some reengineering capability which will extend the life well beyond the point where these aircraft will come into production.

Senator WARNER. So we do not have any gap?

Mr. HEBER. Right.

Senator WARNER. That is fine.

Senator Bryan, did you have a question?

Senator BRYAN. I think that these systems, when they become fully operational, if I understood your testimony, will supersede both the SR-71 and the U-2, is that right?

Mr. HEBER. It is still probably a little bit premature to say that specifically. We have done some studies over the past couple of years where we have looked at joint operation of these systems with U-2's, and it is clear that there are unique roles and missions for each of the platforms. I would also hesitate to say that we would want to replace any system at this point in the development of these programs, given that we have really only got one 18-minute flight under our belts at this period of time. But certainly I think that these types of unmanned aircraft are going to be the wave of the future.

Senator BRYAN. With respect to that 18-minute flight, what can you tell us about that?

Mr. HEBER. I guess you were probably out of the room when I described it for Senator Warner.

Senator BRYAN. I will ask you to repeat it.

Mr. HEBER. Well, I could go through it quickly for you, but basically it was a little bit more than a Wright brothers- type flight. It took off from the air base, made a broad circle, headed back in the other direction, circled again, and then came in for a landing. As I mentioned before, it was basically looking at ensuring that there were stable aerodynamics in the configuration and that we could in fact maintain all the communication links with the aircraft.

Senator BRYAN. With respect to Dark Star and Global Hawk, do all of the indications at this point in the development indicate no problems, that the systems will proceed as anticipated in terms of development schedule in the case of Global Hawk, and the operational schedule with respect to Dark Star?

Mr. HEBER. Absolutely. We are still early on in the development of Global Hawk, obviously, but everything so far looks good, and this flight that we had today I think just clinches where we are in terms of Dark Star.

Senator BRYAN. I am sure we can count on you, Mr. Heber, to make our chairman aware of any problems that might occur in the future and address the committee.

Mr. HEBER. Absolutely. I would be happy to do that.

Senator BRYAN. Thank you, Mr. Chairman.

Senator WARNER. Thank you very much.

Does that conclude much of your presentation?

Mr. HEBER. For the most part. There were a couple of points I wanted to make regarding differences between the HAE's and tactical UAE's, if I could be permitted to do that, and then I just have some wrap-up comments.

Senator WARNER. Good.

Mr. HEBER. As I was talking about the differences between the two systems, the HAE's are also fully autonomous vehicles, and by that, as I described previously, from the time the aircraft rests at the head of the runway till the time it completes its landing rollout, it can operate without any man in the loop whatsoever. Now, we have provisions obviously to allow for communication between the ground station and the aircraft during its flight for mission updates and such. But basically it could literally fly completely hands up, hands off.

On the other hand, the tactical systems have a much more man-in-the-loop type of command and control involved. So what that tells you is there are some inherent differences in the way the ground control station, for example, needs to be configured for the two aircraft systems.

The HAE's provide extremely high bandwidth data. As I indicated, 1600 square nautical miles of imagery per hour is a lot of data to pipe down. While the tactical systems are providing data at somewhat reduced bandwidths from that, and I am sure Admiral Strong will talk more to that, one of the other big differences that you need to keep in mind as you hear about these two different systems is that the HAE systems are designed to be relocatable. By that I mean I can pack these things into a C–17 and transport them into theater and set up operations at an air base, but I am probably not very likely going to move that base of operation around very much. It is going to be fixed in that location.

Whereas the tactical systems that Admiral Strong is going to talk about really are designed to be fully deployable, and I am sure the Army would probably like to see a ground control station for some of the tactical UAE's reside in the back of a Humvee. So it is a much more transportable system.

Both systems, however, I think offer unique capabilities that can be exploited in a very, very complementary way, and an example of that is in terms of queuing. A high altitude system like this with its huge view of the battlefield can literally que the location of a number of these more focused surveillance assets. So there are a number of different ways they can work together.

Basically, that concludes my comments. In summary, the HAE system is well underway to providing the war-fighter and the Nation with what I think is a new, powerful, and much- needed capability. Continuing progress over the next few years will demonstrate and define the capabilities of the system, and ultimately prove the military worth of its implementation in a variety of roles and missions.

Thank you very much, Mr. Chairman and members of the subcommittee. I am happy to take any additional questions you might have at this time.

[The prepared statement of Mr. Heber follows:]

PREPARED STATEMENT BY MR. CHARLES HEBER, DIRECTOR OF HIGH ALTITUDE ENDURANCE, UNMANNED AERIAL VEHICLE, ADVANCE RESEARCH PROJECTS AGENCY

Mr. Chairman and Members of the Subcommittee, thank you for inviting me here today. With your permission, I will provide my written statement for the record and briefly summarize my comments. If I may, I would like to use these two models as displays for my discussion.

I was invited to provide you with a description and status of the High Altitude Endurance (HAE) Unmanned Air Vehicle (UAV) Program. The HAE UAV system is an advanced airborne reconnaissance system comprised of two complementary air platforms, the Tier II Plus Global Hawk and the Tier III Minus DarkStar, and a common mission ground control station. This system is currently under development by the Defense Advanced Research Projects Agency (DARPA) in a Joint Program Office with the Departments of the Air Force, Navy and Army, for the Defense Airborne Reconnaissance Office (DARO). The HAE UAV system addresses several service mission needs validated by the Joint Requirements Oversight Council of the Joint Chiefs of Staff for long range surveillance and broad area coverage imaging capability supporting the theater commander. Each mission-optimized vehicle is to have a Unit Flyaway Price (UFP) of no more than $10 million (fiscal year 1994) averaged over vehicles 11–20. The UFP of $10 million is driven by a desire to have a capability that can be considered as an attributable asset. The Global Hawk vehicle is optimized for supporting low-to-moderate threat, long endurance surveillance missions in which range, endurance and persistent coverage are paramount. The DarkStar vehicle features an incorporation of low observables, or stealth, and is optimized for a moderate endurance, high altitude reconnaissance mission in which assured, survivable coverage is more important than range and endurance. This dual approach provides a flexible and cost-effective mix of platforms. The Chairman of the Joint Chiefs of Staff, in fact, strongly recommends pursuing both the Global Hawk and DarkStar systems to achieve this mix.

The Global Hawk, being developed by an industry team led by Teledyne Ryan Aeronautical and E-Systems, is considered the "workhorse" of the HAE UAV mix. It is a conventionally designed, wing/body/tail, jet-powered aircraft optimized for payload, range and endurance. It is a 24,000 pound vehicle capable of operating at an altitude of 65,000 foot with up to 42 hours of endurance. In terms of physical size, it has an overall wing span of 116 feet and a length of 44 feet. It's overall size is comparable to a U-2 but one-half the weight. The DarkStar, being developed by an industry team led by Lockheed Martin Skunk Works and Boeing Military Aircraft, is more of a special purpose targeted for use in high threat environments prior to the suppression of hostile air defenses. It is a more unconventional design and, as mentioned, is optimized for low observability or stealth for survivability. It has a gas weight of 8,600 pounds, or, about a third of that of the Global Hawk, and can operate at an altitude of just over 45,000 foot for more than 8 hours. Physically, it's a little over half the span and a third the length of the Global Hawk aircraft. The Common Ground Segment, being developed by E-Systems, combines mission planning, command and control, communications and imagery quality control for both systems into a transportable system housed in two ruggedized shelters.

In terms of payload, both systems are being developed to support the collection of high quality radar and optical imagery at high collection rates. The Global Hawk system offers a 2,000 pound payload capacity and carries both Synthetic Aperture Radar (SAR) and Electro-Optic/Infrared (EO/IR) Sensors. With the SAR payload, the Global Hawk will be able to survey up to 40,000 square nautical miles per day per aircraft at better than three-foot resolution, or form 1,900 one-foot spot images, each two kilometers by two kilometers, at one-foot resolution. Hughes Aircraft is developing both of the Global Hawk sensor payloads. The DarkStar offers a 1,000 pound payload and carries either a Low Probability of Intercept (LPI) SAR or EO sensor, one at a time, and offers collection rates and imagery resolution similar to that of the Global Hawk, though the DarkStar capacity per mission is less due to its reduced endurance. Northrop Grumman Electronic Sensors and System is developing the DarkStar SAR and Recon Optical is developing the EO sensor. The common ground station will disseminate the imagery product from the two air vehicles to existing exploitation systems.

The HAE UAV system is taking advantage of a number of unique acquisition practices in order to achieve an affordable system solution. First of all, cost is the single requirement for both of these aircraft. The contractors are being driven to a $10 million UFP requirement, and all other system attributes, including performance, are traded off against this requirement. We refer to this as "cost as an independent variable" and the intent is to arrive at a system solution which is not the best we can imagine but rather good enough to do the job. Second, the HAE UAV program is one of the Department's Advanced Concept Technology Demonstration (ACTD) programs, and, as such, takes advantage of early user involvement in the program to insure that user needs and desires are being addressed, as a way of streamlining the downstream transition of the program into operational use. Our prime customer and user, the United States Atlantic Command (USACOM), is currently working closely with us and the service components to tailor requirements and develop a concept of operations, building upon related work done for the Predator UAV, for ultimately employing these systems in a variety of military roles. In later phases of the program, these users will be directly involved in operational demonstration and evaluation of HAE UAV capabilities, will assess the overall utility to the warfighter, and will provide critical input to production transition decisions to be made near the turn of the century. Thirdly, DARPA is executing the current phase of the program using Section 845 Agreements Authority. This allows tremendous flexibility in how we develop and acquire these systems and provides the mechanism for insuring that we can achieve our $10 million UFP goal. Finally, we are executing the current phase of the program within an Integrated Product Development (IPD) environment. This has created a unique a atmosphere between the Government and industry that promotes teamwork and trust and provides complete visibility into program progress.

Both the Global Hawk and DarkStar developments are in Phase II of a four phase program. Phase I was the concept definition phase and resulted in the selection of our current contractor teams. Phase II, the current phase, is focused on developing, fabricating and flight testing both systems. The flight testing will include both airworthiness and payload performance testing, as well as some limited field demonstrations. During Phase II, two Global Hawk and four DarkStar vehicles and one common ground station will be built and tested. This phase is currently expected to run through December 1997. Phase III focuses on operational demonstration and user evaluation of the two systems through field demonstrations and military exercises. During this phase, eight additional air vehicles, in a mix to be determined, and two common ground stations will be fabricated. Phase III will run through December 1999. The completion of Phase III will support a decision to enter into full production in Phase IV.

The DarkStar program is currently entering a very exciting period in its development. The first two of the four DarkStar air vehicles to be built in the current phase have been fabricated and have undergone ground testing. Technical problems associated predominately with the integration and test of flight control software has delayed the flight testing of the DarkStar air vehicles by about 5 months from the original October 1995 date. Taxi tests are currently underway on one of the aircraft. It is anticipated that first flight of the DarkStar system will occur within days. Initial flight tests will be conducted without payloads to assess the airworthiness of the system. Payloads will be integrated and tested starting with the fifth flight. Following completion of these early flights, the fabrication of air vehicles 3 and 4 will be initiated, to be completed during fiscal year 1997. The Global Hawk program entered development almost a year after the DarkStar program, so, understandably, it is not as far along. Design of the Global Hawk is nearly complete and fabrication and software development has begun. Integration and ground testing of the first of the Global Hawk systems will begin about mid-summer and taxi testing should commence around November. First flight of the Global Hawk is currently projected for the second quarter of fiscal year 1997. As with DarkStar, early flights will be airworthiness tests with payloads integrated afterward and performance testing continuing through the end of Phase II in December 1997.

Following completion of Phase II, and shortly after the initiation of Phase III, DARPA is scheduled to transfer management of the program to the Air Force. Six months ago, the Air Force established a Systems Program Office (SPO) at the Aeronautical Systems Command at Wright Patterson Air Force Base for this purpose. Planning for this transition as well as the transition to production at the end of Phase III has already begun. The Deputy Under Secretary of Defense for Advanced Technology, Mr. Jack Bachkosky, has initiated a process for working out the transition of ACTD programs into production and is leading the discussions currently ongoing regarding the HAE UAV transition.

The HAE UAV System differs in many ways from the UAV system described by RAdm Strong. These differences involve both technical and operational considerations. The HAE UAVs are theater-level assets and are to be controlled by the Joint Task Force Commander. The tactical UAVs will come under the control of lower echelons. The HAE UAVs provide broad area surveillance over the battlefield while the tactical UAVs provide much more focused coverage. The HAE UAVs will provide high resolution digital imagery while the tactical UAVs provide predominately video. The HAE UAVs will provide extremely high bandwidth data; the tactical systems will provide data at much lower band-widths. The HAE UAV systems are designed to be relocatable but basically operate from fixed bases. The tactical systems are designed to be fully deployable. Both systems offer unique capabilities that can be fully employed in a complementary and interoperable way.

In conclusion, the HAE UAV system is well underway to providing the warfighter and the nation with a new, powerful and much needed capability. Continuing progress over the next few years will demonstrate and define the capabilities of the system and ultimately prove the military worth of its implementation in a variety of roles and missions.

Thank you very much, Mr. Chairman and Committee Members. I would be happy to answer your questions.

Senator WARNER. We might defer that and hear from Admiral Strong.

STATEMENT OF REAR ADM. BARTON D. STRONG, PROGRAM EXECUTIVE OFFICER FOR CRUISE MISSILES AND UN-MANNED AERIAL VEHICLES

Admiral STRONG. Thank you, Mr. Chairman and Senator Bryan. I am Rear Admiral Bart Strong. I am the Program Executive Officer for the cruise missiles, Navy cruise missiles, and tactical UAV's. It is a pleasure to be here today. I have a written statement I have proposed for the record.

Senator WARNER. Without objection, the entire statement will be included.

Admiral STRONG. Thank you. I have a short summary of my statement. I would like to go through and give you a quick update of the program.

The Joint Program Office is one of my two series of programs. I work for Mr. Douglass, the acquisition executive for the Navy. We do a lot of interfacing with the Department of Defense, particularly DARO, and all our requirements come from the JROC. My office is very joint. We have just about an equal number of Army and Navy people, and a little bit smaller ratio of Air Force.

I would like to now, sir, give you a brief overview of our four tactical programs.

The first is Pioneer. It has been operational for about 10 years in the Army, Marine Corps, and the Navy. The Army just transferred their last unit back over to the Navy. We have nine systems, and I will give you more detail in that later.

This performed extremely well in Desert Storm for all services. The Navy used it for gunfire support with great effect. The Army used it for Special Operations and other effects, and the Marines used it for general reconnaissance, also.

Senator WARNER. How many systems have we lost to operational or other means?

Admiral STRONG. We had one shot down, sir, and I can look this up and give you the number that we have lost total, here. We have had a fairly high mishap rate on the Pioneer through the years. We are very pleased that——

Senator WARNER. Why do you not give me the year it was introduced and the total number of production models?

Admiral STRONG. Sir, with Pioneer we have had 45 Class A mishaps that we have lost. That is a mishap rate of 6.5 per 1000 hours.

Senator WARNER. What year was it introduced?

Admiral STRONG. 1986.

Senator WARNER. The total number of units built?

Admiral STRONG. We have had nine systems and a total of about 45 air vehicles, plus the ground stations that go with those.

Senator BRYAN. Mr. Chairman, I was not following that. You are saying a total of 45 were in production of the Pioneer?

Admiral STRONG. The Pioneer, we have currently in the inventory, Senator, 45. We have an order of 30. We have taken deliver of about five of those, but approximately 25 more to be delivered.

Senator BRYAN. Your response to the chairman's question—I may have missed it—what is the total production to date of the Pioneer?

Admiral STRONG. Nine systems, sir.

Senator BRYAN. You say nine systems?

Admiral STRONG. Nine systems. A system includes the air vehicle and the ground control systems that communicate, control it, and show the video, sir.

Senator WARNER. How many actually rolled off production?

Admiral STRONG. I will get that for the record, sir.

Senator WARNER. How many losses have we had? In other words, I mean, we are getting new ones, but I am trying to get a grasp of the total number of vehicles.

Admiral STRONG. Well, we have 45 air vehicles.

Senator WARNER. In operation today?

Admiral STRONG. In operation.

Senator WARNER. In order of 30, is this a second generation with considerable upgrade?

Admiral STRONG. I would not say that. No, sir. For cost reasons we expected to take this out of the inventory here in the next few years, and so we did not put a lot of money into upgrading it.

I will move on. On the Predator, I know you are very familiar with this. This is the first ACTD UAV. It has been very successful, as you noted earlier in your comments, sir. This vehicle can fly over 40 hours, and operate up to a 500-mile radius. Last year we operated it in Bosnia out of Albania where it did some very good work. We just redeployed it this month back to Hungary, and it has flown about a dozen flights since there. In fact, we got word this morning that they got some very good synthetic aperture radar pictures back from Sarajevo in a snowstorm. We were very pleased to see that.

Senator WARNER. How did it help to relocate in Hungary?

Admiral STRONG. We are deployed out of Hungary, sir, and working over the Bosnian area.

Senator WARNER. I am trying to think—I guess it is classified. OK.

Admiral STRONG. The plans are—the requirements are to build 16 more operational systems and a research and development system, for a total of 17, and the Department currently is planning an LRIP—limited production—to start in 1997.

The next chart addresses our current source selection. We are conducting a competition for a tactical UAV. This will also be an ACTD model based very much on the Predator experience. At the right there is a lot of data there, but those are the requirements that the JROC established. These are designed to meet both maritime and the shore Marine Corps requirements.

The cost, you will notice, is an aggressive cost figure per air vehicle. We plan to buy quite a few of these, so we have established that. That is the most important requirement we are looking for in the competition. The other technical performance, we hope to meet them. But the JROC defined to meet those as close as possible.

I would point out next to the bottom on the right the mandatory options for a CARS system, which we think is very important to put on all our tactical UAV's, and a heavy fuel engine.

Senator WARNER. You might address how these can be integrated with carrier operations.

Admiral STRONG. The plan is towards the end of the ACTD to do a marinization. It is very important to the Navy that this system meet the tactical requirements for the Navy off of our ships.

In the lower left is the number of quantities. Currently that total is 61 for the three services.

Senator WARNER. How does the Navy use this? That is for future planning?

Admiral STRONG. That is future. This is in source selection right now. We hope to be flying some vehicles within 6 months, and have them aboard ship in a year and a half to 2 years.

Senator WARNER. What does the Navy use in terms of the Predator?

Admiral STRONG. We have run some feasibility operations where we are interconnected from the ship, sir. We are looking at three levels of marinization use of the Predator. One is to receive signals from the Predator; the second would be to control as well as receive, control the vehicle; and the third, which would be a big jump, is to operate it actually off the ship, and we have a study looking at how feasible that would be.

Senator WARNER. That would be the carrier.

Admiral STRONG. That would be the carrier, large deck amphibs.

Senator WARNER. What about on the helo ships?

Admiral STRONG. Not on the small boys. It needs to have an arrested landing.

Senator WARNER. So it only can be integrated into the attack carrier system, is that correct?

Admiral STRONG. Or a large amphib deck.

Senator WARNER. That is the point I was trying to make. They are looking at the large amphib deck?

Admiral STRONG. Certainly.

Senator WARNER. You might have to incorporate a similar arrest gear on that deck, then?

Admiral STRONG. There are several technical things we want to look at, the structure, the engine, the controls, and EMI/EMF corrosion. All those things we will be looking at, sir.

The Hunter program, this last fall the JROC recommended that this system be allowed to expire with the expiration of the current contract. Dr. Kaminski in January wrote a decision memorandum that is summarized here, basically saying to let that contract expire, provided for the Army to operate one system which is operating now at Fort Hood, and to store the remaining systems.

General Fain, who was asked to comment on this last year, was asked to review the program early in 1995. The summary of his comments are there. He made several recommendations to improve UAV management in the procurement phase. Most were implemented, and we have carried many of those over into our other programs like predator and our current tactical UAV. The Hunter was grounded last fall. We had three mishaps. We did an extensive review of those mishaps and found two problems which were corrected. We started flying again in December, and it is approaching 200 hours now. It seems to be doing quite well. It will be participating in Force 21.

The next chart addresses a concept we are very enthused about, and that is the common tactical control system. Our concept here simply is to use a ground control system that we can operate any of the air vehicles that we have now or in the future, whether they be ashore, on the beach with the marines, or out to the sea with the Navy.

Senator WARNER. Admiral, would you take note my boss has come. The Secretary of the Navy has arrived, and the Secretary is going to consult with me on a different matter. [Pause.]

That relationship started 26 years ago, and it has never changed, Senator. Once a deputy, always a deputy. Now, I am number two on the Environment Committee, so here we are.

Go ahead.

Admiral STRONG. Thank you, sir.

Our concept here, shown by the bubble, is to be able to interoperate with any of the air vehicles.

Senator WARNER. Did we jump over Hunter? I know you put it up and it down, is that right?

Admiral STRONG. Yes, sir. Would you like me to return to discuss that more?

Senator WARNER. Are there some future plans for the Hunter system?

Admiral STRONG. Yes, sir. We are operating one Hunter system which is eight vehicles, and the ground system out at Fort Hood in the Army, and we are funded to support that one system. There is a total of seven systems that were bought in an LRIP. The other systems will be put into storage. We will be using a partial system for training and support of the operational system.

Senator WARNER. So we will retrieve some value?

Admiral STRONG. Yes, sir, and we have learned a great deal in operating these.

Senator WARNER. All right. Thank you very much. Excuse me.

Admiral STRONG. Back to the tactical control system. I think to summarize it what I would say is I look at our tactical system here as giving us the position of having one tactical UAV system that is comprised of a common ground control system and multiple air vehicles. It has many attributes that are summarized up in the right corner. I would say one of the key ones is it allows us to very easily introduce a new air vehicle. We have found that the control systems usually comprise about two-thirds the cost of a UAV system. So we already have this common control system in place. We can obviously introduce a new air vehicle if needed in the future at a much lower cost.

Of course, interoperability is I think the key to success for tactical UAV's, and that is what this stresses. It will allow the sailor out at sea to tune in what is going on, the Marines going over the beach, and when necessary, to turn the images over to the Army.

Senator WARNER. Well, now, if we were to bring such a system into a surface Naval ship, would not the existing equipment aboard the ship be able to perform a number of these functions?

Admiral STRONG. Exactly.

Senator WARNER. So you would not have the total kit that was used on the ground deployed at sea?

Admiral STRONG. You are exactly right, sir. Our concept is that this would be software. We would take some software alone out. They could use it on the TAC 3's and TAC 4's that the Navy are using. In fact, we demonstrated that capability.

Senator WARNER. All right, thank you.

Admiral STRONG. Just in brief I wanted to summarize the number of systems that are currently planned, next to the right-hand column, and the number of air vehicles that would be associated with those. Of course, this shows the jointness of all of the tactical UAV's. I think mixed interoperability is a very important parameter for success here, sir.

In summary, I would just like to state that I think UAV's have proven themselves in combat and in the peacekeeping mission over in Bosnia, and I think we are going to see an explosion of the use of UAV's in defense, as well as in commercial areas. UAV's are certainly up front on jointness, are very affordable, and what we like the most about it, allows us to do a lot of very sensitive missions that used to risk a lot of lives now without risking any lives.

[The prepared statement of Admiral Strong follows:]

PREPARED STATEMENT BY REAR ADM. BARTON D. STRONG, PROGRAM EXECUTIVE
OFFICER FOR CRUISE MISSILES AND UNMANNED AERIAL VEHICLES

Mr. Chairman and Members of this committee: I am pleased to have this opportunity to come before you this year for my first time as Program Executive Officer for Cruise Missiles and Joint Unmanned Aerial Vehicles (PEO(CU)) to discuss the status and future plans of tactical Unmanned Aerial Vehicles (UAV).

Over the past year much progress has been made in improving UAV capability to the Warfighters, and plans have been established that will provide increased future capability in an affordable manner. Decisions have been made to reduce the number of UAV systems and to consolidate ground control stations. Perhaps most gratifying, the immense potential of UAV systems has become widely recognized and supported. Also, all Services have agreed to a joint approach to procuring and operating tactical UAVS. The Joint Requirements Oversight Council (JROC) and all Services agree that interoperability, jointness, affordability, rapid introduction and most importantly, military utility, are the foundations of our UAV programs.

This paper provides information on the spectrum of tactical UAVs and how we work to meet Service requirements by using off-the-shelf technologies to ensure interoperability and commonality. It provides a brief overview of each of our UAVs and discusses our vision for a Tactical Control System (TCS).

ORGANIZATION

In response to congressional direction to consolidate the management of the Department of Defense (DOD) nonlethal UAV programs, the Under Secretary of Defense established the UAV Joint Program Office (JPO). The DOD chartered the UAV JPO to be the central manager for all systems development and acquisition programs for nonlethal tactical UAVS. The UAV JPO is a small, customer-oriented organization composed of a Common Systems Directorate and four Program Offices all jointly manned to ensure Service needs are met. The UAV JPO maintains a continuous, close relationship with the user community throughout all phases of the acquisition life cycle.

Requirements for UAVs are set by the JROC; the Navy is the Executive Service for the acquisition of DOD UAVS. The PEO(CU) has responsibility and accountability for designing, developing, and procuring UAVS, and for transitioning UAV systems to the Services.

In fiscal year 1994, the Defense Airborne Reconnaissance Office (DARO) was established to provide oversight and guidance to all airborne reconnaissance efforts including all UAVS. Funding for the UAV JPO projects is provided within the DARO budget line.

The DOD is currently preparing a report on UAV management as requested by the Congress.

UAV MISSIONS

In developing affordable and effective UAVs and ground control systems we need to prepare for both core and specific UAV missions. The core missions include day or night reconnaissance, surveillance and target acquisition (RSTA); combat assessment (CA); and battlespace management. As new payloads become available, more specific UAV taskings will evolve to include adjusting indirect fire; close air support; deception operations; search and rescue (SAR); and mine detection. Our list of potential "real-time or near real-time" UAV missions is growing.

UAV INTEROPERABILITY STRATEGY

Common subsystems are important to our overall UAV interoperability strategy. Usually when we think of a UAV system, we envision only the air vehicle. While the air vehicle must meet requirements, many of the keys to successful operations and drivers of increased costs reside in the ground systems and subsystems used to operate the spectrum of UAVS.

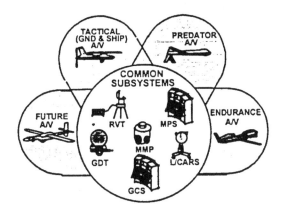

Common subsystems include remote video terminals (RVT), mission planning systems (MPS), modular mission payloads (MMP), ground data terminals (GDT), UAV common automatic recovery system (CARS), ground data terminals (GDT), and ground control stations (CiCS). Having ground systems which incorporate an open architecture, receive payload information from any UAV regardless of service, properly control the air vehicle and are comprised of existing/proven hardware for reliability and affordability are key ingredients of success and are the foundation of our programs.

TACTICAL UAV REQUIREMENTS

The availability of tactical UAVs to the warfighters is increasing. Pioneer and Predator are currently deployed, a Hunter system is being used at Fort Hood to refine concept of operations. We are in source selection for the Tactical UAV. The following table identifies Service requirements:

Air vehicle	Services	System quantities	Air vehicle quantities
PIONEER [1]	USMC, USN	9	45
PREDATOR	USA, USN, USAF	[2] 17	66
TUAV	USA, USN, USMC	61	244
HUNTER	USA	1	8

[1] These systems will be replaced with TUAV systems as they come on line
[2] Includes one research and development system

PIONEER UAV PROGRAM

The Pioneer has been operational about 12 years and may be in our Navy and Marine Corps inventories past the year 2000. As the TUAV system comes on line, Pioneer systems will be retired. The Army transitioned its one Pioneer system to the Navy in July 1995. Pioneer provided highly successfully reconnaissance support for Persian Gulf Desert Shield/Desert Storm operations in 1990–1991.

Army, Navy and Marine commanders lauded Pioneer's operational effectiveness. Six operational units flew over 300 combat missions over the course of the operation. Only one air vehicle was shot down. U.S. Navy Pioneer assets were extremely successful in target selection, naval gunfire spotting, and damage assessment as the battleship's 16inch guns destroyed enemy targets and softened defenses along the Kuwait coastline. The Marines used Pioneer to direct air strikes and provide near real-time reconnaissance for special operations. The Army conducted combat assessment, area searches, route reconnaissance, JSTARS threshold settings and target confirmations, and target locations. The success of Pioneer in supporting these combat operations established the utility and importance of UAVs in combat.

Between 1985 and 1995, Pioneer units logged over 12,000 flight hours and supported worldwide operations in Africa, Northern Europe, the Western Pacific, Korea, the Mediterranean, the Persian Gulf, Haiti, the Balkans, Somalia, and recent operations in Bosnia.

The Pioneer is powered by a reciprocating, pusher-propeller engine and can carry payloads weighing up to about 100 pounds. Payloads include either electro-optical (EO) or infrared (IR) sensors.

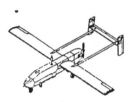

Pioneer is operated from our Navy amphibious ships, primarily the Landing Platform Dock (LPD). We currently conduct shipboard launch by rocket assisted take-off (RATO). Shipboard recovery is into a net, which is rigged on the aft part of the ship. We currently are on contract to procure and install the UAV CARS on all Pioneer systems. This system will significantly decrease the risk of mishaps during the critical recovery operation. When operating from land, we have the capability for pneumatic-launch, rocket-launch, or using unprepared areas for launch and recovery.

TACTICAL UAV SYSTEM ACTD PROGRAM

The Tactical UAV (TUAV) program is being initiated as DOD's most recent Advanced Concept Technology Demonstration (ACTD) program and currently is in source selection. The ACTD process was selected in order to ensure early and active participation of the military user in evaluating military utility and developing the concept of operations that will permit the most effective utilization of this new capability. We expect to provide the Army, Navy and Marine Corps with a single UAV system that can deliver timely, accurate and complete targeting and other battlefield information to combat units in near-real-time. Our TUAV concept of operations supports the Division/Brigade/Battalion, and Marine Expeditionary Force (MEF) needs, and includes employment of the TUAV from aircraft carriers (CVs) and large deck amphibious ships (LHAs/LHDs).

A Request for Proposal (RFP) was issued February 1, 1996 that provides for the basic ACTD, an option for six low rate initial production (LRIP) systems, and appropriate transition to production. Industry responses were received 18 March and contract award is planned for April or May of this year. Cost is a primary consideration. The target costs are $350,000 for the 33rd and $300,000 for the 100th air vehicle (A/V), to include costs of sensor payloads. JROC performance goals for the TUAV ACTD are presented in the below table.

JROC PERFORMANCE REQUIREMENTS [1]

Cost	$350K @ 33rd and $300K @ 100th A/V and Sensor
Range	200 km
Target Location Error	Best Possible Using State of the Art GPS (not to exceed 100 m)
On Station Endurance	3 hrs
Launch and Recovery	Unprepared Surface/Large Deck Amphibious Ships
System Mobility	2 HMMWV/1 Trailer
System Deployability	Single C–130 (4 A/V and Ground Equipment)
Payload	EO/IR
Integration	EMI Shielding/Corrosion Inhibition
Data Link	Compliant with JII (200 km LOS at sea level)
Propulsion System	As provided by Contractor
Mandatory Options	UAV CARS/Heavy Fuel Engine
Options	Common Data Link/Synthetic Aperture Radar

[1] As close as possible

We allow bidders to trade-off various performance parameters in their proposals. The potential buy is for 61 TUAV systems. Each system includes four air vehicles. Plans are to modify 12 Navy ships to operate the TUAV. The Army would operate

38, the Navy 8, and the Marine Corps 11 systems. Four systems are planned for the Joint UAV Training Center.

HUNTER UAV PROGRAM

Acquisition of the Hunter program began in fiscal year 1989 with full and open competition resulting in the September 1989 award of two firm-fixed-price contracts. After extensive technical evaluation testing and limited user testing, a prime contractor was competitively down selected on 30 June 1992. A January 1993 Defense Acquisition Board (DAB) review approved the program for low rate initial production, block enhancements, the acquisition strategy, and established exit criteria for production. Subsequently there were contractor delays in system deliveries to the Government and several hardware and software problems were experienced that required correction.

FAIN REPORT

In December of 1994, the Assistant Secretary of the Navy (Research, Development and Acquisition) requested LtGen Fain, USAF, to lead an Independent Review Team (IRT) to review the Hunter program. The IRT formal report was completed in March of 1995 and contained many useful recommendations. All received serious consideration and most were adopted by Hunter and other UAV programs. The IRT concluded that there were no known technical problems.

One of the IRT's recommendations was to adopt a fly-fix-fly approach for addressing hardware and software issues. The fly-fix-fly program has progressed as planned and has resulted in improved safety and flight procedures. The use of Integrated Product Teams was emphasized and employed by the contractor and Government with success. As a result, several management positions were strengthened within the contractor and govenment program offices. Although operating UAVs has proven to be safe, the air vehicles can be expected to experience occasional mechanical, electrical and human procedure problems that can result in a mishap. Constant vigilance enables us to quickly identify trends and propose fixes when necessary.

HUNTER DECISION

The JROC on 13 October 1995 recommended that the Hunter contract be allowed to expire. On 31 January 1996, USD (A&T) released an acquisition decision memorandum (ADM) which directed us to allow the contract to expire after accepting the last two of seven systems; that the Army operate one system with its operating forces to refine UAV concepts of operation; support the operating system with the necessary training and logistics; store the remaining Hunter systems; and to continue commonality and interoperability initiatives that apply to the on-going tactical UAV efforts. Acceptance of systems six and seven is scheduled to occur in the summer of 1996.

Lessons learned from hunter and other UAVs beyond the LtGen IRT are categorized as follows:

— Reaffirmed the need for a timely and accurate picture of the battlefield.
— UAVs must be reliable, survivable, and maintainable.
— Interoperability of ground stations is of critical importance.
— Discipline and operational procedures, developed over the years for manned platforms, must be applied to the operation of UAVS.

PREDATOR UAV SYSTEM ACTD PROGRAM

The Medium Altitude Endurance, or Predator UAV, system was the first UAV ACTD and has been highly successful. Responding to a JCS need, the Predator provides a continuous coverage, long-dwell, fully autonomous, and attritable UAV capability. The ACTD spans 30 months and includes exercise participation and field deployment. The ACTD ends 30 June 1996 and will transition to an operational system. Transition to production is expected in fiscal year 1997. The first aircraft was delivered for testing 6 months after contract award. In 1995 the U.S. deployed Predator to Albania in support of UN Peacekeeping Operations in Bosnia. In March 1996, Predator returned to the Bosnian theater equipped with electro-o tics/infrared sensors, synthetic aperture radar (SAR), and ice detection capabilityp Predator is presently providing vital support from its base in Taszar, Hungary in support of the peacekeeping mission.

A typical Predator UAV system consists of three or four air vehicles, a ground control system and the Trojan Spirit communications system. The Predator has a 49 foot wingspan and can stay airborne for over 40 hours. In addition to its EO/

IR and SAR sensors, it also has the capability for satellite command and control, and data transfer using a Ku band satellite communications data link.

TACTICAL CONTROL SYSTEM

A key element of providing affordable and effective tactical UAVs to the warfighters is the Tactical Control System (TCS), often referred to as the ground control system. We are creating a single TCS that will be interoperable with all tactical UAVS. In essence we will have a single interoperable tactical UAV system that will include a control system with multiple air vehicles as required. This approach promotes commonality, interoperability, affordability, jointness, and easy introduction of new air vehicles when needed. Software is the key to this approach. The concept is to define the fundamental architecture and system interfaces between the various air vehicles and their control systems and to use common/transportable software. By having core software that supports the common elements to all of our UAVs and also having a software interface at the subsystem level as established and controlled by our Joint Interoperability Interfaces (JIIs), we can port this software to any number of tactical control system hardware configurations. The TCS, whether on the ground or at sea, will work across the spectrum of UAVs including the full-sized ground control system used by Corps and Division, the Navy Shipboard/Submarine/MEF control systems hosted on TAC3/4 systems, and the downsized ground control systems used by the Brigade, MEF, and Battalion.

The DOD and all Services have reviewed and agree to this approach. The user's benefitsaretruejointness,reducedcostandinteroperability. The TCS approach provides seamless integration with Joint Command and Control and offers a common, effective, future for all of our UAV systems. We expect to achieve interoperability across the TCS architecture by fiscal year 1998.

TACTICAL CONTROL SYSTEM

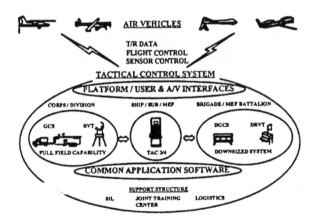

CONCLUSION

Jointness and interoperability are the keys to developing affordable and effective UAV systems to support our warfighting commanders. To achieve these important goals, focus must be on both the air vehicle and the control systems. We have established an architecture for the TCS that will benefit our users and provide seamless integration with Joint Command and Control mechanisms that are also under development.

UAVs are essential warfighting assets-extremely flexible and capable of dynamic tasking and retasking while avoiding the risk to human life. UAVs are proving themselves around the world in operations today.

TACTICAL
UNMANNED AERIAL VEHICLES

BRIEFING TO:
SUBCOMMITTEE ON AIRLAND FORCES
SENATE ARMED SERVICES COMMITTEE

MARCH 29, 1996

RADM BART STRONG
PROGRAM EXECUTIVE OFFICER
CRUISE MISSILES AND JOINT
UNMANNED AERIAL VEHICLES

1996 / 03-26-96

TACTICAL UAV ORGANIZATION

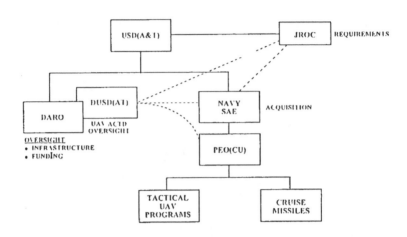

PIONEER

CHARACTERISTICS

ENDURANCE	5 HOURS
RADIUS OF ACTION	100 NM (185 KM)
MAX ALTITUDE.	15,000 FT
PAYLOAD	ELECTRO-OPTIC OR INFRARED
SYSTEM.	5 AIR VEHICLES 1 GROUND CONTROL

STATUS

SYSTEMS.	9 (5 NAVY, 3 USMC, 1 TRAINING)
ACQUISITION.	ATTRITION AIR VEHICLES, SPARE PARTS
OPERATIONALLY DEPLOYED	AUSTIN, DENVER, SHREVEPORT (LPD)
STATISTICS:	AS OF 21 MAR 96 - 12,244 FLIGHT HOURS - 2,738 COMBAT HOURS - 835 COMBAT SORTIES

(FY) 97 98 99 00 01

UAV CARS INSTALLATION

TUAV TRANSITION

PREDATOR
ACTD

CHARACTERISTICS

ENDURANCE	> 40 HOURS
RADIUS OF ACTION	500 MILES (SATCOM)
MAX ALTITUDE	25,000 FT
PAYLOAD	ELECTRO-OPTIC INFRARED SYNTHETIC APERTURE RADAR
SYSTEM	3 OR 4 AIR VEHICLES 1 GROUND CONTROL

STATUS

DEPLOYMENTS	FY95 BOSNIA (ALBANIA) FY96 BOSNIA (HUNGARY)
STATISTICS	AS OF MAR 96 - 2,277 FLIGHT HOURS - 770 OPERATIONAL HOURS - 85 OPERATIONAL SORTIES
MARINIZATION	UNDER STUDY
TRANSITION & PRODUCTION	IPT 17 SYSTEMS - 11 USAF - 3 NAVY - 2 ARMY - 1 R&D

(FY) 94 95 96 97 98 99

ACTD / LRIP / PRODUCTION

TACTICAL UAV
ACTD

SCHEDULE
(CONTRACT AWARD: 3RD QTR FY96)

ACTD (6 SYSTEMS)
- 6 MONTHS — 1ST FLIGHT
- 12 MONTHS — 1ST SYSTEM DELIVERY
- 18 MONTHS — 6TH SYSTEM DELIVERY
- 24 MONTHS — LAND/SHIPBOARD DEMO ACTD COMPLETED

PLANNED PRODUCTION TRANSITION
- LRIP OPTION (FY98)(6 SYSTEMS)
- FOLLOW-ON PRODUCTION PLAN

SYSTEM REQUIREMENTS

SERVICE	QUANTITIES
ARMY	38
MARINE CORPS	11
NAVY	8 DETS/12 SHIPS
TRAINING BASE	4

COMBINES CLOSE AND SHORT RANGE MISSIONS FOR SEA & LAND FORCES

JROC PERFORMANCE REQUIREMENTS*

COST	$350K @ 33RD AND $300K @ 100TH A/V AND SENSOR
RANGE	200 KM
TARGET LOCATION ERROR	BEST POSSIBLE USING STATE OF THE ART GPS (NOT TO EXCEED 100m)
ON STATION ENDURANCE	3 HRS
LAUNCH AND RECOVERY	UNPREPARED SURFACE/ LARGE DECK AMPHIBIOUS SHIPS
SYSTEM MOBILITY	2 HMMWV/1 TRAILER
SYSTEM DEPLOYABILITY	SINGLE C-130 (4 A/V AND GROUND EQUIPMENT)
PAYLOAD	EO/IR
INTEGRATION	EMI SHIELDING/CORROSION INHIBITION
DATA LINK	COMPLIANT WITH JTI (200 KM LOS AT SEA LEVEL)
PROPULSION SYSTEM	AS PROVIDED BY CONTRACTOR
MANDATORY OPTIONS	UAV CARS/HEAVY FUEL ENGINE
OPTIONS	COMMON DATA LINK/ SYNTHETIC APERTURE RADAR

* AS CLOSE AS POSSIBLE

UNCLASSIFIED

HUNTER

HUNTER DECISION

JROC RECOMMENDATION (13 OCT 95):
- ALLOW CONTRACT TO EXPIRE

USD(A&T) DECISION SUMMARY (31 JAN 96)
- ALLOW EXISTING CONTRACT EXPIRE
- ARMY OPERATE ONE SYSTEM
- STORE REMAINING SYSTEMS
- CONTINUE COMMONALITY & INTEROPERABILITY INITIATIVES

LTGEN FAIN REPORT RELEVANCE
- EXPECT UAV ATTRITION/MISHAPS
- USE INTEGRATED PRODUCT TEAMS
- SCRUTINIZE OFF-THE-SHELF SYSTEMS FOR RISK/VALIDITY. USE FLY-FIX-FLY
- STRONG CONTRACTOR & GOVERNMENT MANAGEMENT NEEDED

FUTURE
- HUNTER RETURN TO FLIGHT DEC 95
  - 177 FLIGHT HOURS (21 MAR 96)
  - CONTINUE NEEDED SUPPORT

- III CORPS OPERATIONS/ASSESSMENT
  - FORCE XXI PARTICIPATION

(R3)/TACTAVI/Dnk 1996/03.26.96

UNCLASSIFIED

UNCLASSIFIED

TACTICAL CONTROL SYSTEM

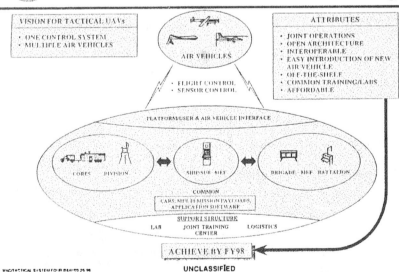

MAC/TACTICAL SYSTEM COLR/R&W/03.25.96

UNCLASSIFIED

SERVICE REQUIREMENTS

AIR VEHICLE	SERVICES	SYSTEM QUANTITIES	AIR VEHICLE QUANTITIES
PIONEER*	USMC, USN	9	45
PREDATOR	USA, USN, USAF	17**	66
TUAV	USA, USN, USMC	61	244
HUNTER	USA	.	~

* THESE SYSTEMS WILL BE REPLACED
WITH TUAV SYSTEMS AS THEY COME
ON LINE

** INCLUDES ONE RESEARCH &
DEVELOPMENT SYSTEM

SUMMARY

- UAVs PROVIDE PROVEN COMBAT & PEACE KEEPING CAPABILITY

- UAVs ARE:
  - JOINTLY ACQUIRED & OPERATED
  - AFFORDABLE
  - SAVING LIVES

Senator WARNER. Tell me a little bit about the commercial application.

Admiral STRONG. The commercial industry is just starting to look into it, but oil exploration, Border Patrol, forest fires, forest monitoring, environmental.

Senator WARNER. You could have manned fixed wing for those operations.

Admiral STRONG. They have them, sir.

Senator WARNER. The theory of the UAV is to reduce the threat to the operators, more or less.

Admiral STRONG. We are finding that you can develop a vehicle, for instance, the Predator, that is quite inexpensive compared to what the design of a manned aircraft would be, and can do many of those jobs. Certainly not all of them, but I was recently talking with the individual who is selling UAV's or proposing UAV's to Third World countries where they have difficult kinds of communications. They put up phone lines and they are torn down. So they expect to use UAV's to relay telephonic communications.

Senator WARNER. What interest comes from our allies?

Admiral STRONG. We have recently met with the Brits and the Germans on the tactical UAE's, particularly the control system. They are very enthused with that, and we are in the initial discussions of how we can work together with that. I think we have quite a future there, sir.

Senator WARNER. Good.

Senator Bryan.

Senator BRYAN. Thank you very much, Mr. Chairman.

Admiral, let me focus your attention on the chart that I think preceded that, where you indicate service requirements, the 45 Pioneer, the '66 Predator, the 244 TUAV, and the 8 Hunter, using the definitional criteria for air vehicle, how many of those do we have currently in the inventory and deployed in the field, of that total category?

Admiral STRONG. Sir, starting from the top, we have those 45 air vehicles are in the Navy and the Marine Corps.

Senator BRYAN. That would be the Pioneer you have referenced, is that right? That is the Pioneer?

Admiral STRONG. Yes, sir, the Pioneer.

Senator BRYAN. OK, so 45 are actually fully deployed?

Admiral STRONG. Yes, sir. We have Predator, we bought 10, we have lost two, one in combat, and we have eight currently in the inventory.

Senator BRYAN. Currently in the inventory.

Admiral STRONG. Right. The tactical UAV is in source selection. We have none of those.

Senator BRYAN. Right. I understand that. The Hunter?

Admiral STRONG. The Hunter, we have all eight of these plus those in storage.

Senator BRYAN. So eight that you currently have operational and deployed.

Admiral STRONG. Yes, in the 3rd Corps.

Senator BRYAN. So if my math is correct, we have got 61, is that right? 53 and 8, 61 that are currently actively deployed?

Admiral STRONG. That is correct, sir.

Senator BRYAN. Admiral, can you tell us generally where those are deployed?

Admiral STRONG. Certainly. Predator is deployed in Hungary. We have one of the groups there where we are working, and the other one, one of the other systems back with the contractor. The Pioneer is deployed off of LPD's around the world. We have three LPD's that are configured, and we are configuring three more. The Hunter system is at Fort Hood in Texas.

Senator BRYAN. Generally in terms of its operational control, as you are contrasting the difference between the HAE and the tactical, you indicated the full level would be much more focused as opposed to a theater command, who has the operational control? In other words, who makes the decision where these vehicles are to be deployed, whether it is in Hungary or Fort Hood, or wherever it may be? What level of a command structure is that?

Admiral STRONG. Those are made at the top levels of the operational command authority, sir.

Senator BRYAN. Then once they are given to the various commands, at what level is the actual practical deployment made? I mean, at the—help me out. Who actually would have that.

Admiral STRONG. Sir, as a general statement, sir, and I will get you a more complete answer, but the tactical forces, the tactical commander on site, is the one we are trying most importantly to get the data to.

Senator BRYAN. That could be either Air Force, Army, Navy, or Marine Corps, depending upon the circumstances?

Admiral STRONG. I hesitated because it will be Air Force as well as the others soon, because they will be operating the Predator system.

Senator BRYAN. Tell us a little bit more about the CARS system. You mentioned that very briefly, but what are the plans for the development, back to the UAV?

Admiral STRONG. We are on contract now to equip all nine Pioneer systems with CARS. CARS on the tactical UAV is a mandatory option. WE did not want to require it in the original configuration in the competition, but they will have to propose that, and our intent is to put it in.

The Predator, we are doing a feasibility study with Predator we think would be very useful to put on that aircraft also, sir.

I guess that covers the four of them, sir.

CARS will—in my view it will reduce the mishap rate so it will save us money; it will reduce the training, and probably the number of people we will need with the detachment; and it will certainly expand the envelope of the UAV's by allowing us to operate in more marginal weather and various conditions.

Senator BRYAN. If your development plan proceeds on schedule, how many of these air vehicles will we have in the inventory and actually deployed, say, 10 years from now, or any other baseline year that you would choose to use? Because as I understand it, the program is to phase out the Pioneer, once the TUAV systems come on line. Am I right on that?

Admiral STRONG. Yes, sir. That is the plan.

Senator BRYAN. So how many would we have a decade from now under the current projections of the development schedule, assuming now complications or unforseen problems develop?

Admiral STRONG. Well, sir, the JROC has established the requirements that I showed on the right of the chart there, sir, and that is what we would be working towards here over the near term. I would hate to have to guess 10 years from now, but I would think this type of number is where we would be.

Senator BRYAN. I guess my confusion, Admiral, and I will turn and yield to the chairman after this——

Senator WARNER. No, you go right ahead, Senator. I have pretty well completed my questions.

Senator BRYAN. I thank you, Mr. Chairman. I will just be a couple of minutes.

The reason I am a bit confused there, if indeed the TUAV, the 244 vehicles, are ultimately produced and deployed, then presumably the Pioneer would be retired, so that those numbers, if you add them up, and tell me if I am wrong in this assumption, you are not going to have 45 and 66 and 244 and 8. If the TUAV is fully developed, I take it that some of the other vehicles will either be retired—if that is an incorrect assumption, please correct me.

Admiral STRONG. Sir, I would correct myself here. Certainly the long-term plan is to have the tactical UAV, if it is successful, and the Predator. Those two vehicles would comprise the tactical UAV for the three services.

Senator BRYAN. I see.

Admiral STRONG. We would keep Pioneer around until we made sure we had the capability.

Senator BRYAN. How about the Hunter?

Admiral STRONG. I think a decision will be made on the disposition of Hunter after it has operated a while and we see if the tactical UAV and the Predator will suffice. If one of those should fall short, perhaps they would reconsider the Hunter.

Senator BRYAN. OK. So ultimately, if everything works out, it is the predator and the TUAV that will be the tactical UAV's, am I correct?

Admiral STRONG. That is the plan, sir.

Senator BRYAN. I thank the chairman.

Senator WARNER. Do you have further questions?

Senator BRYAN. No.

Senator WARNER. Well, we have had an excellent hearing. We may submit some questions for the record.

The subcommittee is adjourned.

[Questions for the record with answers supplied follow:]

QUESTIONS SUBMITTED BY SENATOR STROM THURMOND

JOINT SURVEILLANCE AND TARGET ATTACK RADAR SYSTEM (JSTARS) COMMON GROUND STATION (CGS)

Senator THURMOND. Last year, Department of Defense provided a demonstration of the JSTARS capability to North Atlantic Treaty Organization (NATO) officials aboard the U.S.S. *Mount Whitney*. What has the Administration done since that time to promote JSTARS for the NATO Alliance Ground Surveillance mission?

Mr. DECKER. Last October, at the U.S.S. *Mount Whitney* demonstration, we demonstrated the ability to downlink JSTARS data from the E-8 aircraft to the deployed Rapid Reaction Force Command element aboard the U.S.S. *Mount Whitney*.

The demonstration went extremely well. Since that time, we have deployed a proto-type Common Ground Station to the Supreme Headquarters Allied Powers Europe (SHAPE), Technical Center at the Hague. This system, supported by Motorola, is assisting NATO in identifying and developing the various technical interface re-quirements between JSTARS and the NATO command and control system.

QUESTIONS SUBMITTED BY SENATOR JOHN W. WARNER

HUNTER UNMANNED AERIAL VEHICLES

Senator WARNER. It is my understanding that the problems encountered by the Hunter Unmanned Aerial Vehicle (UAV) have been corrected and that the systems are currently operating effectively at Fort Hood and Fort Huachuca. Would you please bring the subcommittee up to date on the current operations at both Fort Hood and Fort Huachuca?

Mr. DECKER. As of 15 April 1996 since Hunter's return to flight on December 20, 1995 at Fort Huachuca and January 6, 1996 at Fort Hood, there have been a total of 93 flights, for 192.8 total flight hours. There have been 503 touch and go land-ings. There have been no major anomalies. Night training began last week at Fort Hood with extensive touch and go landings. Three night flights were conducted without incident.

Senator WARNER. Since the Government has invested in seven systems and asso-ciated infrastructure, and they seem to be operating well, what are your plans for utilizing some or all of the remaining systems?

Mr. DECKER. Fort Hood will retain the one operational system for Force XXI sup-port and contingency operations, as needed, commonality and limited training ef-forts would continue, and the remaining six systems would be stored. Two systems have yet to be accepted by the Government; that is expected to occur this summer.

JOINT SURVEILLANCE AND TARGET ATTACK RADAR SYSTEM (JSTARS) COMMON GROUND STATION (CGS)

Senator WARNER. I understand that the JSTARS system has been deployed to Bosnia to support Implementation Forces (IFOR) troops. How has that system been performing in Bosnia?

Mr. DECKER. The GSM's have been extremely effective in providing JSTARS data, correlated with Signals Intelligence data received through the Commander's Tactical Terminal (CTT). We are very pleased with the support provided and comments re-ceived from the Air and Ground Component Commanders. The JSTARS system is deployed as part of the Implementation Force (IFOR) in support of operation Joint Endeavor. We have a combined Army and Air Force Provisional Squadron based at Rhein Main Airbase, Germany, which serves as the Squadron and aircraft's main operating base with 13 Ground Station Modules (GSM) deployed with the ground and air component commanders in Bosnia and supporting locations. The GSMs con-tinue to provide intelligence through the CTT when the JSTARS aircraft is not on station. We were able to field the Light GSM's much earlier than planned based upon the increased emphasis and funding provided by Congress in 1993.

Senator WARNER. I understand that the Army has recently awarded the contract for the Common Ground Station Module for JSTARS. What additional capabilities will this provide the tactical commander and will this include additional sensors such as the Predator unmanned aerial vehicle (UAV), Advanced Synthetic Aperture Radar System—Two (ASARS II), and Airborne Reconnaissance—Low (ARL)?

Mr. DECKER. We have, in fact, awarded a competitive contract for the Common Ground Station (CGS) to an industry team led by Motorola which will greatly en-hance the capabilities of the Joint STARS GSM. The CGS design incorporates the latest in commercial technology and employs an open system architecture that will ensure rapid insertion of technology into the system. The CGS design will allow ad-ditional sensor products to be received and correlated with current products. Motor-ola, as part of the Government/industry team, has demonstrated links to the Preda-tor UAV and is also working with Hughes on the ASARS IIE and California Micro-wave, the ARL contractor, to have a direct downlink into the CGS. We expect to add these capabilities to the units in support of Operation Joint Endeavor, if re-quired.

ARMY AND UNMANNED AERIAL VEHICLE (UAV) MODERNIZATION

Senator WARNER. Last year, the Army announced the decision to withdraw the OV-1s from the Army inventory by the end of this year. How is that effort proceeding, and how do you plan on providing Intelligence and Warning support to the Commander of U.S. Forces Korea after the withdrawal of OV–1s is completed?

Mr. DECKER. In 1991, Congress directed the retirement of all OV–1 aircraft be completed by September 30, 1996. As a result, OV–1 retirement plans are proceeding according to schedule. To date, there are two remaining operational OV–1 units. One is located in the XVIII Airborne Corps, and the other is located in Korea. The OV–1s assigned to XVIII Airborne Corps provide contingency force coverage while the OV–1s in Korea are currently providing daily Intelligence and Warning support. Both of these remaining units are scheduled to be retired by June 30, 1996 and September 30, 1996 respectively.

As a replacement for the retired OV–1s in Korea, the Army is deploying two RC–7 Airborne Reconnaissance Low-Multifunction (ARL–M) aircraft, equipped with Moving Target Indicator (MTI)/Synthetic Aperture Radar sensors. A third ARL–M aircraft will be equipped with a MTI/SAR sensor to support world-wide contingencies as needed.

The November 1994 Joint Staff decision to use the U.S. Air Force U–2R exclusively for the daily reconnaissance mission in Korea remains valid. However, the demanding world-wide U–2R operational tempo necessitated an Army solution to supplement the U–2R capability in Korea.

ARMY FORCE STRUCTURE

Senator WARNER. General Griffith, I note in the DOD budget documents that the end strength for the Army is indicated as a range of 475,000 to 495,000—a difference of 20,000—more than a heavy division equivalent. I understand that the Army may retain up to 495,000 only if they can find the resources to pay for the additional 20,000 soldiers. This decision is clearly resource driven—not based on strategy or warfighting requirements. General Griffith, based on the strategy in the Bottom-up Review, current OPTEMPO, and warfighting requirements, should the end strength of the Army be 475,000 or 495,000—or higher?

General GRIFFITH. Active Army end strength of 495,000 represents the minimum level for a force of 10 Active Component (AC) divisions to be able to execute the National Military Strategy (NMS) at an acceptable level of risk. Our rigorous Total Army Analysis process validated the capability, and attendant risks, of the 495,000 AC force to execute the Bottom-Up Review strategy of two Major Regional Contingencies. To my knowledge, the warfighting and sustainment capabilities of a 475,000 AC force have never been modeled or analyzed in any way. In fact, below 495,000 the ability of the active Army to execute the National Military Strategy becomes problematic, particularly given our current operational deployments. At lower levels, the Army would undoubtedly require more time and resources to win the conflict and the cost to the Nation would be higher. For these reasons, we feel that 495,000 is the right active Army end- strength.

RESOURCES

Senator WARNER. General Griffith, the Chairman of the Joint Chiefs of Staff recently stated that procurement needs to reach a $60 billion a year level in the Department of Defense. What levels of funding does the Army need to ensure critical modernization needs are met?

General GRIFFITH. The Army has significant shortfalls in Research Development Acquisition (RDA) accounts due to chronic underfunding in the past. 'Me Army requires $14 to $16 billion annually in its modernization accounts in the Future Years Defense Program to fund them at a level commensurate with other Army programs. Funding for full recapitalization would require annual resources in the $15 to $20 billion range. We are only funded for approximately $11 billion in fiscal year 1997.

Senator WARNER. Using current projections for future years, what modernization requirements will not be met?

General GRIFFITH. Due to the overall anemic nature of our modernization accounts, we have a number of high priority unfunded requirements in fiscal year 1997 and the out years. We have developed a 1–N List which prioritizes our unfunded requirements. Areas where we have significant shortfalls include Logistics Automation; Combat Support/Combat Service Support; Soldier Enhancements; Night Vision devices; Command, Control Communications, Computers, Computers and Intelligence (C⁴1); Force XXI, and various high priority weapons systems. Lack of modernization funds also make it difficult for us to invest in economically efficient strategies such as buying out programs early.

Senator WARNER. How does the Army balance modernization requirements against force structure realities? Can you equip the total force or just a core force?

General GRIFFITH. We cannot modernize the total force with the current level of funding, and the active force at 495,000 is about as small as it can get and still accomplish our currently assigned tasks. So, in an era of declining resources the Army has had to balance the allocation of resources to maintain near-term readiness, improve quality of life for soldiers and continue to modernize the force. Current production rates do not allow efficiency nor total modernization of even Force Package 1 until 2015. Furthermore, we have had to make tough decisions about some systems in order to realign the balance between readiness and modernization. This has resulted in the termination of lesser priority programs in order to reinvest in more critical modernization needs. We must maintain the delicate balance of readiness and modernization in order to meet current and future threats.

ARMY MODERNIZATION

Senator WARNER. General Griffith, Army modernization has been identified as a critical problem. Certainly, this problem will affect the future warfighting capability of the Army. Has the Joint Requirements Oversight Council (JROC) addressed this problem? If so, what was the JROC position?

General GRIFFITH. Although the JROC has not specifically addressed Army modernization, they have recognized that modernization is a Department of Defense (DOD) wide issue. Their review resulted in a recommendation to set a DOD procurement al of $60 billion. I'm confident that level would fulfill the Army's modernization needs.

ADDITIONAL FUNDING

Senator WARNER. General Griffith, if additional funding becomes available, what would be the Army's priorities and in what amounts? Please be as specific as possible.

General GRIFFITH. Should additional funding become available, our requirements would be modernization, infrastructure revitalization, and near-term readiness. From the modernization perspective, we would use additional funding to buy out programs early to get economic efficiencies. We'd also use additional funds for logistics automation; combat support/combat service support (CS/CSS); upgrades to the command, control, communications, and computer infrastructure (C⁴1) network; night vision improvements; Force XXI; critical modernization shortfalls; the Reserve Components (RC); and soldier enhancements. In the infrastructure revitalization area, we need funding in barracks revitalization; real property maintenance (RPM); family housing construction and operations; power projection command, control, communications, and computer infrastructure, (PPC⁴I); and to accelerate construction projects. If we were provided additional resources for near-term readiness, we would invest in end-item management, ammunition management, strategic mobility, Defense Message System (DMS), and Title XI requirements.

AVIATION CAPABILITY

Senator WARNER. General Griffith, do you believe we have sufficient Army combat and combat support aviation capability?

General GRIFFITH. The Army has sufficient quantity of combat and combat support aircraft and units to satisfy the Defense Planning Guidance. The Army Aviation Modernization Plan addresses the requirement to modernize our aviation fleet to keep pace with technology and threat capabilities and provides the strategy to meet those requirements. Key to our modernization plan is the continuation of three critical aviation programs: Apache Longbow (including Fire Control Radar), UH–60 Black Hawk, and Comanche. In addition to the aircraft, the Aviation Modernization Plan also identifies requirements of the Hellfire missile program. The one modernization shortfall the Army recognizes is for the cargo (CH–47D) aircraft, which will be approaching 40 years of age by the turn of the century. As a result, the Army has identified the Improved Cargo Helicopter (ICH) as a top priority in the fiscal year 1998–2003 Program Objective Memorandum (POM) development.

MODERNIZATION OBJECTIVES

Senator WARNER. General Griffith, what are the top modernization objectives for the Army?

General GRIFFITH. The threat-based Army of the Cold War is giving way to the capabilities-based Army of the 21st Century, capable of land force dominance across a continuum ranging from conventional warfare to military operations other than war. We have developed a series of modernization objectives which provide a capabilities based foundation for the Army to meet its many diverse missions. The following are the Army Modernization Objectives:

Project and Sustain the Force
Protect the Force
Win the Information War
Conduct Precision Strike
Dominate Maneuver

Today's environment and future environments demand the capabilities to project continental United States based forces quickly and to sustain those forces for extended periods of time. This is the tenet of the first modernization objective, Protect and Sustain the Force.

The second tenet, Protect the Force, has two elements—protection against fratricide and protection from opponents' missiles and nuclear, chemical, and biological capabilities. Both require situational awareness.

The third tenet of the Army modernization objectives says that the Army seeks to Win the Information War. Information warfare capabilities harness advances in information technologies in order to collect, process, disseminate, and use information. The goal is to provide future forces with the operational advantages of information dominance.

The fourth tenet, Conduct Precision Strike, is critical to assist the future force commander in the accomplishment of his mission. He must have the organic capability to conduct deep attacks against the threat. To successfully attack targets with precision at extended ranges requires the capability to see deep then transmit that information/intelligence in near real time to firing units employing advanced weapons and munitions systems.

In order to succeed in its fifth and final tenet, Dominate Maneuver, the Army must be able to control and dominate the fight in order to achieve swift, decisive victory with minimum casualties. Modernization of maneuver forces aims toward making them more deployable, tailorable, and lethal.

QUESTIONS SUBMITTED BY SENATOR DAN COATS

TACTICAL WHEELED VEHICLES (TWV)

Senator COATS. I share your belief in the importance of Tactical Wheeled Vehicles (TWV). I also share our often stated opinion that we must make effective use of limited funding by procuring a combination of new and remanufactured vehicles to meet the soldiers needs. The 2½ ton Truck Extended Service Program (ESP) has been a model program in establishing how remanufactured vehicles enhance fleet readiness and I was greatly pleased that the 2½ ton Truck ESP "First Unit Equipped" (FUE) occurred in what must be record time. I am sure you will agree that even with these accomplishments that much remains to be done to meet our truck needs. In this connection, I have a few questions on some critical programs: The High Mobility Multipurpose Wheeled Vehicles (HMMWV) remains essential to both current and future program requirements. The Army conducted a study that established manufacturing capability could be maintained with a Department of Defense production rate of 10 vehicles a day. The Congress provided $72 million in additional funds to the last year's request. I understand that $24 million of those funds were diverted to meet emergency Bosnia requirements. What steps has the Army taken to recover those funds diverted to ensure continued production of HMMWVs?

Mr. DECKER. The Army is considering requesting reprogramming authority to supplement these funds.

Senator COATS. What shortfall exists in this year's budget request in order to achieve the required Department of Defense-wide 10 per day production rate?

Mr. DECKER. To fund the required 1,750 vehicles the Army asked for $41 million on its "1–N List." Since the list was published, the manufacturer, AM General, and O'Gara Hess & Eisenhardt Armoring Company (OGE) came to the Government stating that the most economical rate for Uparmor HMMWVs is 360 per year. This would allow the Government to amortize the facilitization costs over more vehicles and continue the production momentum built up for Bosnia that peaks at 70 per month. The constrained Army Acquisition Objective of the M1114 is over 2,000 vehicles. In order to buy a total 1,750 HMMWVs (including a subtotal of 360 Uparmor HMMWVs), the Army needs $21.6 million over and above the "1–N List" figure of $41 million.

HIGH MOBILITY MULTIPURPOSE WHEELED VEHICLES (HMMWV)

Senator COATS. The extreme threat of mines in Bosnia has required that the Army ramp up their production of armored High Mobility Multipurpose Wheeled Vehicles (HMMWV) and I understand that the request provides for only 127 Up Armored HMMWVs. What are the requirements for Up Armor HMMWVs? What level of funding would be required to maintain a reasonable production of Up Armored HMMWVs to meet urgent requirements?

Mr. DECKER. The constrained Army requirement for Uparmor HMMWVs is over 2,000 vehicles. As I stated earlier $62.6 million would allow for the production of 360 Uparmored HMMWVs in a total yearly production of 1,750.

Senator COATS. The Congress provided $2.0 million in Research and Development (R&D) funds to initiate a HMMWV Extended Service Program (ESP) for HMMWVs approaching their useful service life. I understand the Marine Corps has already released funding to initiate this program. Will the Army harmonize their efforts with the Marine Corps and why have the Army funds not been released?

Mr. DECKER. The Army and Marine Corps are harmonizing their requirements for a HMMWV remanufacture effort. The Marines have been working with the Army's Program Executive Office for Tactical Wheeled Vehicles on this program and have agreed to let the Army manage the entire program. The Marine Corps provided $90 thousand in fiscal year 1995 R&D funding to conduct preliminary studies and has provided an additional $80 thousand in fiscal year 1996 R&D funds in support of this effort. The fiscal year 1996 funding will be used to conduct a limited teardown of two vehicles to determine which parts may be reused during a rebuild and which parts can not. No Army funding has been provided to date, the $2.0 million in funding is currently on Office of the Secretary Defense (Comptroller) withhold. No further action can be initiated by the Army without additional funding.

Senator COATS. What does the Army require to accelerate this program to ensure availability of High Mobility Multipurpose Wheeled Vehicle Extended Service Program (ESP) production in fiscal year 1998?

Mr. DECKER. In order to accelerate the HMMWV remanufacture program to ensure a production contract award in fiscal year 1998 both Research and Development (R&D) and procurement funding would have to be adjusted in fiscal year 1997 and fiscal year 1998. The $2.0 million in fiscal year 1996 funds currently on Office of the Secretary of Defense (Comptroller) withhold would have to be immediately released, and an increase of $3 million in fiscal year 1997 (R&D) funding would be required. This funding would be applied to develop a remanufacturing approach, produce prototypes and conduct testing. The current budget has Army production funding starting in fiscal year 1999 and United States Marine Corps funding starting in fiscal year 2000. Both funding streams would have to be accelerated to fiscal year 1998.

Senator COATS. The 2½ ton Truck has exceeded all expectations on reliability and will achieve Operations and Support (O&S) cost savings at 91 percent less than those vehicles in the field. What steps does the Army plan to provide 2½ ton Truck ESP vehicles to appropriate active units, specifically Korea?

Mr. DECKER. In the Future Years Defense Programs (FYDP) submitted with the President's Budget, there is outyear funding for 2½ ton Truck ESP. The outyear funding is under consideration to support Army forces in Korea.

MEDIUM TACTICAL TRUCK REMANUFACTURING (MTTR)

Senator COATS. The draft Request For Proposal (RFP) for the Medium Tactical Truck Remanufacturing (MTTR) to remanufacture 5-ton Truck Extended Service Program (ESP) and Marine Corps has been released. However, it cites the Army program as only an option. What does the Army require to ensure execution of the 5-ton Truck ESP and eliminate its position as only an option in this solicitation?

Mr. DECKER. First and foremost the Army needs the $6 million in Research and Development (R&D) requested on the "I to N" list for this effort in fiscal year 1997 and the fiscal year 1996 dollars are on withhold. With both years funding in hand, the Army could then exercise the option to the contract in fiscal year 1997. To eliminate its position as an option, the Army program would require an immediate infusion of an additional $5 million in fiscal year 1996 which exceeds our reprogramming authority and would delay the release of the RFP.

Senator COATS. Congress provided $1.2 million in additional funds for the Army 5-ton ESP program. Why have those funds not yet been released and applied to the solicitation?

Mr. DECKER. No funding has been provided to date. The $1.2 million in funding is currently on Office of the Secretary Defense (Comptroller) withhold. No further action can be initiated by the Army without additional funding.

M113 CARRIER MODIFICATION PROGRAM

Senator COATS. I am concerned over the reduced funding levels the Army has allocated to the M113 Carrier Modification Program. Last year, the Committee fully supported the fiscal year 1996 Carrier Modification program and directed the Army to restore a previously cut $20 million in fiscal year 1997. Service testimony and Committee findings point out the advantages of mobility and crew safety factors of the M113A3 over older versions. It seems clear that the Army's Force XXI combat units require the distinct maneuver capabilities that a modernized vehicle could offer. What are your plans to restore funding to the M113A3 Carrier Modification Program?

Mr. DECKER. Modernization of the M113 Family of Vehicles (FOV) has been an important, long-term Army effort for a number of years. Our present goal is to modernize approximately 200–250 vehicles per fiscal year. This effort requires average funding of between $45–50 million per year. This roughly modernizes one heavy division every 3 years.

The Army is working to restore the funding that was cut from the carrier modification effort in fiscal year 1999 through 2000 in the current fiscal year 1998–2003 Program Objective Memorandum. Due to limited modernization resources and current Army priorities in the near-term, however, the Army has been unable to restore the fiscal year 1997–98 shortfall. The fiscal year 1997 shortfall of $27 million is presently listed as an unfinanced requirement. Given additional funding, the Army would seek to reestablish previous funding levels in these 2 years.

PROGRAM FUNDING

Senator COATS. The Army has maintained that the digital battlefield is crucial to its efforts to maintain a modern, but smaller, force capable of decisive victory. While perhaps mundane in comparison to major weapons systems, computers, digital communication equipment, and data management software are integral to battlefield digitization efforts. Are you satisfied with the progress and funding of component programs supporting Force XXI?

General HARTZOG. Yes and no. The Force XXI process has many more component programs than materiel and digitization of the battlefield. The process of changing the Army is having a direct impact on warfighting doctrine, organizational structures, training and leader development programs, and, as always, the center piece of the Army, quality soldiers. As the Army makes key technological advances, there must be timely and balanced change in these other component programs.

We must balance change in each of the component programs of Force XXI to ensure we successfully field Army XXI shortly after the turn of the 21st Century. While I am satisfied with what we've gotten so far, we estimate an additional $100M per year, beginning in fiscal year 1997 and through 2004, will allow us to leverage and exploit existing programs and emerging technologies. The existing streamlined acquisition reform will facilitate this endeavor.

SIMULATIONS

Senator COATS. "Simulation" has played a major role in the Army's battlefield digitization efforts—looking at how evolving technologies can help tie together various weapons platforms, and even replacing prototype systems because of limited modernization funds. Despite the top priority the Army places on battlefield digitization and the merits of simulation, I understand the Army may be eying simulation efforts as a potential bill-payer to avoid cutting troop strength. Could you elaborate on how stable funding levels are in the simulation arena?

General HARTZOG. There have been cuts to Army models and simulations programs; however, I am not aware of a move to use resources programmed for simulation efforts specifically as a bill-payer to avoid cutting troop strength. I can tell you that the Army has many difficult decisions to make—between critical, near-term readiness requirements and transitioning today's Army toward the Army of the 21st Century. Our challenges are being driven by shrinking resources, unforeseen and unbudgeted commitments such as Bosnia, and continuous downsizing.

The worlds of simulations and simulators provide worthwhile means of experimenting with new ideas and conducting training. There is a role for both in today's Army as well as the Army of the 21st Century. Simulations, which allow us to experiment with scenarios, environments, and conditions, are a great analytical tool. Meanwhile, simulators, particularly training simulators, fill a gap in training that is being created by decreasing resources, increasing range and lethality of weapons systems, and environmental constraints. Thus, simulators enhance the Army's long-standing training goal of tough, realistic field exercises as the primary means of training. The Army must leverage the rapid growth in technology to offset these challenges.

Smart use of simulations and simulators, in both analytical efforts and in the right mix with live training exercises, will help offset the challenges of broad, force projection missions, rehearsal capabilities, digitization of the force, training proficiency, and training to standards under realistic conditions.

ENSURING THE VALIDITY OF 21ST CENTURY FORCE REQUIREMENTS

Senator COATS. General Hartzog, recognizing the number of changes over time, how can you be sure that the requirements you established today will be valid for the 21st century force?

General HARTZOG. We cannot be 100 percent certain. The ever increasing rate of technological change makes this task even more daunting. That's why we must give careful consideration to how we establish requirements, and then continually reexamine both the requirements and underlying assumptions. We review the National Security and National Military Strategies, confirm our missions, update our intelligence estimates, examine our Lessons Learned, refine our warfighting concepts, and explore potential technologies in Army Warfighting Experiments (AWEs), simulations, and analyses.

The Chief of Staff of the Army has recently given TRADOC the job of approving all Army requirements. To make this work, we are establishing Integrated Concept Teams to bring Army, industry, and academia together to develop concepts and examine "the art of the possible."

Senator COATS. How do you prioritize future warfighting requirements?

General HARTZOG. Once our Integrated Concept Teams determine what is possible, we will conduct experiments, simulations, and analyses to determine what combinations of requirements would improve our ability to accomplish our missions. We will assess the warfighting contribution of these requirements and seek out solutions that provide the greatest capability to the soldier. Prioritization would take into account the life cycle cost, as well as versatility and warfighting contribution.

Senator COATS. In light of rapid change as given, what types of programs should we avoid?

General HARTZOG. We want to avoid programs that are tied to obsolete or soon to be obsolete technologies, particularly information technologies. We must avoid those programs that are more manpower intensive than those which they replace especially as it applies to crews, maintenance, and logistics.

ARMORED GUN SYSTEM (AGS) CANCELLATION

Senator COATS. Can you explain the recent cancellation of the Armored Gun System (AGS) in light of our experience in Somalia and likely future roles for the Army? The Congress has been provided little detail concerning this decision.

Mr. DECKER. The Army's decision to terminate the AGS program was based on operational and affordability considerations. The requirement for which AGS was developed still exists. The Army requires a direct fire capability to support early/light entry forces. The system, or systems to meet this operational need must be air transportable, provide mobile, protected firepower and an effective anti-armor capability. There are alternative means available to meet this requirement. The Army will perform this mission with currently fielded forces (Abrams and Bradley equipped forces), as well as by accelerating Javelin into early deploying forces. Additionally, the recent decision to procure 120 C–17 aircraft increases the capability to put armored forces into an airhead more quickly. In summary, from an operational perspective the decision to terminate the AGS is consistent with previous experiences, like Somalia, and anticipated future requirements.

Because of continuing budgetary pressures, the Army reviewed its modernization programs to identify systems which have alternative operational solutions, and therefore might be terminated to free-up resources for reinvestment into other high priority modernization programs. The AGS was a low density program (237 vehicles) and was costly ($6.5 million per vehicle). By terminating AGS, the Army will be able to reinvest approximately $1 billion over the next 6 years.

ARMORED GUN SYSTEM (AGS)

Senator COATS. How will the Second Armored Cavalry Regiment (ACR) be equipped? Will a heavier configuration of the units that were to get the AGS cause a great requirement for C–17s as we equip these units with heavier systems? Have all the costs involved with the cancellation of the AGS been considered?

Mr. DECKER. Heavying up the second ACR will entail equipping it with tanks, fighting vehicles, armored personnel carriers, and attack helicopters and organizing the second ACR in the same manner as the third ACR.

By reconfiguring the second ACR into a heavy organization, the lift requirements for that specific unit will be affected, given its current equipping status as a wheel mounted organization. This, however, will not increase C–17 airlift requirements, since sealift is the mode of transportation for second ACR in the Mobility Requirements Study-Bottom Up Review Update (MRS–BURU), Time-Phased Force Deployment List (TFPDL). Our power projection strategy takes a heavy cavalry regiment (third ACR) into account with regard to lift requirements. Additionally, another heavy cavalry regiment would not change this requirement, since the two regiments, the second and third ACRS, would be similar organizations in terms of manning and equipment.

The Army has considered all costs in the cancellation of Armored Gun System.

JOINT FORCE OPERATIONS SUPPORT

Senator COATS. General Hartzog, how does the Army ensure that as requirements are determined these requirements support joint force operations?

General HARTZOG. For the past 3 years, the Army has explored new ways to determine requirements. We now begin with a holistic future warfighting concept based on desired Joint and Army capabilities. We study and review the Joint Warfighting Capabilities Assessment (JWCA), lessons from recent operations, and the results of experiments using future conflict scenarios, as well as other forms and forums of analysis.

Initially, TRADOC headquarters and its schoolhouses prepare materiel requirements, determine changes needed in warfighting doctrine, and validate necessary joint and Army-unique training. We forward these to all the Armed Services, other major Army commands, and the Department of Army for review and comment.

In determining requirements, TRADOC, after comprehensive staffing, forwards the approved materiel requirements to the Department of the Army who prioritizes the funding and acquisition. Throughout this process, there is close work in 10 study areas of the JWCA process to ensure that requirements generated are addressed in the joint context. This process ensures applicability and reduces duplication.

MODERNIZATION REQUIREMENTS AND MARINE INTERFACE

Senator COATS. How does the Army interface with the Marines in establishing future modernization requirements?

General HARTZOG. The Army and Marine Corps use similar systems to determine future warfighting requirements. The Army and the Marine Corps exchange Liaison Officers (LNO) at our respective Headquarters and Combat Developments Commands. These liaison officers strive to reduce redundancies and keep each service informed of mutually beneficial initiatives in development or production. Service LNOs are also assigned to four Army Battle Labs: the Mounted Battlespace Battle Lab at Ft Knox; the Dismounted Battlespace Lab at Ft Benning; the Depth and Simultaneous Attack Battle Lab at Ft Sill; and finally, the Battle Command Battle Lab at Ft Leavenworth. Army LNOs are assigned to the Marine Corps Combat Development Command (MCCDC) for the same reason. Finally, the staffs at HQ TRADOC and HQ Marine Corps Combat Development Command share continuous dialogue, working issues daily. Routinely the CG TRADOC and the CG MCCDC host coordination and information briefings ensuring all phases of requirements are reviewed for mutual interest and benefit.

EXAMPLES OF JOINT REQUIREMENTS

Senator COATS. Can you give this committee some examples of joint requirements in development or production?

General HARTZOG. Examples of joint requirements in production or development are:

1) AAW–S (JAVELIN)—replacement for the DRAGON, medium anti-armor weapon.

2) MPIM/SRAW—multipurpose and short range light armor and bunker defeating system

3) TOW/Follow-on to TOW (FOTT)—Heavy armor antitank system.

4) M1A2 Tank

5) ATCAS—light 155mm Howitzer.

6) ANTPQ–36—Counter-Mortar Radar.

7) GLPS—Gun Laying Positioning System.

8) AFATDS—Digitization links for the Commander's control of fire support.
9) 120mm Light mortar.
10) V–22 Osprey tiltrotor aircraft.
11) 155mm ammunition family
12) Replacement Truck Fleet
13) Stinger—short range, ground to air air defense weapon system
14) Land Warrior System—soldier field equipment set.

FORCE XXI/SEA DRAGON

Senator COATS. How does Force XXI (Army) tie in with Sea Dragon (Marines)?
General HARTZOG. Force XXI is the Army's process for building the 21st Century Army. Sea Dragon is the Marine Corps' parallel program moving the Marine Corps into the 21st Century. As with the Army, the Marine Corps has established the Commandant's Warfighting Lab (CWL) to organize and direct concepts-based experiments. Marine liaison officers (LNOS) to the Army Battle Labs are also part of the CWL, which provides direct ties between the two services' development efforts. The Marine CWL has lead for its participation in the Advanced Concept Technology Demonstration (ACTD) process and interfaces directly with TRADOC and the Battle Lab activities.

The Marine Corps will conduct their first advanced warfighting experiment in the SEA DRAGON series (SEA DRAGON ACTD) in Feb 97 at the 29 Palms Training Facility. They are participating with the Army at the NTC during the Task Force XXI AWE. Goals are to demonstrate digital interoperability between the services.

The Army and the Marine Corps have a Memorandum of Agreement (MOA) to maintain interoperability throughout digitization developments. Additionally, HQ TRADOC and CWL have established a Joint Working Group to provide oversight for these issues. Both TRADOC and Marine Corps Combat Developments Command are represented on the Joint Digitization of the Battlefield Council of Colonels/Captains and Joint Digitization General Officer's Working Group.

ARMAMENT RETOOLING AND MANUFACTURING SUPPORT INITIATIVE

Senator COATS. Secretary Decker, the Armament Retooling and Manufacturing Support (ARMS) program has been relatively successful in its initial, 3-year implementation phase. Two ammunition plants are now being maintained at zero cost to the taxpayer; four more are approaching zero cost. ARMS seems to be an excellent alternative to the layaway of Facilities that could be critical in a time of war, and seems to be an excellent defense conversion program. Why doesn't the Army support this program?

Mr. DECKER. The Army has supported this program by aggressively exploring alternative incentive arrangements and executing it with funds available. However, the program has thus far been an experiment and must compete for resources with other Army priorities, such as readiness, modernization, and bills for current operations. This forces us to make tough choices when deciding which items to include in the budget request, or proposing billpayers. Placing ARMS on the rescission list was not an easy one. Doing so should not be considered evidence of lack of confidence in or commitment to the program. We are looking hard at ARMS during our long range planning.

CRUSADER

Senator COATS. I am concerned how long it took and the amount of money spent ($200 million) to decide that liquid propellant (LP) technology had some serious problems, and that the Crusader would cost significantly more ($500 million and slip the program 2 years) just to continue its development. Why did it take so long to determine this technology would not yield the results we were looking to obtain?

Mr. DECKER. While it took several years and considerable resources to establish conclusively that LP was no longer an acceptable risk, we made the decision to shift from LP as soon as we were confident that continued investment of time and resources in conjunction with the Crusader program would be injudicious. In fact, we decided to transition to solid propellant in advance of the July 1997 milestone originally scheduled to evaluate the propellant issue. We learned a great deal about the characteristics of LP and the regenerative liquid propellant gun (RLPG) since we made the decision in 1991 to develop them for Crusader. The technology did not mature as we expected. The armament maturation efforts during demonstration and validation revealed that, to meet Key Operational Performance Parameters (KPPs), the risks became unacceptable. The Army Science Board confirmed this in their findings early this year. From October 1995 through March 1996, the Army Science Board evaluated the Feasibility of the Crusader with an LP-based armament system. The board concluded that although an LP-based Crusader is "doable", the development program would entail significant cost, schedule and technical risks. Additionally, the board determined that the RLPG/LP would require additional technology base efforts to address the critical challenges of controlling pressure oscillations and spiking, automatic ignition, and material compatibility.

Senator COATS. What were the lessons learned from this program?

Mr. DECKER. From our recent experience with liquid propellant (LP), we have relearned the importance of having a solid, alternative strategy in place to turn to in the event pursuit of a high technology solution fails. We had the best available Government and contractor team on the job and resourced them to accomplish the mission. Nevertheless, unforeseen technical difficulties with LP persisted; and because we had a solid propellant (SP) development program in place to mitigate LP's risk, we were able to transition seamlessly to SP and keep Crusader's fielding schedule on track.

Senator COATS. Will using a solid propellant change the performance of this system?

Mr. DECKER. The solid propellant Crusader will meet all of the Key Operational Performance Parameters (KPPs)—range, rate-of-fire, resupply and mobility. The solid propellant Crusader only partially meets the multiple round simultaneous impact (MRSI) requirement. This shortfall can be offset by completing development and fielding of the XM982 projectile. With the XM982, Crusader can meet all user requirements. A comparison of the ability of a liquid propellant (LP) or solid propellant (SP) Crusader to meet critical requirements (without the XM982 Projectile) follows.

Critical Requirements

	Parameters	Paladin (I)	PzH 2000	Crusader SP	Crusader LP
KPP's	40 KM Max Range	40	40	40	47
	10 Rds/min Rate Of Fire	6	8	10	10
	12 Minute Howitzer Rearm	No	12*	12	12
	67 KPH Highway Speed	60	60	72	72
	39 KPH X-Country Speed	32	25	47	47
Other	60 Round Capacity	39	60	60+2	60+2
	3 Man Crew	4	5	3	3
	4 to 8 Rds MRSI (8-36 km)	No	No	8-25 km	6-44 km
	20 Second Response Time	22	30	15	15
	55 Ton Combat Loaded Weight	34	60-62	55-60	65-72

* 30 minutes, based on military judgement

Only Crusader alternatives meet user requirements

Specifically, a solid propellant-based Crusader, without the XM982 projectile, win provide 90 to 98 percent of the operational effectiveness of an LP-based Crusader.

UNFUNDED ARMY MODERNIZATION

Senator COATS. Secretary Decker, using the administration's inflation projections, Army Procurement will not experience any real program growth until fiscal year 2000 or later. If the inflation projections are wrong, and the inflation projections are closer to the Congressional Budget Office's projections, then even this modest growth may disappear. Will the Army be able to execute its modernization plan at its current level of funding?

Mr. DECKER. The Army has significant shortfalls in Research, Development and Acquisition (RDA) accounts due to chronic underfunding in the past. The Army requires $14 to $16 billion annually in its modernization accounts in the Future Years Defense Program to fund them at a level commensurate with other Army programs. Funding for full recapitalization would require annual resources in the $15 to $20 billion range. However, we are only funded for approximately $11 billion in fiscal year 1997. Congress provided us some help last year, and the Office of the Secretary of Defense helped us this year. We are also taking actions internally to free-up funds to reinvest in our modernization accounts. We are instituting acquisition reform, attempting to procure at economic rates and buy-out systems early; we are retiring overage and obsolete vehicles in order to save operations and maintenance costs, we are using modeling and simulations where possible to save funding; and we have taken action to terminate the Armored Gun System (AGS) program in order to free-up funding to reinvest into our anemic modernization accounts; but these actions are insufficient to solve our modernization problems. We have developed a 1–N List which prioritizes our requirements for additional funding. With additional funding the Army could invest in economically efficient strategies including buying-out more programs early. We could also invest in areas where we have significant shortfalls such as Force XM, Logistics Automation; Combat Support/Combat Service Support; Soldier Enhancements; Night Vision Devices, Command, Control, Communications, Computers, and Intelligence (C⁴1); and other critical modernization shortfalls, including various high priority weapons systems.

TOTAL ARMY ANALYSIS (TAA) AND DIVISION REDESIGN

Senator COATS. General Hartzog, with the completion of the Total Army Analysis (TAA) and the Division Redesign, what was the level of requirements that came from these studies?

General HARTZOG. The Total Army Analysis (TAA) concluded with a briefing to the Deputy Secretary of Defense on November 8, 1995; however, the Division Redesign is still in the decision process. However, promising concepts, ideas, systems, and technologies for near-term implementation across the Force have emerged. Some of these, if fielded today, would provide the Force a significant battlefield advantage. One of these is the Land Warrior System that we demonstrated here today. Other systems with immediate impact include the Apache/Longbow, M1A2, Javelin, and the Patriot PAC III. In the often overlooked area of logistics, the Movement Tracking System (MTS) and the enablers that provide Total Asset Visibility will give the Force a significant battlefield advantage. Any of the mature, modernized command, control, communications, computers, and intelligence (C⁴1) systems, such as the Army Battle Command System, will also have an immediate impact.

RE-EQUIPPING ARMY UNITS

Senator COATS. How will the Army re-equip the units affected by these studies?

General HARTZOG. Resources tend to drive all options. Given current resources, we will have to equip units incrementally over 10+ years. This creates interoperability concerns, such as operational tempo. The window of opportunity is now because the threat is low. Over time, risks increase based on the potential rise or resurgence of a near-peer competitor.

The ideal situation would be to digitize entire divisions—combat, combat support, and combat service support—including RC units that are part of these divisions. In addition, we would need to digitize all corps units that support the division. The bottom line is we need to equip the Total Force—not just the active force—in a coordinated and appropriate manner, over time. Analysis of our Advanced Warfighting Experiments (AWE) will allow us to identify those key enablers that contribute directly to enhancing a soldier's warfighting capability.

BATTLEFIELD DIGITIZATION

Senator COATS. One of the focal points of the Army's modernization effort is Battlefield Digitization. The Comanche seems to be an essential element of that effort, but funding support in past has appeared to be wanting. How important is this requirement to the Army's effort to digitize the battlefield?

General HARTZOG. The Army fully recognizes that our current ability to exploit the technological capability of the digital battlefield is limited. Comanche is a missing link in a complex chain to get precise and timely tactical combat information into the hands of soldiers on the ground. Comanche represents the centerpiece of equipment modernization that will enable the Army's transformation to the future "information-age" force—Army XXI. Comanche can directly and digitally receive timely and accurate combat information from satellites, J–STARS and AWACS aircraft. When fielded, Comanche will fulfill its role as a technological overmatch combat system on the digital battlefield. It has the digital processing power for connecting the sensors, shooters, and joint tactical commanders. Thus, the force will be able to receive and transmit a three dimensional situational picture of the battlefield, connect to the joint digital architecture, and deliver precision fires throughout the width and depth of the battlefield.

ARMY MODERNIZATION

Senator COATS. How does the Comanche fit with other systems and modernization efforts?

General HARTZOG. The U.S. military has recognized the direct correlation between precise and timely reconnaissance and, ultimately, battlefield success. Over the past two decades, a multi-billion dollar effort has been underway to upgrade all levels of reconnaissance and early warning systems. This effort includes satellites, fixed and rotary-wing aircraft, ships, armored vehicles, and the soldier, sailor, and airman on the front-lines. They all require timely combat information to ensure victory. Reconnaissance planning and execution precede all successful combat operations.

The RAH–66 Comanche is a top long-term modernization program. It will be a key Army link on the digital battlefield. The Comanche will have digital processing power to provide immediate connections between sensors, shooters, and joint tactical commanders.

Additionally, it provides critical combat power to light and contingency forces during early, forced entry operations and is designed to close undetected when scouting for the heavily armed AH–64 Apaches. Fielding of the Comanche will also meet the requirements for the Special Operations Aviation light attack platform and improve the Army's ability to: 1) see the battlefield (night, adverse weather) with 2nd generation Forward Looking Infrared (FLIR) and millimeter wave radar fusion in time to allow ground force dominance; 2) maintain total battlefield awareness for the ground commander; and 3) reduce fratricide.

IMPACT OF NON-DIGITIZATION

Senator COATS. General Hartzog, digitization of the battlefield is an important battlefield enhancement, what would be the impact of not having all systems in the battlefield digital capable?

General HARTZOG. We are convinced that digitization will allow our forces to make decisions faster than the enemy, making our operations more lethal and survivable. If we digitize only part of the force, we can expect limitations. Our Division XXI Advanced Warfighting Experiment (AWE), scheduled for November 1997, will give us a better understanding of the challenges we would face when digital and non-digital units fight together. Findings from previous AWEs have revealed the following:

a. Reduced Operational Tempo (OPTEMPO). Non-digitized units are unable to share near real-time information and awareness of where friendly and enemy forces are situated. Therefore to ensure success when a digital and non-digital units fight adjacent to one another, the pace of operations must accommodate the slower organization. This slower OPTEMPO would reduce flexibility of the commander and decrease lethality and survivability.

b. Slower Distribution of Information. Within digitized units, information is available to anyone upon demand. Inability to receive, process, and distribute this information rapidly takes away a commander's advantage of engaging the enemy at will.

c. Decreased Split-Based Operations. Digital technology applied to all systems will reduce the need for deploying units to transport large amounts of supplies. Sensors will automatically trigger a resupply before reaching critical levels. Since this total asset visibility would not be available to non-digitized units, they would have to transport more supplies and move them around within the area of operation; thus, increasing vulnerability and requiring more time and precious resources.

d. Increased Manpower Requirements. In the absence of complete digitization across the force, there is a likely need for adding digitized liaison teams to serve within non-digitized units.

NEAR-TERM MODERNIZATION INITIATIVES AND CAPABILITIES

Senator COATS. General Hartzog, what are some near-term modernization initiatives and critical capabilities that support Force XXI?

General HARTZOG. Regardless of which initiatives we choose to implement, in order to produce a trained and ready Army, it must be balanced across the six imperatives of doctrine, force mix, materiel, unit training, leader development, and quality soldiers. We are pursuing initiatives that address each of these imperatives. Some of these initiatives, such as digitization, the experimental division design, new weapons, and command and control systems have already been addressed.

The near-term critical capability that supports Force XXI is real-time situational awareness that falls within the digitization initiatives. This capability and the work being done to achieve battlefield visualization through digitization is critical to the attainment of an information-age army.

Equipping units with digitized systems such as appliqué (486 computers) allows for real-time information sharing and situational awareness throughout the fighting force. This will occur both horizontally and vertically, and to any joint or coalition force with the capability to function in the digital environment. Real-time situational awareness also has sweeping ramifications on the six imperatives mentioned above. We, therefore, must provide balanced change and continuity throughout all initiatives in the Force XXI campaign. Other near-term initiatives include:

a. Unit Training. Distributed, integrated simulations and fully embedded training devices, which will reduce the heavy load on training areas and ammunition, enable more units to participate in a given training event, and provide more efficient, effective, and standardized After Action Reviews.

b. Leader Training. CD–ROM readers and CD training packages, which would replace the paper packages and doctrinal manuals of the past—saves space and provides for more efficient updating.

c. Quality Soldiers. Distance learning will lead to savings in travel, per diem, PCS costs, base operations, and instructors, while increasing the number trained and the ability to reach soldiers in distant or isolated locations. This will greatly affect RC so diers.

LAND WARRIOR

Senator COATS. General Hartzog, technology, including Land Warrior Program, will provide the commander and the individual soldier a great amount of information. How will the Army keep the amount of information to a manageable level?

General HARTZOG. Advanced Warfighting Experiments and other user evaluations will quantify what amount of information is manageable by the soldier. Computer software can then be tailored to prevent cognitive overload and limit the scope of information provided to the soldier. Leader training with emphasis on information management will address the type, content, and form of information required by soldiers involved in various combat operations.

QUESTIONS SUBMITTED BY SENATOR CARL LEVIN

PRIORITY OF OH–58 CONVERSIONS

Senator LEVIN. The Congress has been adding conversions of the OH–58 helicopter to the budget over previous years. I have asked the Army in previous years about the relative priority of these conversions of the OH–58As and OH58Cs to the newer configuration. Without fail, the Army has assessed this priority as being much lower than other aviation priorities. I note that in the Army priority funding list, totaling over $7 billion, includes some upgrades for the OH–58, but not a single dollar is requested for the previously funded conversion program. Should the committee infer that these conversions continue to enjoy lower priority than other Army needs, not just in aviation?

General GRIFFITH. The Army has converted a total of 382 OH–58A/C model aircraft to the upgraded OH–58D configuration. The original conversion program converted 201 OH–58As to the OH–58D Army Helicopter Improvement Program (AIEP) unarmed configuration. In 1990, the Secretary of the Army approved a plan to convert the 201 AHIP aircraft to the armed OH–58D Kiowa Warrior configuration. The Army fully funded the retrofit of the AHIPs to the Kiowa Warrior configuration in prior budget years. However, budget decrements in fiscal years 1994, 1995, and 1996 reduced the retrofit program and a total of 16 AHEPs remain unfunded for the OH–58D Kiowa Warrior upgrade. The retrofit of the 16 AHIPs is an unfunded requirement of $38.4 million on the fiscal year 1997 Army 1–N list. Congressional support has provided added funding for the conversion of an additional 181 OH–58As to the OH–58D Kiowa Warrior configuration.

The conversion of the OH–58D AHIPs to the Kiowa Warrior configuration is an Army Aviation priority and, is depicted on the Army prioritization list. However, current conversion priority is influenced by higher priority items, such as safety enhancements for the Kiowa Warrior fleet and Army commitment to Comanche as the objective armed reconnaissance aircraft. The safety enhancement program includes incorporation of crashworthy crew seats, an integrated body and head restraint system, and the R3 engine upgrade that includes a full authority digital electronic fuel control (FADEC) for engine reliability. The safety enhancement program is an unfunded requirement of $86 million for fiscal year 1997. The OH–58D Kiowa Warrior is recognized as an interim armed reconnaissance aircraft that has reached its maximum growth potential. It is scheduled for replacement by the RAH–66 Comanche commencing in fiscal year 2006.

[Whereupon, at 12:10 p.m., the hearing was adjourned.]

○

ISBN 0-16-054023-2

9 780160 540233

CPSIA information can be obtained
at www.ICGtesting.com
Printed in the USA
BVHW041449160119
537984BV00009B/327/P

9 781332 257744